Mastering Foreign Exchange and Money Markets

A step-by-step guide to the products, applications and risks

PAUL ROTH

An imprint of **Pearson Education**

London · New York · San Francisco · Toronto · Sydney
Tokyo · Singapore · Hong Kong · Cape Town · Madrid
Paris · Milan · Munich · Amsterdam

To my parents, my family and my partner
for their patient support and encouragement.

PEARSON EDUCATION LIMITED

Head Office:
Edinburgh Gate
Harlow CM20 2JE
Tel: +44 (0)1279 623623
Fax: +44 (0)1279 431059

London Office:
128 Long Acre, London WC2E 9AN
Tel: +44 (0)171 447 2000
Fax: +44 (0)171 240 5771

First published in Great Britain in 1996

ISBN 0 273 62586 1

British Library Cataloguing in Publication Data
A CIP catalogue record for this book can be obtained from the British Library

10 9 8

Typeset by Pantek Arts, Maidstone, Kent.
Printed and bound in Great Britain by Bell and Bain Ltd, Glasgow.

The Publishers' policy is to use paper manufactured from sustainable forests.

CONTENTS

Part 1: THE MARKET CONTEXT

1 Market overview   3

2 Review questions   39

Part 2: SPOT FX

3 Market concepts   43

Contents

Contents

FOREWORD

Traditionally, much of the knowledge and skills of professionals in the wholesale financial markets has been learned on the job. This approach has varied from the simple "sit by Nelly" approach to the sophisticated mentoring systems used by some large financial institutions. It is true that such training has always been supplemented by formal training programmes; until recently, however, the traditional approach was dominant. A side-effect of this emphasis on "on-the-job-training" has been the difficulty experienced by outsiders in understanding what insiders do.

The ratio of "on the job" training to other training techniques is now declining. The reason is that the markets have changed dramatically over the last 20 years: increased use of technology (computers and communication systems) and new theoretical ideas (option pricing) have increased the number of products, many of them very complex, and increased the linkages between markets. In order to communicate knowledge and skills in this new world every educational tool and technique needs to be used.

This is where the work of the ACI Institute becomes important. The ACI Institute is the educational arm of the ACI. It was founded in London in 1994. The ACI is the Financial Markets Association, an international professional body with more than 25,000 members in 54 countries, which began life in 1956.

The task of the ACI Institute is simple to state: it is to use the skills of its members to make a clear statement of what a market professional needs to know, and to what level they need to know it. The Institute is benchmarking the acquisition of knowledge in the rapidly changing wholesale financial markets – a task which is both challenging and exciting. To this end we encourage authors, publishers and tutors to provide as wide a variety of routes to our exams as possible.

For this reason I am delighted that Paul Roth and Pitman

Publishing have produced *Mastering Forex and Money Markets*. It captures, in text and computer simulation, the professional knowledge necessary to pass the ACI's first level examination: *Introduction to Foreign Exchange and Money Markets*. Also, we think that the volume will be appreciated by a wider audience as a source of information about the activities of participants in the foreign exchange and money markets.

Michael J Osborne
Director, ACI Institute

GUIDE TO THIS BOOK

It is often said that one is born a trader, and by and large our own experience bears this out. People who make it in this business tend to possess certain competencies which allow them to cope – and thrive – under pressure, and these skills are very difficult to develop in someone who does not already have some of the neccessary "instincts."

Having said that, we don't have a model of the ideal trader. Every trader is an individual with a unique style, and of course different markets require different approaches: the mercurial spot FX trader may find the technical complexity of the fixed income markets rather dry and dull; the more analytical trader may not take too well to the relentless pace of spot FX.

Whatever their inclinations, every budding dealer must go through two necessary stages in their training:

- they must acquire a technical understanding of how the markets work and – very importantly today – how they interlink;
- they must gain some practical exposure to a variety of markets, to discover the area which suits them best.

Many potentially good traders have come unstuck, either because they lacked the necessary technical skills, or because they simply landed on the wrong desk.

The text of this book should help you gain the basic technical understanding of the FX and money markets, up to the level required by a professional qualification such as the ACI *Introduction to Foreign Exchange and Money Markets* examination. And the *Risk Manager* simulation will give you some useful practical exposure to the dynamics of the markets.

This book is divided into four major sections:

- **Part I** is a general overview of the FX and money markets: its structure and evolution, its major participants and also some key bits of jargon.

- **Part II** covers spot FX: interpreting market rates, quoting prices in major currencies and crosses, position-keeping and understanding the risks involved.

- **Part III** introduces the main money market instruments: Euro-deposits, certificates of deposit and various types of discount securities. It also covers money market derivatives such as forward rate agreements and interest rate futures. We look at the key characteristics of each instrument as well as their uses in trading and risk management.

- **Part IV** builds on the money market concepts developed in Part III to explain the structure of the forward FX contracts – outrights and FX swaps. We look at the pricing of forward FX, its uses and how it "arbitrages" against the underlying money markets or their derivatives.

At the end of each major section you will find some test questions in the style of the ACI *Introduction to Foreign Exchange and Money Markets* exams. Passing this exam is very largely a matter of developing technical speed and accuracy, and to get the maximum benefit from these drills you should adhere to the recommended timing benchmarks. You will find the answers to these tests in Appendix 3, at the end of the book.

Parts II, III and IV, together with the associated exercises and simulations, form self-contained units. This is so that you can focus on particular market sectors if you so wish.

The Simulation

Associated with each section of this book is a dealing simulation exercise which you should attempt *after* you have completed the section and performed the paper exercises. For each simulation run, you are given specific dealing objectives, and you will be able to measure your own performance against established benchmarks. The benchmarks are based on the performance of qualified traders working on *Risk Manager*, but of course a good result in a simulated environment is no guarantee of success in the real world.

Nothing can replace the experience of real trading; the simulation is not a replication of the real world. It is a generic *model*, and as such it is designed to capture some of the real-world dynamics while abstracting from others. Time is accelerated, market events are compressed and, in this stand-alone version of *Risk Manager*, you cannot fully reproduce the "buzz" of the dealing room. Most importantly, you are not risking real money!

What *Risk Manager* can do is take you one step closer to the real world, and help you gain additional insights into the art of market making and risk management. No textbook can provide this. If *Risk Manager* can help you develop some fundamental dealing skills and avoid making the wrong career moves, the product will have achieved its objectives.

Please consult Appendix 4 (pages 391–392) for instructions on how to install *Risk Manager for Windows* on your PC.

The version of *Risk Manager* included with this book is only a subset of the full system we have developed, which covers debt capital market products (e.g., bonds and swaps) as well as options and many more advanced risk management analytics. The full system can also be networked into a complete "dealing room" and we can send you more details of its capabilities on request.

Please mail or fax us your feedback – critical or otherwise – and you can visit our website for further information. You will find our company details in the **About Risk Manager . . .** section of the program's **Help** menu, and in Appendix 5 on pages 393–394.

Enjoy!

ACKNOWLEDGEMENTS

This book and the associated software did not come together in one Big Bang: they are the result of more than ten years of my company's professional training and development work with banking clients. Much of the text and exercises contained in this book is derived from classroom materials that we developed to prepare trainees for the ACI *Introduction to Foreign Exchange and Money Markets* examination. The dealing simulation itself goes all the way back to 1984, and has been through many versions, culminating in *Risk Manager for Windows*; a subset of the software comes with this book.

Although I have been the anchor point throughout this process, many other people have played a vital role in it. First and foremost is Andrew Chisholm, my partner for six of the past ten years, who has since left the firm to take up the post of Head of European Training at JP Morgan. Andrew's contribution to the text and exercises in this book has been significant, and his revenue-generating activities within the firm made it possible for us to fund the development of *Risk Manager for Windows* – a very costly exercise, as anyone who is involved with Windows programming will appreciate!

My special thanks also to Steve Hemingway and Nisar Mohammed, two of our analysts responsible for much of the software design and coding, and to Steve Dagleish and Paul Mayhew, who between them have brought nearly half a man-century of market experience to bear on this book.

These are just some of the key people behind the product but the total cast is much more extensive: it includes Carolyne Locher, our trouble-shooting office manager, who ensures that things happen just in time; Alex Lawler, our sub-editor, who polished more of the book's rough edges; and Martin Glyn Jones, our software developer, who recently took on the unenviable task of maintaining and further developing the half a million lines of code which constitute *Risk Manager for Windows*.

My grateful thanks go to all the other people whom I have not mentioned – staff and consultants at Chisholm Roth, as well as clients – for their valuable comments and contributions over the years. Responsibility for any errors, omissions or shortcomings rests, of course, with the chief orchestrator.

Grateful acknowledgement is also made to Dow Jones Telerate, Hambros Bank Limited, Reuters Limited and Richard Irwin Inc. for allowing us to reproduce copyright material.

Paul Roth, Chisholm Roth & Company Ltd, London, 1996

Windows is a trademark of Microsoft Corporation

ABOUT THE AUTHOR

Paul Roth is Managing Director of Chisholm Roth & Company Ltd., a London-based training and development consultancy with an outstanding track record. Since he co-founded his company in 1989, Paul has developed and presented in-house training programs in Treasury, Capital Markets and Derivatives for many client organizations, including Banque Indosuez, Banque Nationale de Paris, Bankers Trust, Barclays de Zoete Wedd, Deutsche Morgan Grenfell, I.S.M.A., JP Morgan, Lehman Brothers, Mercury Asset Management, Mitsubishi Finance, NatWest Markets, NM Rothchild, Reuters, Robert Fleming, S.A.M.A. and Schroders.

Chisholm Roth's business is spread equally between training and software development, having been involved in the production of valuation models and risk management systems for major financial sector clients. Paul is the architect of *Risk Manager for Windows*™, a suite of computer trading simulations and leading-edge valuation models which are used for dealer training by more than 70 banks worldwide.

Paul gained an MSc in Economics at the London School of Economics and lectured at the University of Reading and the Open University before moving to the City of London, in 1980, to work as Senior Analyst with the Henley Centre for Forecasting, and later with the International Division of Williams & Glyn's Bank. He is a Visiting Fellow at the I.S.M.A. Centre, University of Reading.

Part 1

The Market Context

■ ■ ■

*"... international
trade, the exchange
of currency and
the borrowing and
lending of money
have always been
closely linked."*

Market Overview

Overview This introductory chapter outlines some of the major factors behind the growth of the FX markets and the associated international money markets. We trace the evolution of exchange rate systems through the Gold Standard, Bretton Woods and the European Exchange Rate Mechanism. We also outline the factors behind the growth of the Eurocurrency markets, and the pivotal role played by London as a financial centre.

The focus is mainly on FX although we also introduce the main money market instruments which are covered in more detail in Part III of this book.

You don't need to know about the origins of a market in order to trade in it successfully, and you can safely skip this chapter if you are in a hurry to get on. But if you are new to this business you may find that a little background knowledge is a good thing: it may help you gain a better perspective on why the industry is the way it is.

The Framework

A foreign exchange – or FX – transaction involves the purchase of one currency against the sale of another currency for settlement or delivery on a specified date. The rate of exchange is the price per unit of one of the currencies expressed in units of the other currency.

About US$30 billion of goods and services are traded across international borders every day. To help fund this trade, banks around the world lend to their prime customers in almost any currency. In turn, the banks make a market amongst themselves in multi-currency funds – banks short of one currency borrow or buy it from banks which are long (have a surplus) in that currency.

Although precise figures are not available, comparable sums of investment funds cross borders every day in search of higher returns, safer returns or both. However, the great bulk of FX operations nowadays is not directly related to international trade or investment. Approximately $1.2 trillion worth of currency

Turnover in major centres

Fig 1.1

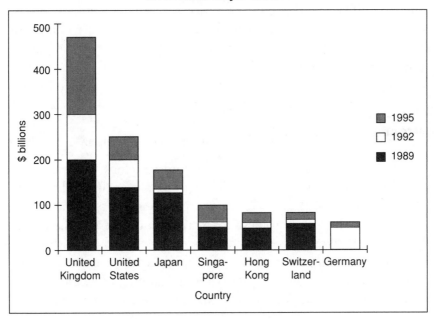

Source: Bank of England, March 1996

changes hands every day (according to *The Economist*, 30 March 1996).

The typical interbank dealer does not normally initiate large speculative positions for their own sake. This is the preserve of a few senior dealers. He responds to market opportunities created by large customer transactions somewhere in the system.

The objectives of a bank dealing room are:

● to make profit given an acceptable degree of risk;
● to enhance the institution's standing in the professional (interbank) market and with its clients.

Trading volume in FX has grown steadily since the 1980s. The bulk of trading is booked in London, Tokyo and New York. The market is:

● fairly easy to enter (for an international bank);
● extremely liquid;
● and generally operates in an orderly manner.

The FX and the associated money markets are primarily "over-the-counter" (OTC) markets. In other words, currency denominations, amounts, settlement dates and price are all nego-tiable. This information is confidential to the parties concerned and there is no obligation to disclose it. There are no fixed contract sizes or dates as in futures exchanges, although for indication purposes, market makers quote rates for various "fixed" settlement dates and conventional "market amounts."

> **"Modern telecom-munications allow the almost instantaneous transfer of funds almost anywhere in the world."**

FX dealers are linked round-the-clock via telephone, computer networks and, to a lesser extent nowadays, by telex. There is no physical marketplace, but there is always at least one money centre open for business at any time somewhere in the world. Through a network of correspondent relationships, banks transfer payments from importers to exporters, and exchange the currency of these payments. Modern telecommunications allow the almost instantaneous transfer of funds almost anywhere in the world.

Market Structure

Most FX dealers specialize in one or a small group of closely related currencies. In fact, there is not just one FX market, but groups of more or less interrelated currency pairs. Some of the main "traffic" routes are:

- US dollar/D-mark/Swiss franc
- US dollar/Japanese yen
- Sterling/US dollar (known as "cable")
- Member currencies of the European Exchange Rate Mechanism
- The Scandinavian currencies
- The Middle Eastern currencies

Liquidity in the major currencies is good, but the more "exotic" currencies can be thinly traded and treacherous for the inexperienced trader.

> **Market liquidity refers to the ease with which a trade may be executed without causing a significant movement in the price.**

Annual foreign exchange turnover in major centres, by currency

Fig 1.2

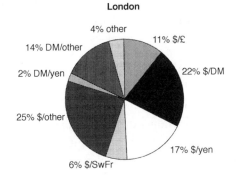

London

4% other
11% $/£
14% DM/other
2% DM/yen
22% $/DM
25% $/other
17% $/yen
6% $/SwFr

New York

11% DM/other
8% $/£
2% DM/yen
31% $/DM
21% $/other
7% $/SwFr
20% $/yen

Tokyo

2% other
4% DM/yen
12% $/DM
6% $/other
76% $/yen

Source: Bank of England, November 1995

Figure 1.2 shows the currency composition in FX turnover in the major traded centres in 1995.

US Dollar as the Major Trading Currency

Since the end of World War II, most countries have settled their trade debts by purchasing or selling currencies against dollars. The following example illustrates how this would have worked.

Example A British company importing goods from Germany has to pay for these in D-marks. The company asks its British bank to make a payment in D-marks and to debit its UK sterling account with the costs.

To complete this transaction the British bank obtains the D-marks in the interbank foreign exchange markets. It buys them from another bank and credits the dollars to that bank's account in New York. The British bank then buys the dollars back from the market and pays for them in sterling by debiting its customers sterling account in London.

The exchange of sterling for D-marks by "passing through" the dollar is termed a cross-currency transaction. With about 90% of world trade still being settled this way, the dollar remains the major traded currency in the FX markets.

Market Origins

As we shall see throughout this book, international trade, the exchange of currency and the borrowing and lending of money have always been closely linked.

In societies where money does not exist, the rate of exchange for goods and services is settled by tradition, law, or through barter. As trade expands and the variety of goods available increases, the barter system becomes increasingly chaotic and unwieldy. The solution is to create a common medium of exchange – money.

> "... international trade, the exchange of currency and the borrowing and lending of money have always been closely linked."

The great advantage of money is that it enables producers to specialize. The division of labour would be impossible if people had to spend a large proportion of their time and energies bartering. For barter to take place the two parties must have exactly complementary needs; with money this is not necessary. As one famous economist put it, in order to buy a suit, the farmer does not need to find a hungry tailor!

The Romans tried to establish their monetary system throughout their Empire not only to make trade flow more easily, but also to establish a manageable system of taxation. Their coinage was often used alongside the currencies of individual countries within the Empire: an early attempt at a common European currency. The gold content in the coinage varied considerably and many were not made of gold at all. A system of exchange parities between the different currencies therefore had to be established.

The idea of obtaining money in advance of the sale of goods also developed early on, which led to the business of borrowing and lending money at interest. The rudiments of banking were already in place.

The City of London

In 1694, the English King William III urgently needed money to finance his wars against France. It would have taken too long to raise the funds through taxation, so William Paterson, a Scottish merchant, suggested founding a bank which would then lend its share capital to the government.

In the spring of that year, Parliament passed an Act which provided for the incorporation of the Bank of England, and the world's first central bank came into being. The public were invited to invest in the company, and within 11 days a total of £1,200,000 had been subscribed to Bank of England Stock.

Private and joint-stock banks had already been in business all over the trading world for many centuries. What was unique about the Bank of England was its Royal Charter, which excluded the operation of any other bank within a 60-mile radius of the City of London.

The effect was that from then on governments had to negotiate with the Bank of England in matters of taxation and the minting of coin. The idea developed of a central bank with a powerful say in the management of the currency, as well as a role in setting domestic interest rates.

The relative freedom of the City of London from government interference, together with the expansion of the British Empire through trading companies and wealthy merchants, provided the perfect environment for "the City" to become the financial capital of the world.

It was not until 1832 that the Bank of England lost its monopoly, giving way to a boom in banking and financial services. New London banks were set up to provide loans for shipping, commodity finance and insurance. Foreign banks also moved in to find the best prices for commodities and the keenest rates of interest.

The 19th century saw the rise of sterling as a world trading currency. The key factors were:

- rapid industrialization in Europe and America, dependent on imported raw materials such as iron ore and steel;
- great advances in transport and communications, permitting expansion of world trade and the international flows of capital to finance this trade.

The Gold Standard

Before World War I and again briefly in the inter-war period most of the major trading countries adhered to the International Gold Standard. This required a country to define its monetary unit in terms of a specific quantity of gold. Central banks supported this by allowing free convertibility between gold and paper currency. Governments had to allow unrestricted export/import of gold.

These conditions kept exchange rates stable. International flows of gold kept official exchange rates ("mint parities") close to the gold price. Each country's money stock grew or contracted in line with its gold stock.

Wars, Booms and Slumps

World War I dislocated the major economic powers in different ways. Some nations were left heavily indebted, while others experienced an unprecedented economic boom, until the Wall Street Crash in 1929. During the ensuing period of economic depression the Gold Standard came under pressure and was eventually abandoned.

One by one the major European countries left the Gold Standard in an attempt to undercut their trading competitors with a weaker currency. Rampant inflation destroyed the value of currencies such as the German Reichsmark.

Soon after, with Europe engaged in another war, the US consolidated its position as the world's economic powerhouse. Government and financiers bank-rolled the Allied forces, while US industry had the rest of the world as its customer and demanded payment in US dollars. The dollar displaced sterling to become the main currency for international trade settlements.

The Bretton-Woods Agreement

After World War II, the Allied governments were determined to avoid a repetition of the currency chaos and economic depression of the 1920s and 1930s. The first step was the reconstruction of the world monetary system. The United Nations Monetary and Financial Conference held at Bretton Woods, New Hampshire, in July 1944 sought to do this by designing an adjustable peg system of exchange rates, and by establishing the International Monetary Fund (IMF) and the International Bank for Reconstruction and Development (the "World Bank").

The objective of the IMF was to create monetary stability and remove exchange restrictions that hampered international trade. New rules were established for maintaining and adjusting exchange parities. The value of each national currency was expressed in fixed amounts of gold; but it was the dollar's official convertibility into gold, at a fixed price of $35 an ounce, which underpinned the whole system.

Exchange rates were kept within a narrow band (+/− 1%) around an officially declared parity. For example, from 1949 to 1967, the pound was pegged at a parity value of GB £1 = US$2.80.

The Bretton-Woods system helped to promote a much more rapid recovery in world trade than after World War I. However, other factors were also at work. One was the US-sponsored Marshall Plan, a $12 billion program of financial aid for both Western and Eastern Europe.

The Eurodollar Market

It was during this period of post-war reconstruction that the Soviet Union accumulated huge reserves of US dollars which were held by

New York banks on behalf of Banque pour l'Europe du Nord in Paris, and Moscow Narodny Bank in London. These institutions were the foreign trading arms of the Soviet central bank. As the Cold War escalated, fears mounted that the US might freeze these Soviet assets.

To pre-empt such a move, the Soviets transferred their dollar deposits to European banks, which in turn placed them in New York. The same dollars could no longer be considered to be Soviet assets. The main depositors of Soviet dollars were the French nationalized banks based in London.

The choice was partly because France had a large Communist vote at the time, and partly because of the freedom of operation allowed in the London market. Also, London had already in place an efficient mechanism for clearing dollars in New York which had been developed for the settlement of Lloyds insurance premiums and claims. This is how the so-called Eurodollar market came into being.

What are Eurodollars?

Eurodollars are dollar banking operations which are not subject to the same regulations as apply in domestic US dollar banking.

Dollar deposits held on account with European banks are matched by equal amounts held by those banks with their correspondents in New York. The actual dollars are physically in the United States, but are held on account for foreign banks.

The "Euro" prefix does not mean that Eurodollars must be held by European banks or in Europe. Offshore bases for Eurodollar business have developed in such exotic places as the Cayman Islands, Hong Kong and Singapore (the so-called "Asia-dollar market"), Bahrain and many other financial centres.

Since the implementation of the US International Banking Act in 1981, even banks operating in New York have been allowed to handle Eurodollar business.

Whatever the booking centre, the fact remains that any Eurodollar transaction between two offshore banks must ultimately be mirrored by equivalent transactions between a paying agent and a receiving agent in New York. The agent banks, in turn, clear the funds transfer through the Federal Reserve System (by "Fed Wire").

Market Growth

Quite naturally a market in Eurodollars flourished in London during the two decades following the end of World War II, during which institutions with surplus dollars lent to banks and corporations which were short of dollars. Alongside the banking business a lively foreign exchange market flourished.

Other factors contributed to the growth of the Eurodollar market. One was the various restrictions imposed on domestic dollar interest rates, in particular the Federal Reserve's Regulation Q. This restriction placed a ceiling on the interest rates which US banks could pay on domestic term deposits.

This encouraged depositors of dollars to place in London, taking advantage of the interest rate differential between New York dollars and Eurodollars.

Another factor was the gradual reappearance of inflationary pressures in the USA (and Britain), with consequent balance of payments problems under a rigid system of exchange rates.

Both excesses in domestic spending and the outflows of capital from the deficit countries would have been dampened, if not reversed, under a regime of high interest rates. But in the post-war climate, this option would have been politically suicidal.

Instead, from 1957 and throughout the 1960s, successive British governments experimented with measures which attempted to control the supply of money by physically restricting the amount of sterling which banks could lend. British banks were openly encouraged to use the dollar as a means of financing trade and foreign investment.

In the US the Kennedy administration singled out the Yankee bond market (bonds issued in the domestic market by foreign borrowers) and other dollar lending to foreigners as the principal cause of the country's balance of payments problems. In 1964, the authorities introduced an Interest Equalization Tax (IET) which effectively eroded any cost advantage that could be had from raising dollars in New York.

This was followed in 1965 by the introduction of Foreign Credit Restraint Program Guidelines, which physically restricted domestic dollar lending to foreign borrowers. At the same time, US multi-nationals were actively encouraged to use the Eurodollar market rather than the domestic market as the funding vehicle for inter-national trade and expansion.

To summarize, the picture that emerges from this period is one in which domestic banking in the USA was increasingly starved of opportunities through a combination of lending restrictions and artificially low interest rates. The Eurodollar market, where the control of lending operations was virtually left to each individual bank, flourished steadily.

Market trends

Throughout the 1960s many US banks established representative offices in London which were quickly converted to full-scale opera-tions. Figure 1.3 illustrates this growth.

Fig 1.3

US banks in London 1966–72

End of Year	No. of Banks with Branches	No. of Branches
1964	11	180
1966	13	244
1968	36	373
1970	79	532
1972	107	627

Because most of the business in London was dollar-based, the vol-ume of foreign exchange business also increased dramatically in New York.

In the 1950s a foreign exchange dealer in London or New York would have quoted a rate of exchange in the interbank market and expect to deal in an amount of $10,000. By the end of the 1960s the accepted market amount was at least $1,000,000 – "one dollar" in dealers' jargon. Today "one dollar" is the minimum amount, with deals of $5 and $10 millions being normal, although many banks remain within the $1–5 million range.

These trends also went hand-in-hand with the development of a whole new family of international financing instruments – Eurobonds, Euronotes and Euro-commercial paper, as well as back-to-back loans which were the precursors to what today we call currency swaps. We shall outline the characteristics of some of these instruments briefly later on in this chapter, and we'll discuss them in more detail in Part III.

Figure 1.4 shows the total amounts outstanding in the major debt categories. Eurobonds and Euronotes alone now match in size the entire US government bond market – the largest borrower in the world. Notice also the large proportion of interbank deposits within international bank claims. The vast majority of these have maturities of 12 months or less.

Whenever a debt instrument matures, the beneficiary has the option of reinvesting the money in another instrument bearing a different currency denomination, and this gives rise to a foreign exchange transaction.

Eurocurrency debt

Fig 1.4

Estimated net financing in international markets in billions of US dollars[1]								
Components of net international financing	1994	1995					1996	Stock at end Dec.
	Year	Year	Q1	Q2	Q3	Q4	Q1	1995
Total international[2] bank claims	272.9	651.7	318.4	166.1	92.0	75.2	..	9,223.6
minus: interbank redepositing	82.9	336.7	158.4	91.1	47.0	40.2	..	4,578.6
A = Net international bank lending....	190.0	315.0	160.0	75.0	45.0	35.0	..	4,645.0
B = Net euronote placements	140.2	192.4	36.0	52.6	57.8	45.9	56.6	593.8
Completed international bond issues[3]	373.6	359.9	74.5	79.9	101.9	103.6	129.9	
minus: redemptions and repurchases	228.1	239.2	54.7	58.2	60.4	65.8	74.5	
C = Net international bond financing[3]	145.5	120.8	19.8	21.7	41.5	37.8	55.5	2,209.6
D = Total international financing[4]	475.7	628.2	215.9	149.4	144.3	118.6	..	7,448.3
minus: double-counting[5]	65.7	118.2	40.9	39.4	29.3	8.6	..	1,008.3
E = Total net international financing	410.0	510.8	175.0	110.0	115.0	110.0		6,440.0

1 Changes in amounts outstanding excluding exchange rate valuation effects for banking data and euronote placement; flow data for bond financing.
2 Cross-border claims in all currencies plus local claims in foreign currency.
3 Excluding bonds issued under EMTN programmes which are included in item b.
4 A + B + C.
5 International securities purchased or issued by the reporting banks, to the extent that they are taken into account in item A.

Source: Bank for International Settlements, June 1996.

From Fixed to Floating Currencies

By the mid-1960s, West Germany and Japan were again challenging the economic supremacy of the US. In 1971, under the strain of unrelenting capital outflows and widening trade deficits, the US was forced to abandon the official convertibility of dollars into gold (which until that point was officially still pegged at $35 per ounce).

The upshot of this unilateral decision by the Nixon Administration was a period of intense negotiation to establish a new and more viable system of exchange rates. The US wanted to preserve the dollar's parity against gold, while allowing market forces temporarily free reign to find a new set of equilibrium exchange rates. In contrast, most European countries and Japan, mindful of the fact that this would undoubtedly cause their currencies to rise against the dollar (making their exports less competitive) preferred a more managed and gradual devaluation of the dollar, both against their currencies and against gold.

On 17 December 1971, the Group of Ten (USA, Britain, Canada, France, West Germany, Italy, Holland, Belgium, Sweden and Japan) met at the Smithsonian Institute in Washington DC, where they agreed on a compromise. The dollar was devalued against gold, from $35 to $38 an ounce, while the other currencies were officially revalued by around 10% in relation to the dollar. There was also a provision for a wider band, within which market rates would be allowed to fluctuate, by up to 2.25% around the new "central rates."

The Smithsonian Agreement proved to be only a temporary measure to alleviate the US balance of payments problems, and in February 1973, the dollar was devalued again. Soon after, the rest of the G10 countries allowed their own currencies to float freely, thus ending the Bretton Woods system of fixed parities.

The regime of floating exchange rates started the boom in foreign exchange trading as a profit-making activity in its own right, which has continued to this day. It was coincided with the start of the European Monetary System (outlined on pages 30–33) and the movement towards European monetary integration.

The devaluation of the dollar and higher domestic interest rates stimulated a flow of dollars back to America. Up to a third of

Eurodollar business was believed to have returned to the US during the following five years. Some of the funding vacuum was filled by surplus D-marks, Swiss francs, Japanese yen, Dutch guilders, sterling and other currencies. Their role in international finance has increased steadily since then.

Oil Crises and Debt Problems

The oil price rises imposed by the Organization of Petroleum Exporting Countries (OPEC) in 1974 changed dramatically the pattern of international debt flows. Almost overnight the price of oil rose from just a few dollars per barrel to over $25.

Industries in North America, Europe and Japan suffered considerably higher costs as a result. However, the oil-producing countries (mainly those centred around the Gulf) were now dollar-rich. The most attractive home for those funds appeared to be the Eurocurrency market.

Banks receiving the dollars lent them on to countries in Western and Eastern Europe, Latin America and Asia to pay for oil imports and to finance economic development.

Many of the dollars lent thus returned to the oil exporters as income. They were again placed with offshore banks who re-lent them to oil importers, and so on. Dollars recycled from the Gulf in this way became known as "petrodollars."

The same petrodollar merry-go-round occurred in the wake of the second OPEC price hike, in 1979. It saved the borrowing countries from the very severe recession that would have ensued had they been forced to cut their oil consumption. But it left the Eurocurrency market with an overhang of non-performing debt which threatened the stability of the whole system.

Other Eurocurrencies

Figure 1.5 shows the currency composition of the international debt totals shown earlier in Figure 1.4.

SWIFT (The Society for Worldwide Interbank Financial Telecommunication) is a multinational facility for the transfer of interbank

Fig 1.5

Currency composition of international bank lending

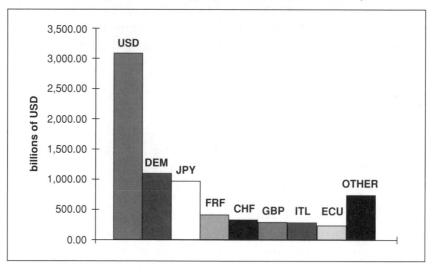

Source: Bank for International Settlements, June 1996.

funds based in Belgium and the Netherlands. Payment instructions are transmitted instantaneously by entering tightly formatted and password-controlled messages into the SWIFT computer network. Currencies are identified by ISO codes (see Figure 1.6).

You can see from the chart in Figure 1.5 that the US dollar remains the main international debt currency, but nowadays D-marks, Swiss francs and Japanese yen have become increasingly significant in new debt issues. The role of sterling in international bonds markets

Fig 1.6

SWIFT payments system ISO codes

USD	=	US dollars
DEM	=	D-marks
CHF	=	Swiss francs
FRF	=	French francs
GBP	=	British pounds
JPY	=	Japanese yen
ITL	=	Italian lire
ECU	=	European Currency Units

Note: **ISO** (The International Organization for Standardization) is a body based in Geneva responsible for, among other things, designating a common language of currency codes.

has increased since the liberalization of the early 1980s, while the role of the ECU has declined dramatically since 1991.

The ECU is a "cocktail" unit of account composed of fixed amounts of various European currencies. This is discussed in more detail in a later section.

The Main Debt Instruments

FX involves the sale of a financial asset denominated in one currency and the purchase of another financial asset denominated in a second currency. Below is a brief summary of the main Eurocurrency instruments available. Some of these will be discussed in detail in Part III of this book.

Eurodeposits

Demand Deposits and Call Money

Non-interest-bearing or low-yielding facilities kept mainly for international money transfers. Balances are normally kept to an operational minimum. Funds can be withdrawn by the depositor at short notice and without penalty. A bank trading US dollars against D-marks must have a US$ account with an agent ("correspondent") bank in the US and a D-mark account with a bank in Germany.

Fixed Deposits

Interest-bearing deposits for a fixed term, in US dollars or another Eurocurrency traded primarily between banks in London. Mostly for an original maturity, or "tenor", of 12 months or less, deals are typically for amounts of over US$ 1 million or equivalent. A principal source of short-term funding for international banks. The London Interbank Offered Rates (LIBOR) are the finest interest rates which banks charge for lending (offering) funds to top quality names. LIBOR is widely used as a benchmark rate for other Eurocurrency lending instruments.

> "FX involves the sale of a financial asset denominated in one currency and the purchase of another financial asset denominated in a second currency."

Certificates of Deposit (CDs)

Receipts for Eurocurrency fixed-term deposits. These are mainly in bearer form and therefore easily negotiable in a secondary market, unlike fixed deposits which are non-negotiable. Typically for minimum denominations of $25,000 or equivalent and maturities 12 months or less. Interest payable is typically fixed at the time of issue, although for paper with longer maturity, it may be reset periodically in line with a reference rate such as the three- or six-month LIBOR. This is a convenient short-term "home" for spare cash. For the convenience of being negotiable CDs typically yield 10–20 basis points (0.10%–0.20%) below the LIBOR for comparable fixed-term deposits.

> **Bearer securities: financial instruments in which the name of the beneficiary does not appear on the paper, so ownership is automatically bestowed upon its holder. This makes them easy to negotiate (buy or sell) in the secondary markets.**

Discount Paper

This covers a category of financial instruments in which the rate of interest an investor earns is not stipulated explicitly, as in a bank deposit or CD, but is implied in the difference between its price at the time of purchase and its value at maturity. Before maturity these instruments trade at a discount to their maturity value (also known as face value or par value).

Bankers' Acceptances

Known in the UK as "bank bills", these are commercial bills of exchange which have been drawn on or "accepted" by a recognized bank. These instruments have been used for hundreds of years to finance international trade.

A bill of exchange is simply an IOU typically signed by an importer in favour of an exporter; when the bill has been endorsed or accepted by a bank, the bank then guarantees its payment at maturity, which makes the bill easily negotiable in the secondary market – i.e., tradeable as a commodity.

Treasury Bills

Short-term IOU's issued and fully guaranteed by the government.

Commercial Paper

Unsecured promissory notes issued in bearer form by international companies with good credit ratings, typically with maturities of one to nine months. There is a well-established and highly liquid CP market in the US and a newer, more specialist market for Euro-CP mainly in London.

Medium-Term Instruments

The money markets cover financial instruments with an original maturity of 12 months or less. Instruments with longer maturities are termed capital market paper.

Most money market paper has an original maturity of 12 months or less, and it is here that the links with the FX markets are strongest. However, the money markets are only the short end of the debt capital markets spectrum and it is useful to be aware of some of the medium-term financing instruments available.

Syndicated Credits

Medium-term (5–10 year) direct loans to sovereign or large corporate borrowers. Interest is variable, adjusted every three or six months, based on a fixed margin ("spread") over LIBOR or US Prime Rate. Very large amounts are typically involved – $500 million and upwards. The loans are parcelled out among banks participating in the syndicate to reduce credit risk to any one institution.

Eurobonds

Unsecured medium-term negotiable debentures issued as bearer certificates by major corporates and governments outside the regulating umbrella of any domestic stock exchange. Maturities typically range between three and seven years. Interest or "coupon" payments are paid regularly during the term of the debt and these are either fixed at the time of issue ("straight bonds") or adjusted periodically in line with a LIBOR or US Prime reference rate ("floating rate notes").

Treasury Bonds

Medium-term certificates of debt issued by governments, with terms ranging from one up to 30 years. Coupon payments are typically fixed and paid semi-annually.

Strictly speaking, treasury bills and bonds are domestic rather than international (Eurocurrency) instruments: they are closely regulated by their central banks. However, some of the treasury markets (notably in the US, Japan and many European countries) are very large and open to international investors, which makes the distinction nowadays between domestic and Euro very blurred. Because of their importance, they are often used as a reference for the pricing of many Eurocurrency instruments such as Eurobonds and interest rate swaps.

Market Participants

Central Banks

Central banks play two key roles in the FX and money markets:

- market supervision
- control over money supply and interest rates.

Central banks intervene to smooth out fluctuations in the markets for freely convertible currencies by using their stock of foreign currency reserves, or by influencing interest rates through money market operations. Among the most active central banks are the Federal Reserve System (the "Fed"), Deutsche Bundesbank, Bank of Japan, Bank of England, Banque de France and Banque Nationale Suisse.

Banks

Commercial banks provide integrated FX, deposits and payments facilities for customers. They also make an active market in currencies and deposits amongst themselves.

Banks, acting as market makers, continuously alter their prices so as to balance the supply and demand for each currency within their own books, hopefully for a profit.

The interbank rate of exchange is the wholesale price for a currency, in substantial amounts. The commercial rate of exchange is the retail price, for smaller amounts. The difference between the two depends on a number of factors:

- the value of the customer to the bank;
- the size and type of transaction;
- the settlement date (when the two currencies are actually exchanged).

Market volatility caused by changes in economic conditions, international conflicts, natural disasters, or change in government policy.

Market Information Vendors

In London, there are over 500 banks from all over the world involved in FX operations, but less than 50 of these are active market makers. This is still a sufficiently large number to cause the market user a problem in deciding which of the major dealing banks is quoting the best rate of exchange. One solution is provided by the market information vendors, who may not be considered market participants as such but nonetheless play a vital role in the whole process. Terminals supplied by Reuters, Telerate and other vendors show the latest "indication" rates being quoted by the major banks within a given time zone.

Reuters FXFX page

Fig 1.7

```
Reuters : Quotes : FXFX
Function  Edit  Screens  Format  View  Setup  Help

1013 CCY PAGE NAME * REUTER SPOT RATES      * CCY HI*EURO*LO FXFX
1013 DEM BCIX B.C.I.         MIL 1.5279/84  * DEM  1.5306  1.5260
1013 GBP MMDB HSBC MIDLAND LON 1.5514/21    * GBP  1.5547  1.5486
1013 CHF DRBX DRESDNER       FFT 1.2532/42  * CHF  1.2550  1.2508
1013 JPY UBZA UBS            ZUR 108.70/80  * JPY  108.80  108.25
1012 FRF MMDB HSBC MIDLAND LON 5.1725/75    * FRF  5.1797  5.1695
1013 NLG BAXX BARCLAYS       LON 1.7106/16  * NLG  1.7127  1.7092
1013 ITL BAXX BARCLAYS       LON 1542.80/4.30* ITL 1545.42 1539.58
1013 ECU XIMU IMI BANK       LUX 1.2387/90  * ECU  1.2403  1.2360
------------------------------------------------------------------
XAU CSBL 390.15/390.55 * ED3  5.37/ 5.50 * FED   PREB * LGVS 30Y
XAG CSBL  5.37/ 5.38   * US30Y YTM 7.01  * 5.50- 5.75 * 87.14-15
```

Fig 1.8

Telerate page 256

PAIR	BID ASK	PAGE	GMT	SOURCE	CTR	GMT	HIGH LOW	GMT
06/06	14.54 GMT		WORLDWIDE FX	SPOT DEM				256
DEM/JPY	71.39-42	3438	14:53	U B S	LUG	06:57	71.51-71.19	09:44
GBP/DEM	2.3594-04	3609	14:53	DEUTSCHE	FFT	23:18	2.3705-2.3539	14:14
DEM/CHF	0.8212-16	4863	14:50	MARSHALL	N Y	05:38	0.8214-0.8210	09:46
XEU/DEM	1.8896-01	20321	14:41	I M I	LUX	10:03	1.8918-1.8898	14:08
DEM/FRF	3.3894-99	3341	14:54	SE BANKEN	STK	12:07	3.3922-3.3804	13:46
DEM/ITL	1011.90-12.30	3830	14:53	SE BANKEN	LDN	12:08	1013.30-1009.95	01:04
DEM/NLG	1.119150-9250	4863	14:51	MARSHALL	N Y	06:17	1.119275-1.119175	11:07
DEM/BEF	20.5667-72	4805	14:52	MARSHALL	LDN	11:51	20.5690-20.5645	06:43
DEM/ESP	84.58-60	20728	14:52	C I M D	MAD	06:58	84.82-84.57	13:43
DEM/PTE	103.26-29	4805	14:52	MARSHALL	LDN	13:18	103.31-103.19	06:53
IEP/DEM	2.4177-97	6566	14:51	ULSTER	DUB	07:01	2.4235-2.4132	09:45
DEM/GRD	157.91-96	4805	14:52	MARSHALL	LDN	13:57	157.95-157.81	05:55
DEM/DKK	3.8611-16	3305	14:41	DEN DANSK	COB	06:57	3.8612-3.8582	10:34
DEM/SEK	4 4040-70	3305	14:46	DEN DANSK	COB	07:56	4.4135-4.3950	00:59
DEM/NOK	4.2783-93	4863	14:33	MARSHALL	N Y	11:54	4.2899-4.2725	23:49
DEM/FIM	3.0705-30	4863	14:33	MARSHALL	N Y	07:00	3.0760-3.0680	06:00

Source: Dow Jones Telerate.

Interbank Brokers

Interbank brokers relay prices received from banks via a telecommunications network to other banks and some large market users. These prices are not merely for indication purposes; they are "live" rates at which the quoting banks must be prepared to deal, usually for an accepted market amount.

> **A broker broadcasts to all its clients the highest rate currently paid by banks buying a currency (the bid rate) and the lowest rate asked by banks selling the currency (the offer rate).**

The illustration in Figure 1.9 summarizes the relationship between brokers and their banking clients.

The banks feed their buying and/or selling prices to the broker using a dedicated communications line. The broker assembles the rates received and broadcast the best buying price (highest bid) and the best selling price (lowest offer), together with the amounts available for trading, if relevant. A subscriber wishing to trade at one of the prices broadcast simply calls the broker using a dedicated communications line.

The broker-client relationship

Fig 1.9

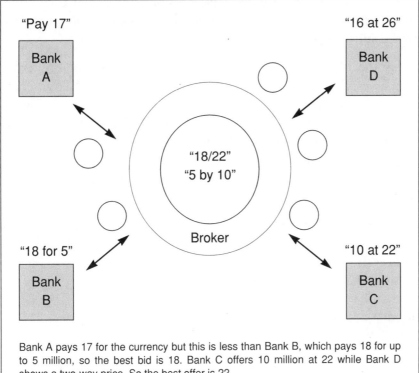

"Pay 17"

Bank A

"16 at 26"

Bank D

"18/22"
"5 by 10"

Broker

"18 for 5"

Bank B

"10 at 22"

Bank C

Bank A pays 17 for the currency but this is less than Bank B, which pays 18 for up to 5 million, so the best bid is 18. Bank C offers 10 million at 22 while Bank D shows a two-way price. So the best offer is 22.

Broking firms cannot "run positions" by quoting their own rates. They do not disclose the name of the parties quoting prices or accepting a price until a positive commitment has been made by both sides. By accessing the market through a broker, smaller banks can transact at prices which they might never be quoted if they went directly to the market maker.

Brokers operate on a commission basis which is related to the amount, size and complexity of deal required.

Typical FX brokerage in major currencies can range from $10 to $50 – up to 1/2 a "pip" – per $1 million dealt (a pip on a USD/DEM rate is 100th of a pfennig). This is a small cost for the infrequent dealer, but not for banks turning over tens of billions of dollars every day. Large clients typically negotiate volume discounts on their brokerage and this makes their business more cost-effective.

Over 40% of all FX business nowadays is channeled through brokers. The market is dominated by a small number of London or New York-based houses operating locally through wholly or partly owned subsidiaries.

Today the FX market is also serviced by two electronic brokering companies (EBS, which is owned by a consortium of large commercial banks, and Instinet, which is owned by Reuters). Under these systems, market makers input their bids and offers into special terminals at their offices, and the whole function of matching bids with offers is handled by a central computer, making the whole process of dealing as simple as pushing on a few buttons.

Up to 25% of all FX business is now believed to be channeled through electronic brokers, although most dealers will not rely exclusively on these systems because they still want to sense the mood of their human brokers or counterparties.

Corporations and Institutions

These are the main end-users of the FX and money markets. Companies use these markets to manage their cash flows in the same or different currencies. Institutional investors, which manage a very large part of the domestic and international financial assets outstanding, use the markets to manage their day-to-day liquidity, and the FX markets to structure their portfolios across a range of currencies.

Changes in the patterns of corporate and institutional cash flows have profound and often lasting effects on market trends, and the banks which detect these changes early stand to make large profits on that information.

Traditionally banks take on currency risk, but corporate and institutional users of the FX markets are normally concerned with covering or "hedging" their foreign currency exposures.

However, the distinction is blurred because some companies – and of course some investors as well – are aggressive players in their own right and actively take positions in currencies. Many of the large multinationals have set up their own in-house banks, complete with dealing rooms and risk control departments.

Government and quasi-government agencies may also be major players, particularly those of developing countries or centralized economies where the traditional import and export business is often channeled through government monopolies. These bodies can enter the FX markets in very large amounts.

Margin Accounts

Buying foreign currency through the retail branches of banks has no effect whatsoever on the market. Private investors who speculate on the currency markets are normally required to place collateral into "margin accounts" with their banks.

The currency futures markets are tiny in comparison with the "cash markets" – the OTC markets for spot or forward FX. However many interbank dealers monitor the futures markets closely and often react to movements there. Occasionally small speculators can provoke a stampede in some futures exchange which is picked up by the banks, and this can have a major effect on the underlying currency markets – a classic case of "the tail wagging the dog" – but this is rare nowadays.

A Zero-Sum Game?

If someone profits, must someone else necessarily lose all FX trade? Overall, the answer is "yes." Looking at the various players in the FX market, it is true statistically that commercial banks tend to profit on FX dealing over all the others.

They tend to be net gainers because they know the markets better than anyone else – they are after all the market makers. They win over central banks simply because profit is not the principal criterion of central bank intervention.

The interbank market has its own "league table" of banks.

> **Division 1: commercial (or "money-centre") banks which handle a large flows of corporate, institutional and personal business and are very active market makers.**

First-division banks can build up large positions which can move markets. They can, for example, execute deals of US$100–500 million or equivalent in major currency pairs at a time.

But their main asset is not financial muscle – it is information. The more active a bank is in the markets, the more business it wins and the more market intelligence it gathers – about who is in the market and in what size. The price to pay for this is a willingness to be a competitive buyer or seller under any market conditions – sometimes at a loss.

Division 2: the smaller European banks, US regionals, Middle Eastern banks, Far Eastern banks.

Second-division banks tend to be much more customer-driven. They will make prices for their customers, but any significant positions will be quickly covered in the market. Sometimes they will line up a third party in the market before giving the customer a price, with a built-in profit margin.

This arrangement may sound like easy money for these banks, but the customer may not be a known name in the market. By intermediating between the customer and the major market makers, these banks provide a valuable service to their customers.

Currency Cocktails

Over the past decade, the use of composite currencies such as the European Currency Unit (ECU) has become significant, both as an investment currency and in international trade. Many international companies operating in, or selling to, Europe nowadays invoice in ECU.

The ECU is made of a number of European currencies. The composition of the ECU is given in Figure 1.10 below. Each currency is given a fixed "weighting" according to the strength of its country's economy and its currency's value against the US dollars on a given base date.

Currency weightings are only changed every so often, whenever there is a currency re-alignment within the EMS (see below) or a new currency joins the basket. The weighting divided by the current USD rate of exchange (for sterling and the Irish punt, the rate of exchange must be *multiplied* by the weighting) gives the current dollar value of the currency within the basket. Having established the

ECU currency composition as at 21 September 1989

Fig 1.10

Currency	Weighting	Rate of Exchange	US$	Percent
German mark	0.6242	1.3906	=0.4489	33.5426%
French franc	1.332	4.8815	=0.2729	20.3915%
British pound	0.08784	1.5801	=0.1388	10.3714%
Italian lire	151.80	1626.75	=0.0933	6.9715%
Dutch guilder	0.2198	1.5571	=0.1412	10.5507%
Belgian franc	3.301	28.60	=0.1154	8.6229%
Danish krone	0.1976	5.4475	=0.0363	2.7124%
Spanish peseta	6.885	120.525	=0.0571	4.2666%
Portuguese escudo	1.393	146.500	=0.0095	0.7099%
Greek drachma	1.44	225.850	=0.0064	0.4782%
Irish punt	0.008552	1.6206	=0.0139	1.0386%
Lux. franc	0.13	28.60	=0.0046	0.3437
TOTAL			**=1.2303**	**100.0000**

total value of the ECU basket in US dollar terms, it is then possible to see the percentage contribution of each currency within it.

The ECU came into being in the early 1970s with the creation of the European Exchange Mechanism (ERM). Currencies which are members of the ERM are allowed to fluctuate within narrow bands around pre-defined "central rates" against the ECU, so the ECU is pivotal within the system. The ERM therefore reinforces the stability of the member currencies against the ECU.

Originally the ECU was only used as a unit of account by European Community institutions and for inter-governmental swap and credit facilities. Gradually it began to be recognized as an ideal invoicing currency (and a natural hedge) by companies operating within the European markets.

The advantage of invoicing in ECU, particularly for European-based firms, is a much lower level of currency exposure. For example, a 1% change in the USD/DEM rate causes only a 0.34% change in the ECU/USD rate: however, a 1% movement in the USD/DEM rate has a greater influence on the ECU/USD rate than a 1% move in the USD/ITL rate. To an extent, fluctuations in constituent currencies will tend to offset each other.

For trading purposes, all the major banks now provide banking facilities in ECUs and offer full services in spot and forward FX between the ECU and the dollar (the most common traffic route) or between the ECU and any constituent currency. A restricted ECU funds clearing system is provided by a handful of banks. Since there are no ECU notes or coins, ECU balances must be converted into a specific currency when these are cashed.

There is also an active market in fixed-interest, short-term deposits in ECU, where the interest rates are again a weighted average of Eurodeposit rates in the component currencies. This provides corporate treasurers in high-interest European countries with a cheaper funding instrument, which carries a much lower exchange risk.

In the capital markets, pan-European companies have found issuing ECU-denominated bonds to fund their subsidiaries preferable to issuing separate, single-currency instruments. Depending on progress achieved towards European Monetary Union the ECU (or "Euro", as it will be called) could become one of the top trading currencies by the next century.

The European Monetary System

The first attempt at European exchange rate management was in 1972, and was known as "the snake in the tunnel," because of the way rates looked as they rose and fell either side of their central rates. At the time, exchange rates were limited to a 1.25% movement either side of a central value against each other.

Due to large movements in currency caused by, among other things, the oil crisis of 1973 and the major variations in inflation rates of indifferent member states, it proved impossible to hold each currency within the confines of these narrow bands, and in 1974 the system fell apart.

When European economic stability returned in 1978, France and Germany made a second attempt at monetary co-operation, and in 1979 a new system came into effect: the European Monetary System, as it is known today.

The two key areas which came out of this revision are:

- the Exchange Rate Mechanism (ERM);
- the European Co-operation Fund (EMCF).

The ERM and Managed Rates

The ERM is a device by which member currencies' exchange rates are fixed against each other, at a bilateral central rate, in order to remove problems of currency instability. When it was first formed, each currency was allowed to deviate within a 2.25% band either side of the central rate which was set against all other member currencies. The ECU is also an ERM currency, but its divergence limits against individual currencies are tighter.

If two currencies move outside the permitted limits against each other, or against the ECU, then each member state's central bank must intervene and meet all bids and offers made to them by the market at the relevant rate. If this, together with domestic policy measures such as the raising of interest rates, has no effect, then the central exchange rate can be realigned, provided all other participants agree.

In order for member states to be able to defend their currency, a credit facility of sorts exists. The European Monetary Co-operation Fund (EMCF), which has now been renamed the European Monetary Institute (EMI), takes 20% of each member state's reserves of gold and dollars and puts them into a central pool, giving in return an equivalent amount of ECU and foreign currencies. If exchange rates come under pressure and central banks need to intervene, they can borrow from the fund to defend their exchange rates on the markets.

Not all currencies were kept within this 2.25% band. Prior to 1990 the Italian lira, Spanish peseta, and Portuguese escudo were allowed to operate within a 6% band, as did the British pound when it joined the ERM in October 1990 at a central rate equivalent to DM 2.95.

In 1992 the British pound and Italian lira found themselves coming under increasing selling pressure. Both currencies hit the bottom of their respective ERM bands in September. The lira devalued on 13 September, and a new central parity was fixed for it at a lower rate.

Over the next three days, the pound was sold heavily, with the Bank of England and other European central banks buying back as much as they could. On 16 September, UK interest rates were increased by 2% in an attempt to rally the pound. The government was determined not to let the pound be devalued.

Despite these attempts, the pound had fallen outside its permitted limit. The pressure on the Bank of England to buy back pounds became too great and the government was forced to act once again by increasing interest rates by another 2%, which took them to 15%. This was not enough, and by evening it was announced that sterling had been suspended from the ERM.

In 1993, there was heavy speculative pressure on ERM currencies, which overwhelmed the system. On 1 August, it was agreed by member states once again to widen the intervention bands, this time to 15% either side of the central rates. At the time of writing only the D-mark and the Dutch guilder still operate within the 2.25% band.

Currency Pairs

Within the ERM, there are few formally linked currency pairs. The D-mark and guilder have a written formal agreement, which makes them strongly correlated within the ERM.

There is evidence of informal links or "shadowing" within the ERM. For example, the Spanish peseta and the Portuguese escudo historically have had a close alliance. If the peseta comes under pressure from the D-mark, the escudo will also weaken to a greater or lesser degree. Other examples of shadowing are the D-mark against the Austrian schilling, and the Belgian franc against the D-mark. Although Britain is no longer confined within the ERM bands, its shadow the Irish punt (due to Ireland's strong economic ties with Britain) has experienced many difficulties staying within the mechanism.

Current Membership of the ERM

As at 6 March 1995, there are nine currencies participating in the ERM:

- Austrian schilling (AUS)
- Belgium/Luxembourg franc (BEL)
- Danish krona (DKK)

- Dutch guilder (NLG)
- French franc (FRF)
- German mark (DEM)
- Irish punt (IRP)
- Portuguese escudo (PTE)
- Spanish peseta (ESP)

The Greek drachma, Italian lira and the British pound, though constituents of the ECU, are all trading outside the ERM at the time of writing. Figure 1.11 details the current central parities of each currency against the ECU and against each other, as well as the intervention levels.

Market Regulation

The Eurocurrency markets have never been greatly regulated. Governments have always feared that without controls a relatively minor "accident" could easily snowball into global financial chaos. This almost happened in July 1974, when Herstadt Bankhaus, a small family bank in West Germany, overtraded in the FX market, forcing the Bundesbank to freeze its operations right in the middle of the day, when payments to and from Herstadt were still being processed.

Panic spread throughout the dealing rooms. Large depositors decided to deal only with the world's top ten or 15 banks, whose balance sheets were comfortably large. The problem was that those banks being offered deposits had no place to invest them, and those – the vast majority – who were not offered the deposits, were desperate for funds. The crisis occurred at a time of high inflation and soaring interest rates. Loan maturities right across the board shortened dramatically, and FX volume contracted.

Central banking authorities, especially in West Germany, have since taken steps to prevent a repetition of the Herstadt incident, but that bank's name has now been immortalized in the technical vocabulary to denote a specific type of risk.

Fig 1.11 **ECU central rates of currencies of EU member states and bilateral central rates and compulsory intervention rates for the currencies of the countries participating in the EMS exchange rate mechanism in force since 6 March 1995**

	ECU 1 =		BEF./ LUF100 =	DKK100 =	DEM100 =
BELGIUM/ LUXEMBOURG: BEF./LUF.	39.396	S C B	– – –	627.880 540.723 465.665	2395.20 2062.55 1776.20
DENMARK: DKK.	7.28580	S C B	21.4747 18.4938 15.9268	– – –	442.988 381.443 328.461
GERMANY: DEM.	1.91007	S C B	5.63000 4.84837 4.17500	30.4450 26.2162 22.5750	– – –
SPAIN: ESP.	162.493	S C B	478.944 412.481 355.206	2589.80 2230.27 1920.70	9878.50 8507.18 7326.00
FRANCE: FRF.	6.40808	S C B	18.8800 16.2608 14.0050	102.100 67.9257 75.7200	389.480 335.386 288.610
IRELAND: IEP.	0.792214	S C B	2.33503 2.01090 1.73178	12.6261 10.8734 9.36403	48.1698 41.4757 35.7143
NETHER- LANDS: NLG.	2.15214	S C B	6.34340 5.46286 4.70454	34.3002 29.5389 25.4385	(130.834)(2) 112.673 (07.0325)(2)
AUSTRIA ATS.	13.4383	S C B	39.6089 34.1107 29.3757	214.174 184.444 156.641	816.927 703.550 805.077
PORTUGAL PTE.	195.792	S C B	577.090 498.984 428.000	3120.50 2687.31 2314.30	11903.3 10250.6 8827.70
GREECE GRD.	292.867 (notional)				
ITALY: ITL.	2108.15 (notional)				
UNITED KINGDOM: GBP.	0.788652 (notional)				

ESP100 =	FRF100 =	IEP1 =	NLG100 =	ATS100 =	PTE100 =
28.1525	714.030	57.7445	2125.60	340.420	23.3645
24.2447	814.977	40.7289	1830.54	293.183	20.1214
20.8795	529.660	42.8260	1576.45	252.470	17.3285
5.20640	132.066	10.6792	393.105	62.9581	4.32100
4.48376	113.732	9.19676	338.537	54.2170	3.72119
3.86140	97.9430	7.92014	291.544	46.6910	3.20460
1.36500	34.6250	2.80000	(103.056)(2)	16.5050	1.13280
1.17548	29.6164	2.41105	86.7628	14.2136	0.976581
1.01230	25.6750	2.07800	(76.4328)(2)	12.2410	0.840100
–	2945.40	238.175	8767.30	1404.10	96.3870
–	2536.54	205.113	7550.30	1209.10	82.9927
–	2184.40	176.641	6502.20	1041.30	71.4890
4.57780	–	9.38050	345.850	65.3545	3.79920
3.94237	–	8.08631	297.661	47.6706	3.27168
3.39510	–	8.96400	256.350	41.0533	2.81770
0.586120	14.3599	–	42.7439	6.84544	0.469841
0.487537	12.3686	–	36.8105	5.89521	0.404620
0.419859	10.8500	–	31.7007	5.07688	0.348453
1.53793	39.0091	3.16450	–	18.5963	1.27637
1.32445	33.5953	2.71662	–	16.0149	1.09920
1.14060	28.9381	2.33962	–	13.7918	0.946611
9.00338	243.686	19.8971	725.086	–	7.97000
8.27008	209.773	18.9629	624.417	–	6.86358
7.12200	180.654	14.8082	537.740	–	5.91088
139.920	3549.00	286.083	10564.0	1691.80	–
120.493	3056.35	247.145	9097.55	1456.97	–
103.770	2632.10	212.836	7834.70	1254.70	–

These buying and selling rates are not operational. Reflecting a bilateral agreement between the German and Dutch monetary authorities, the following rates continue to apply: selling rate NLG 100 in Frankfurt: DEM 90.7700; buying rate NLG 100 in Frankfurt: DEM 86.7600; selling rate DEM 100 in Amsterdam: NLG 115.2350; buying rate DEM 100 in Amsterdam: NLG 110.1675.

S = Selling rate   C = Bilateral central rate   B = Buying rate

Source: European Monetary Institute, Paris

Herstadt risk, also known as settlement risk or clean risk, is the risk of loss arising from the settlement of an FX operation, whereby one of the counterparties to the trade fails after the other one has issued payment instructions.

In Part II, we shall examine how FX risks, including Herstadt risk, are managed in the dealing room. In Britain, major banks that participate in the Eurocurrency markets must work within guidelines set by the Supervisory Office of the Bank of England. They have to report on a daily basis their outstanding foreign currency positions and projected treasury cash flows. They must also satisfy the central bank that they have the internal systems necessary to process the volume of business and monitor the risks involved.

More recently, the Bank for International Settlements established clear guidelines for supervising the capital adequacy of international banks. The aim was to ensure that banks have sufficient capital resources to cover the risks on their operations, including FX.

The supervisors' dilemma remains one of imposing adequate controls to eliminate market excesses without at the same time stifling competition and innovation, which are the hallmarks of the Eurocurrency markets.

Market Integration

The last 20 years have seen an explosion in the use of derivative instruments, such as financial futures and options, which offer protection against the effects of interest and exchange rate volatility.

The net effect of these developments has been to render more transparent the linkages between the domestic and international markets and also between the FX and the money markets. More than ever before, the foreign exchange trader has to be aware of developments taking place in other related markets.

The ACI and the National Forex Associations

The ACI is the Association Cambiste Internationale – the Forex Markets Association. It was founded in France in 1955 by an agreement between the Forex Associations in Paris and London. Other national Forex Associations were soon formed and there are now Forex Associations affiliated to the ACI in 54 countries with a membership totalling more than 25,000 people. The ACI has the largest membership of any of the international associations in the wholesale financial markets. The secretariat of the organization is based in Paris.

The ACI Institute is the educational arm of the ACI. It was founded in London in 1994. It is currently developing a portfolio of examinations aimed at new entrants to the industry. The aim is to provide benchmarks for treasury dealers, and those providing support to dealers, about what they should learn during the first two or three years of their careers. The examinations are designed to be at about the same level of difficulty as that found in the first or second year of an undergraduate degree.

You will find details of the curriculum provided by the ACI in Appendix 6 on page 395.

Summary

In this introductory chapter, we outlined the framework, structure and history of today's FX and money markets, in particular the emergence of the Eurocurrency markets. We traced the evolution of the exchange rate systems from the Gold Standard up to the present-day European Exchange Rate Mechanism.

We then reviewed the major participants in these markets. Finally, we looked briefly at market regulation and the role of the ACI and the national Forex Associations.

Keywords

Before proceeding to the next section, please be sure that you are familiar with the following key terms and their definitions:

- "over the counter" (OTC) markets
- the Gold Standard
- the Bretton-Woods Agreement
- the Smithsonian Agreement
- Eurodollars/Eurocurrencies
- SWIFT and currency ISO codes
- market makers
- interbank brokers
- the Exchange Rate Mechanism
- the European Monetary System
- European Currency Unit
- Herstadt risk
- the ACI.

Review Questions

1. What are Eurodollars?

   a. Dollars held by European banks

   b. Dollars held by banks outside the jurisdiction of the US banking authorities

   c. Dollar transactions which are not subject to the same regulations as those governing domestic dollar transactions

   d. None of the above

2. Which of the following post-war regulations did *not* directly contribute to the growth of the Eurodollar market?

   a. US Regulation Q

   b. US Interest Equalization Tax

   c. US Foreign Credit Restraint Program

   d. The Bretton-Woods Agreement

3. Gold was the traditional means of establishing a currency's value. When did gold cease to be officially "tied" to the US dollar?

   a. Gold ceased to be tied at US$38 an ounce in 1973, when the major currencies began to float.

   b. Gold ceased to be officially tied at US$35 an ounce on 1 August 1971.

   c. Gold was never really tied to the dollar after World War II because an individual could not in practice exchange cash for gold at the official price.

   d. Gold ceased to be tied at US$38 per lb. on 31 March 1972.

4. Which security was developed as a negotiable form of Euro-deposit?

   a. Eurobonds

   b. Treasury bills

   c. London negotiable CDs

   d. Syndicated credits

5. Which of the following groups do not normally take positions in the FX markets?

   a. Brokers

   b. Central banks

   c. Governments

   d. Commercial banks

6. Which of the following currencies is not a member of the ERM (as at 1 May 1996)?

   a. Spanish peseta

   b. French franc

   c. Swedish krona

   d. D-mark

7. Which of the following currencies is not a constituent in of the ECU (as at 1 May 1996)?

   a. Portuguese escudo

   b. Greek drachma

   c. D-mark

   d. Swiss franc

Part 2

Spot FX

■ ■ ■

"The idea of buying and selling money with money seems unnatural to many people."

Market Concepts

In this chapter, we introduce the following fundamental FX market concepts:

- settlement date;
- two-way prices;
- direct and reciprocal quotation;
- the bid–offer spread.

The focus here is on the spot FX markets; Forward FX is covered in Part IV of this book.

Settlement Date

A spot deal is a transaction in which one currency is exchanged directly for another for settlement usually in two working days.

Over two-thirds of all the business transacted in the FX market is for spot settlement or "spot value." The remainder is either for "forward" or "ante-spot" settlement.

Example On Wednesday, the FX dealer at Bank A in London agrees to sell spot US dollars to Bank B's dealer in Frankfurt, in exchange for D-marks. On Friday, Bank A's D-mark account in Frankfurt is credited with the marks; Bank B's US dollar account in New York is credited with the dollars.

If the deal had been done on Thursday, instead of Wednesday, then the spot date would have been Monday: weekends and holidays in either financial centre are skipped over. In some Middle Eastern markets, where Friday is a non-working day, the foreign currency side of the spot transaction may be settled on the Friday ("with recourse"), but the local currency is settled on Saturday which is a working day.

Forward transactions are contracts to exchange one currency for another at some future date, other than spot, at a price or rate of exchange which is determined on the trade date.

The purpose of forward deals is to establish and fix the cost of exchange for a known FX commitment at some future date. Forward deals are covered in detail in Part IV of this book.

Two-Way Prices

The idea of buying and selling money with money seems unnatural to many people. Certainly it can be confusing because, unlike our everyday purchases of goods and services, two prices are quoted rather than one. Despite these complications, you will see that the same basic principles apply.

The buyer of a product or commodity normally tries to obtain it at the lowest possible price. The purchase of foreign currency is exactly the same. The traveler, when buying the currency of the country that he intends to travel to, tries to obtain as much of that currency as possible, while at the same time spending the smallest amount of his own currency. Put simply, he wants to buy the foreign currency at the cheapest available price.

So what is the source of confusion? The fact is that by buying foreign currency you are of course selling your own country's currency at the same time. The process of buying and selling money is an act of exchanging one currency for another.

When the traveler returns from his journey he may still have some foreign currency left over, which in his own country will not be acceptable for normal day-to-day payment. The traveler must therefore sell the foreign currency and buy back his own local currency. Naturally he wants to obtain as much of his own currency as possible. The traveler is now a seller of foreign currency, and a buyer of his own country's currency. The bank, travel agent or exchange bureau must therefore publish two prices. The first price will determine the rate of exchange for a buy–sell transaction; the second will determine the rate of exchange for a sell–buy transaction.

All of this is familiar to any traveler. Similar principles also apply in the professional market, where banks and other operators trade in

Two-way foreign exchange prices

Fig 3.1

Allbank (London) plc		
	We buy GB£	We sell GB£
D-marks	2.6540	2.6545
Japanese yen	240.50	240.75
Swiss francs	2.5035	2.5045

larger amounts: a genuine market maker will always quote a two-way price, regardless of the market conditions. However, confusion may still occur because of the different manner in which exchange rates may be quoted.

Direct and Reciprocal Quotation

In the United States, foreign exchange rates in many bureaus are quoted in the same way as the price of any product or service. That is to say, prices are expressed in dollars and cents. For example, the price of a calculator might be US$29.95, a bar of chocolate might cost 45 cents, and a D-mark might cost 71 cents. When the price of another currency in the United States is expressed in terms of dollars, it is said to be in "American terms." Similarly, when foreign currency in France is expressed in terms of francs, it is said to be in "French terms," and so on. This is the direct method of quoting foreign exchange.

In the United Kingdom, foreign exchange rates are quoted in "foreign terms," using the "indirect" or "reciprocal" method. This shows the foreign currency equivalent of one pound sterling – in effect, the value of the pound abroad (see Figure 3.1).

If the reciprocal method were applied to the example above, in which DM 1 = 71 US cents, then we could calculate the US$1 = DM 1.41. The calculation is as follows:

$$US\$1 = \boxed{\frac{1}{0.71}} = DM\ 1.41$$

The two quotations should express the same thing but from two different perspectives. The rate of exchange USD/DEM 1.41 is the reciprocal of the rate of exchange DEM/USD 0.71.

It should be noted that a quotation is direct or reciprocal depending on the country quoting the rate. Thus, a direct quotation in the USA is considered a reciprocal quotation from the point of view of other countries.

A note on currency pair conventions:

Throughout this book we shall follow the convention adopted by the ACI to denote a currency pair: two currency

SWIFT codes separated by an oblique, the first currency being the base currency.

For example, USD/DEM denotes the dollars against D-marks with the dollar as the base currency (vocalized as "dollar/mark").

GBP/CHF ("sterling/swissy") denotes sterling against Swiss francs, with sterling as the base currency.

The Bid-Offer Spread

When looking at two-way currency rates as in Figure 3.1, two basic rules will help you to avoid confusion.

Rule 1: Establish which is the base currency

The base currency is also known as the reference or unit currency. It is represented by the unit not normally shown in the quotation.

In a USD/DEM quotation of 1.41, for example, the base currency is dollars, since USD 1 = DEM 1.41. The numbers that represent the price and are always shown in the quotation are given in terms of the "counter-currency" or "rate currency." In this example the price is DEM 1.41, so the counter-currency is D-marks.

Rule 2: The market maker buys the base currency at the rate shown on the left hand side.

The market maker is the person who posts the rates; the market user is the person who takes those rates as given.

In a two-way FX quotation the market maker buys the base currency at the first rate shown, the rate on the left as you see it. This is true whether the quotation is direct or reciprocal. The second rate shown is the rate at which he is selling the base currency.

In the interbank market, which normally deals in amounts of US$1 million and more, rates are usually quoted to five or six significant figures. The D-mark, for example, is usually quoted to the nearest 100th of a pfennig.

Suppose an FX dealer is quoting the following rates:

USD/DEM 1.4145–1.4150

RULE 1: The number not shown is USD 1, so the dollar is the unit currency. The numbers represent the amount of DEM per USD.

RULE 2: The dealer will buy one dollar and pay DEM 1.4145, and he will sell one dollar and charge DEM 1.4150.

The rate on the left is called the bid (the rate at which the base currency is bought). The rate on the right is the offer or ask (the rate the base currency is sold).

Another dealer is quoting:

DEM/USD 0.7067–0.7070

RULE 1: The number not shown is DEM 1 so DEM is the unit currency. The numbers represent the amount of USD per DEM 1.

RULE 2: The dealer will buy 1 DEM and sell USD 0.7067 and sell 1 DEM and buy USD 0.7070.

> **If as a market user you are quoted two rates, the higher rate is the amount you will have to pay, and the lower rate is the amount you will receive for the base currency.**

Figure 2.2 shows spot rates as they might appear in page FXFX on the Reuters network. Only the latest quotation identifies the contributor, with the time of entry and a further Reuters page reference for fuller details. The previous quotation is also shown ("small figures" only, see page 50), together with the high and low for the day.

> **The market maker's bid/offer spread is the difference between the rate at which the unit currency is bought and the rate at which it is sold.**

The spread represents the risk of pricing the exchange of two currencies at a given moment in time. The greater the risk, the wider the spread. The time between a price being agreed and the contract being completed (settlement taking place) will have a direct impact on the extent of the risk involved.

Spot rates on Reuters page FXFX

Fig 3.2

```
Reuters : Quotes : FXFX
Function  Edit  Screens  Format  View  Setup  Help

1013 CCY PAGE NAME * REUTER SPOT RATES      * CCY HI*EURO*LO FXFX
1013 DEM BCIX B.C.I.        MIL 1.5279/84   * DEM  1.5306   1.5260
1013 GBP MMDB HSBC MIDLAND  LON 1.5514/21   * GBP  1.5547   1.5486
1013 CHF DRBX DRESDNER      FFT 1.2532/42   * CHF  1.2550   1.2508
1013 JPY UBZA UBS           ZUR 108.70/80   * JPY  108.80   108.25
1012 FRF MMDB HSBC MIDLAND  LON 5.1725/75   * FRF  5.1797   5.1695
1013 NLG BAXX BARCLAYS      LON 1.7106/16   * NLG  1.7127   1.7092
1013 ITL BAXX BARCLAYS      LON 1542.80/4.30* ITL 1545.42 1539.58
1013 ECU XIMU IMI BANK      LUX 1.2387/90   * ECU  1.2403   1.2360
-----------------------------------------------------------------
XAU CSBL 390.15/390.55 * ED3  5.37/ 5.50 * FED    PREB * LGVS 30Y
XAG CSBL   5.37/ 5.38  * US30Y YTM 7.01  * 5.50- 5.75 * 87.14-15
```

Dealer Conversation – Spot Deal

Dealers in the professional FX market have their own specialized jargon. A typical conversation between two dealers is illustrated below (the date is Wednesday, 10 July).

Bank A: "Hi friends, spot dollar mark please?"

Bank B: "45-50."

Bank A: "At 45 I sell five dollars."

Bank B: "OK, done. I buy 5 million dollars at 1.4145 for 12 July and sell you 7,072,500 marks. My dollars to Citi New York, please. For you?"

Bank A: "My marks to Deutsche Bank Frankfurt. Thanks for deal."

This deal would have taken about 20 seconds to execute. There are some key points to note in this conversation:

● Bank B is the "market maker" showing firm rates, and Bank A is the "market user".

- If Bank A felt it could do better elsewhere it might say "nothing there, thank you."

- Bank B is buying dollars at 1.4145 marks and selling dollars at 1.4150. The 1.41 part of the rate is called the "big figure" and is assumed – only the "small figures" are mentioned.

- Dealers in the professional market normally trade the base currency (here, dollars) in round amounts against the quoted currency (here, marks). This makes things simpler: the higher the figure quoted, the more valuable are the dollars being traded.

- The deal has been agreed on Wednesday, 10 July and (since it is a spot deal) it will be settled on Friday, 12 July.

- Once Bank A "hit the bid," the other party took the trouble to spell out exactly what was agreed. A legal contract has in fact been established.

If Bank A has made a mistake – such as hitting the wrong side of the price – Bank B is not obliged to undo the deal, although they may be helpful if the market has not moved too much.

Assuming the deal has been correctly executed, each side will complete a deal ticket such as the one illustrated in Figure 3.3. Or,

Fig 3.3

A typical deal slip

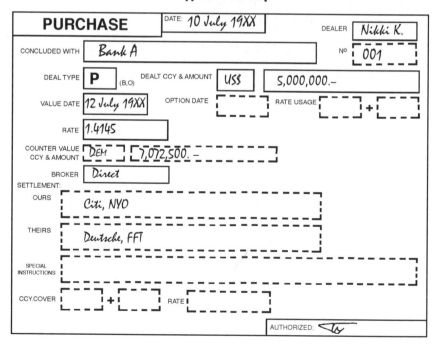

increasingly, they will input the same information into an on-line "front-office" dealing and position keeping system.

Summary

In this chapter, we have examined fundamental FX market concepts such as the types of settlement date and quotation, and two-way prices. We then looked at a typical conversation between two dealers, so as to introduce dealers' jargon.

Before moving on, please make sure that you are familiar with the following terms and their definitions:

Keywords

- spot settlement
- base currency
- direct/reciprocal quotation
- bid/offer spread
- market maker
- market user
- to hit the bid
- take/lift the offer
- big figure
- small figure.

■ ■ ■

*"The focus here
is on the rationale
behind the credit
limits that apply
to FX dealing."*

FX Operations

4

Overview   In this chapter we look briefly at FX operations – what happens after a deal has been made. Besides looking at the various stages of an FX transaction, we will examine trading risks and position limits.

The FX Transaction Work Flow

Figure 4.1 sets out all the steps normally involved in an FX transaction. This follows a deal from the date the contract is made, known as the trade date, through settlement on the value date, to the subsequent reconciliation process.

Fig 4.1

FX transaction work flow

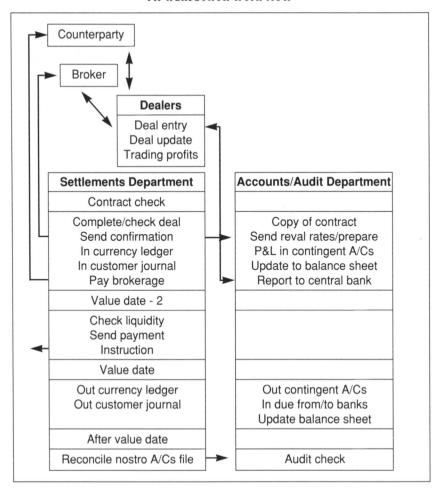

On the Contract Date

- Dealers fill a manual or electronic deal slip.
- Settlements departments check deal slip for inconsistencies, fill in any missing details and send confirmation to the counterparty.
- Settlements check inward confirmation from counterparty.
- If the deal was done via a broker, Settlements credit brokerage account and confirmation to be received from that broker.
- Settlements post two entries in their forex ledgers: IN customer ledger and IN the foreign currency ledger.

Near to the Value Date

- Settlements ensure there will be adequate funding in nostro account on the value date to cover the deal. ("Nostro" account means "our" payments account with another bank. "Vostro" means another bank's account with us).
- Settlements send SWIFT or telex payment instructions to correspondent bank where nostro account is held.

On the Value Date

- Settlements update entries in their forex ledgers: OUT customer ledger and IN nostro ledgers.

After the Value Date

- Settlements reconcile nostro account statement received from agent bank with their own ledgers.
- Throughout the process the bank's Audit Department monitors at arm's length the integrity of the data and makes dual entries in the bank's balance sheet.

The separation of audit from treasury operations, and of dealers from the settlement area, is the key to the control of an area of business which can potentially make significant profits or losses for the bank.

The Settlements Department itself is often viewed as a bureaucratic backwater, far removed from the cut-and-thrust realities of the front office. Moreover, sandwiched as it is between the dealing and control functions, it often gets the blame; rarely any credit. However, deal checking and reconciliation, tedious though they are, are vital to the business as many banks have discovered to their cost. Generating high dealing volumes without the support to ensure prompt and error-free delivery can be more costly than not generating any business at all.

Foreign Exchange Risks

Understanding and managing risk are the key to successful FX dealing. The first two types of risk discussed in this section fall under the broad heading of "credit" (or "counterparty") risk; they relate to what could happen to a position if the counterparty, for whatever reason, were unable to honour its side of a deal.

To a large extent, credit risks are external to the treasury; they must be controlled by limiting the commitments outstanding from any named counterparty, by means of credit limits, country limits or counterparty dealing lines. Credit analysis is the domain of a specialist department outside the dealing room, and the subject is outside the scope of this book. The focus here is on the rationale behind the credit limits that apply to FX dealing.

Delivery Risk

When an FX deal is made, there is a risk that once the payment instruction on your side has gone out, the counterparty might fail to honour its side of the contract. The risk here is on 100% of the contract amount – similar in fact to the risk on a loan. This is also known as "settlement" or "Herstadt risk," after the infamous banking collapse of 1974. (Some people also call it "clean risk.")

Measuring the delivery risk on FX transactions is easy: the problem is that taking 100% of the amount dealt out of a dealing line would very quickly "fill up the line." Because delivery loss in FX operations is in fact extremely rare, it is legitimate to give a lower risk weighting to FX delivery than to loan default. However, rather than fixing an arbitrary weighting, the common practice is to control this risk by limiting the amount which can be settled with a given counterparty on any given date, regardless of when the deal or deals were done.

Replacement Risk

This refers to the risk that a given counterparty may be wound up before a contract reaches its delivery date, in which case you may have to find an alternative counterparty with which to cover your position at the now prevailing market rates. What is at risk here is not the principal amount (since no actual payment will be made to the counterparty) but any profit on the position.

Suppose a bank has made two opposite FX deals to produce a matching position. If one of the counterparties fails before the settlement date, there is a potential loss from having to cover the remaining deal with a new one at less advantageous rates.

The replacement loss will depend on the extent to which the spot rate may have moved since the dealing date. The length of time between dealing date and settlement will clearly have a direct impact on the amount of risk involved. Estimating replacement risk therefore requires the use of statistical techniques to estimate the extent of market price volatility over time.

In the case of spot transactions with only two days to settlement, replacement risk will be a small fraction of the amount dealt. Typical risk weightings vary between 3% and 5%. For example, if your Credit Control Department has established a US$50 million dealing line with Bank A; then, on a 5% weighting, you could theoretically deal up to US$1 billion for value spot, although daily settlement or other limits might in practice not allow you to go this far.

In calculating the risk on spot transactions, different volatility estimates (and therefore different risk weightings) may be given to different currency pairs. For example, deals involving two members of the European Exchange Rate Mechanism (ERM) may be given a lower risk weighting compared with deals involving ERM currencies and the USD, or non-ERM currencies.

Position Risk

Also known as market or price risk, this is the risk of loss resulting from an adverse movement in market rates on an open position. As long as a position remains open, there is a risk that the market rates may move against us and turn a profitable position into a loss – or a loss into an even bigger loss. A dealer who has a square position (total sales equal total purchases) is not subject to position risk.

Example

At 10:00 hours we buy US$5 million spot from Bank A at 1.4145 DEM. We are "long 5 million dollars."

By noon the dollar has weakened and we sell US$5 million at 1.4112 to Bank C, thus "squaring our position" in dollars.

Our profit is given by the following calculation

Profit = –DM5m × 1.4145 + DM5m × 1.4112
= –DM7,072,500.00 + DM7,056,000
= –DM16,500.00

In US dollars:

= –US$16,500.00/1.4112
= –US$11,692.18

The bank's FX position is its net cash flow (long or short) in foreign currency, regardless of settlement date. The net FX position includes not only unmatured spot deals but also net forward FX positions, if any, as well as cleared balances held in foreign currency accounts, such as nostro accounts, which are used for day-to-day settlements. In effect, the FX position broadly defined covers transaction exposures – the FX risk on future currency payments and receipts – as well as translation exposures – fluctuations in the local currency value of foreign currency assets and liabilities.

Within the spot dealing area, position risk is typically controlled by limiting the amount by which a dealer can be short or long in his currency. This limit is set according to how much capital a bank can afford to risk on FX operations. Once a total exposure limit has been established for the bank as a whole, it is then allocated among different currency groups, treasury units and dealers according to the strategic importance of each currency and trading location, the dealers' experience, and other factors.

Position limits are not just a matter of internal concern to a bank. To maintain orderly markets it is imperative that no market player should find itself over-traded. The Bank for International Settlements, which is the main regulatory body in the Eurocurrency markets, requires banks to retain a minimum ratio of 12% of capital to "weighted risk assets" in their balance sheets. Only 1% of the amounts outstanding on FX operations, with a maturity of less than one year, are included in the risk assets total (whereas loans to non-bank private sector entities, for example, must be included 100%). In practice, most banks apply higher risk weightings for spot FX, as we have seen.

Overnight Positions

Both daylight and overnight position limits are typically set for each trader. In London, the Bank of England's report on Net Open Positions is designed to monitor the overnight FX risk of the banks under its supervision. It is defined as the sterling sum of short positions in all currency pairs. The permissible overnight limit is a matter of individual agreement between the Bank of England and each market maker under its supervision.

Banks take different approaches to overnight positions:

- Some square all positions by the end of each day (in some countries this is a central bank requirement).
- Others pass currency books from one money centre which is about to close to another which is still open for business.
- Others still leave open positions overnight but place "stop-loss orders" with correspondent banks abroad, or require dealers to get up in the middle of the night, if necessary, to place orders.

Those banks which either pass or leave open spot positions overnight have to roll these positions over in order to avoid having to take cash delivery or make currency payments. The overnight roll-over of a spot position is discussed in detail in Part IV.

Liquidity Risk

Some allowance must also be made in the position limits for varying degrees of market liquidity in different currency zones, which affect the ease with which positions can be re-matched, or closed in a hurry.

A bank may also break down its total FX position limit for any given currency by value date or range of dates. By imposing limits on the maturity structure of its FX exposure, the bank ensures that not all of its commitments are concentrated in a narrow segment of the market. This is another dimension of the need to spread the risks: it is very important in the structuring of forward books but also it applies to positions which mature the next day, or to positions in cash, as opposed to spot.

Amount/Cash Risk

The interbank market is a wholesale market and it is worth concluding this section with a brief description of certain risks which apply only at the retail end of the market.

For small amounts, market makers tend to widen their spreads to allow for the fact that any contract may have to be combined with other small deals, struck at different rates, before it can be covered in the market. This widening of the spread is partly designed to cover "amount risk." The wider spreads on currency rates at exchange bureaus and bank branches also reflect the high cost of handling and transporting notes and coin (which do not earn interest). So there is a "cash risk" as well.

Summary

In this chapter, we began by looking at the various stages of a typical FX transaction. We then examined the types of risk associated with FX dealing, and some of the techniques used for controlling them.

Before proceeding to the next chapter, please be sure that **Keywords** you are familiar with the following key terms and their definitions:

- nostro account
- vostro account
- counterparty or credit risk
- settlement risk
- replacement risk
- position risk
- liquidity risk.

■ ■ ■

"Changes in the timing of payments for imports and exports can set off major trends in the FX markets."

Reading The Markets

Overview There are a number of background factors which experienced FX dealers take into account when managing their positions. This is part of the skill and discipline of being able to read the market. The treatment here is suggestive rather than comprehensive – reading the markets is a whole science (and art) in itself, and the subject lies beyond the scope of this book.

Leads and Lags in Trade

Changes in the timing of payments for imports and exports can set off major trends in the FX markets.

For example, if the dollar looks fundamentally weak, US importers have an incentive to buy foreign currency sooner to meet future commitments, rather than wait for the payment date when it might be more expensive. But exporters with foreign currency receivables will want to hold on to those currencies rather than convert into dollars.

Conversely, if the dollar looks firm, importers will delay purchasing foreign currency, while exporters will speed up their receivables. FX dealers can ride on the back of such sentiment to conduct profitable trading campaigns.

Example The dealers in a Japanese bank see a surge in customer demand for yen. They decide to sell ("go short") dollars against yen, in anticipation. Selling pressure on the dollar makes for an even stronger yen as the rest of the market begins to turn.

A few hours later the dealers who started the movement buy back their dollars at a lower rate against the yen. They close their position at a profit. This sets off a movement in the opposite direction and the dollar starts to recover.

Speculative campaigns like this one are very risky. The rest of the market may have felt that the dollar remained fundamentally strong, and might have been only too glad to buy dollars. Central banks may intervene in the markets at any time to stabilize the currency. Buying pressure can easily become too great for any single bank to take on.

The most valuable asset in this market is information.

A bank must know when a deal is trade-related, and when it is speculative. A purely trade-related deal with a customer is unlikely to be reversed in the short term, because the currency has been used to make a payment. But a speculative deal may signal a change in market sentiment and may be reversed in minutes.

The keenest market players offer good rates of exchange to customers to see which way they are moving and to gain an insight into corporate thinking. Few corporate deals are wholly trade-related or wholly speculative. Typically a situation arises requiring an FX transaction (such as an export or import order). The treasury function within a corporation then has some leeway over the timing of the FX deal which will cover the business.

Determinants of Currency Rates

At any time there will be people in the market willing to buy and sell currency. The rate of exchange is the price, at which the amount of the currency bought exactly matches the amount sold.

If the demand for yen by dollar holders is greater than the supply, competition between traders will drive the yen rate upwards. Conversely, when the supply of yen is greater than the demand, the dollar value of the yen will fall.

Behind supply and demand lie a variety of factors operating at different levels.

Fundamental Factors

These refer to the underlying economic and financial conditions of the country:

- the balance of payments;
- interest rates and inflation;
- leading and lagging indicators;

- economic growth and capacity utilization;
- fiscal deficits and the money supply;
- reporting delays and market expectations.

Statistics on these items are reported regularly – typically monthly or quarterly. The dates and times of their release are in most cases known to the market and are keenly anticipated.

The dealer must be aware of what the market is expecting. Without this the published statistics have no context. What is important is not what the textbooks say, but how the rest of the market, rightly or wrongly, is likely to react.

The quality of reported statistics is often very poor. Many of the figures which are closely watched are aggregates of a number of components, each of which is subject to error. Some sources publish provisional figures first, based on just a sample of returns. These may be subject to significant subsequent revision.

In some cases, the errors tend to average out. However some figures, such as the trade or fiscal balances, represent differences between some very large quantities. Small revisions in one of the components can lead to major changes in the result. The experienced dealer must also be aware that blatant reporting errors do occur from time to time.

Institutional Factors

This refers to the policy framework surrounding the currency – exchange controls, fixed parities, the European Monetary System, international agreements.

Fixed Exchange Rates

After World War II, rates of exchange between the currencies of the major industrial nations were pegged under the Bretton Woods Agreement. The system worked successfully for many years, during which time currencies traded within very narrow ranges. However fixed parities came under increasing pressure in the late 1960s, as countries pursued divergent economic policies. It finally broke down in 1971 when the US ceased convertibility of the dollar into gold.

Under the fixed-exchange rate system, central banks agree to maintain their currencies within a narrow band of fluctuations. If pressures develop and rates move to the lowest price allowed within the band, the central bank must intervene; it acts as a buffer between the supply and demand of the currency. Therefore a country's official foreign-currency reserves increase when there is strong demand for its currency. Conversely, if demand for foreign currency exceeds the supply available in the open market, foreign reserves will decrease.

Floating Exchange Rates

Under a floating-exchange-rate regime, currencies are freely convertible into one another at rates which are largely determined by market forces. There is no such thing as a pure floating-currency regime. Large amounts of liquid funds can quickly move from one currency to another causing undesirable volatility in the currency which governments will act to avoid; but central bank intervention is limited to maintaining reasonably orderly markets, without any attempt to defend a specific rate. Any imbalance between supply and demand will be settled through changes in the relative value of the currencies. In cases of serious instability, the central bank will adjust domestic financial conditions, for example, by raising or lowering interest rates to make the return on their currency more or less attractive.

Floating exchange rates make international trade much riskier, and inhibit economic growth. After the collapse of Bretton Woods, a group of European nations (notably West Germany, France and Italy) sought to find an alternative mechanism to reduce the volatility of their currencies. The result was the creation of the European Exchange Rate Mechanism (ERM).

Technical Factors

Technical analysis is concerned with the study of the dynamics of market trends, once they are under way, rather than with the supply and demand factors which cause them.

Technical analysis is the study of how the market moves, rather than why it moves.

Technical analysts search for psychological "resistance" and "support" levels in currency prices. They look for recurring patterns in price charts ("head and shoulders," "double bottoms," "triangles," and so on), which may signal a change in market trend. They track the quality and strength of a trend using moving averages and indicators of market momentum.

Summary

In this chapter, we have seen that a key to successful FX dealing is being able to anticipate market trends. We then examined some of the fundamental, institutional and technical factors which dealers take into account when reading the market.

Keywords   Before concluding this chapter, please be sure that you are familiar with the following terms and their definitions:

- trade-related/speculative deal
- fundamental factors
- technical analysis

The exercise in Chapter 6 will give you useful practice in reviewing the material presented so far.

Review Questions

1. If today is Thursday 12 December, what is the spot date?

    a. 14 December
    b. 15 December
    c. 16 December
    d. 17 December

2. When is your delivery risk greatest on an FX deal done for value spot?

    a. Today
    b. Tomorrow
    c. On the settlement day
    d. Always the same each day

3. Deutsche Bank has a sterling account with Midland Bank in London. This account is:

    a. Deutsche's vostro with Midland
    b. Deutsche's nostro with Midland
    c. Midland's nostro with Deutsche
    d. None of the above

4. The Chief Dealer at Bank A sells US$ 10 million from Bank B, and himself issues the confirmation of the transaction.

    a. This is correct because as Chief Dealer he must take responsibility for all trades.

    b. This incorrect because confirmations should be issued independently by the back office.

    c. This is correct because the ACI rules require that Chief Dealers initial all confirmation notes.

    d. This is incorrect because as the buyer, Bank B should issue its confirmation note first.

5. Convert the rates of exchange quoted below into the reciprocal rates of exchange.

    a. GBP/DEM 2.9550 – 2.9555   DEM/GBP _____.

    b. USD/FRF 5.2630 – 5.2645   FRF/USD _____

    c. ECU/USD 1.2325 – 1.2335   USD/ECU _____

    d. DEM/CHF 0.8245 – 0.8248   CHF/DEM _____

    e. DEM/JP 98.75 – 98.85   JP/DEM _____

6. Calculate in each case the amount of US dollars that would be paid or received by a market user for the amounts of foreign exchange currency listed below using the quoted rate of exchange that has been underlined (all rates of exchange are to US$ = 1).

Currency	Amount	Rate of Exchange
DM ·	5,000,000	1.3545 – <u>1.3550</u>
¥	120,000,000	<u>141.75</u> – 141.95
GB£	2,000,000	<u>0.5235</u> – 0.5240
SwFr	10,000,000	1.3257 – <u>1.3263</u>
L	1,000,000,000	<u>1273.8</u> – 1274.8

a. DM5 million would be .... at the rate of 1.3550
    and US$ .... would be ....

b. ¥120 million would be .... at a rate of 141.75
    and US$ .... would be ....

c. GB£2 million would be .... at a rate of 0.5235
    and US$ .... would be ....

d. SwFr10 million would be .... at a rate of 1.3263
    and US$ .... would be ....

e. L1,000 million would be .... at a rate of 1273.8
    and US$ .... would be ....

7. Which of the following is not an objective of position keeping?

    a. Monitoring counterparty risk
    b. Calculating P&L
    c. Measuring market exposure
    d. Calculating average book rate

8. Which of the following is not a limit to control market risk?

    a. Overnight position limit
    b. Stop-loss limit
    c. Forward gap limit
    d. Counterparty limit

9. In this exercise, you are given two-way prices for either US$ or GB£ against a range of counter-currencies quoted by six market makers. You have to identify the best rate available to you as a market user.

    Example:
    USD/DEM
    Dealer A   1.4539/44
    Dealer B   1.4540/45
    Dealer C   1.4538/46
    Dealer D   1.4541/46
    Dealer E   1.4543/48

    From which dealer would you buy US dollars?

    Answer: Dealer A

(1) GB£/US$

Dealer A	Dealer B	Dealer C	Dealer D	Dealer E	Dealer F
1.9505/15	1.9507/17	1.9500/10	1.9502/12	1.9503/13	1.9506/16

To which dealer would you sell GB£?

Answer: _____

(2) US$/JP

Dealer A	Dealer B	DealerC	Dealer D	Dealer E	Dealer F
129.95/10	129.90/05	129.93/08	129.92/07	129.89/04	129.91/06

To which dealer would you sell US$?

Answer: _____

(3) US$/CHF

Dealer A	Dealer B	Dealer C	Dealer D	Dealer E	Dealer F
1.3922/32	1.3920/30	1.3924/34	1.3919/29	1.3926/36	1.3923/33

From which dealer would you buy US$?

Answer: _____

(4) US$/FRF

Dealer A	Dealer B	Dealer C	Dealer D	Dealer E	Dealer F
6.2169/79	6.2160/70	6.2165/75	6.2159/69	6.2161/71	6.2163/73

To which dealer would you sell US$?

Answer: _____

(5) US$/DEM

Dealer A	Dealer B	Dealer C	Dealer D	Dealer E	Dealer F
1.4539/44	1.4540/45	1.4538/46	1.4541/46	1.4542/47	1.4543/48

To which dealer would you sell US$?

Answer: _____

(6) GB£/US$

Dealer A	Dealer B	Dealer C	Dealer D	Dealer E	Dealer F
1.9505/15	1.9507/17	1.9500/10	1.9502/12	1.9503/13	1.9506/16

From which dealer would you buy GB£?

Answer: _____

(7) US$/JP

Dealer A	Dealer B	Dealer C	Dealer D	Dealer E	Dealer F
129.95/10	129.90/05	129.93/08	129.92/07	129.89/04	129.91/06

From which dealer would you buy US$?

Answer: _____

■ ■ ■

" . . . since FX dealing is not a precise science, successful market makers need a combination of information, experience and, of course, the ability to bluff."

Making a Market

Overview   In this chapter we will look at how to make a market in currencies for spot delivery. The question to consider is how to decide what you are prepared to quote to the market.

- A key factor is the nature of your position. If you are long in a currency, you are a potential seller, and this will influence the price you are prepared to quote to attract buyers. If you are short, then you are a potential buyer.

- Another major consideration is what is likely to happen to supply and demand for your currency.

Fundamentals

The FX dealer is constantly bombarded with facts and rumours relating to the state of the economy, changes in prices, indicators of future economic activity, and monetary growth. Success will depend on the ability to sort out the relevant from the irrelevant.

The dealer's position and his interpretation of market forces are very important, but the key factor when making a market is the current market price. Dealers have to consider the market consensus and place their individual price or rate of exchange "around" the market price to achieve their goal.

Quoting a rate of exchange which is out of the market is not normally accepted by other market participants or the central banks, and may cost you your job. After all, dealing at off-market prices could be a way of temporarily hiding position losses by passing the losses to a friend in the market.

Professional market-makers do not charge a handling commission when they deal with other principals directly (although they pay a fee if they act through a broker). Making profits depends entirely on quoting the right rates to create profitable trading positions. The dealer's skill in making a price quickly and profitably is developed by experience. It requires considerable practice to identify the best prices available and then to quote more competitively.

Using the Spread

The dealer's first line of defence is the bid–offer spread. The market maker's spread contains an assessment of the likely cost of reversing an unwanted position, but this time as a market user.

It is late in the day and you have squared your dollar–mark position, when someone calls for a price. The market is 45–50 on a big figure of 1.41.

You do not really want to deal, and you do not know whether the caller is a potential buyer or seller of dollars. So you widen your spread a little to 43–52.

The rationale is this: if you are given dollars at 1.4143 you may be able to sell the dollars back to the market at 1.4145, if you are quick, locking in a 2-pip profit. Conversely, if you sell dollars at 1.4152 you could buy them back from the market at 1.4150, again locking in a 2-pip profit.

Reversing unwanted positions is potentially risky – rates may move against you or the liquidity may not be there to absorb a large deal. The wider your spread – the more defensive your price – the greater is your room for maneuver. The spread is an insurance device which helps the dealer manage his position and liquidity risks.

The wider your spread relative to other market makers, the less inclined the counterparty will be to deal with you. In thin or volatile markets all market makers will tend to widen their spreads.

Different currencies attract different risk considerations, so their spreads will vary. In general the market provides the guidelines for what the acceptable spread will be for any given currency exchange. In a heavily traded market, such as the dollar–mark, spreads are typically less than 5 points or 0.05%. In more thinly traded markets spreads can be as wide as 1%.

Some market makers rely for their profits purely on their ability to read their own market better than anyone else, and therefore do not even quote a spread. When asking for a price in spot dollar–Swissy, for example, the reply might be "30 your choice."

This means that the market maker is willing to buy dollars at (1.45) 30 francs or to sell you dollars at the same rate. Unless you specifically asked for an indication rate it would be very bad form to reject such a price – it is unlikely that you could find a better one!

Shading the Rate

The second line of defence when making a price is to move your rates slightly higher or lower than the market – shading the rate.

Example

You are asked for a dollar–mark price in a market amount. The market is currently quoting 45–50 on a big figure of 1.41, and you would rather be long than short.

So you shade your prices up a little, by quoting 47–52. You are prepared to pay 1.4147 marks for every dollar you take, while others in the market pay 1.4145. But you charge 1.4152 marks for every dollar you sell, against the market price of 1.4150.

If the caller "hits your bid" (you receive dollars), this is what you wanted. But if he lifts your offer (you sell dollars), you may be able to buy the dollars back from the market at 1.4150 and lock in a 2-pip profit.

Shading your prices gives a signal that you are a buyer or a seller. The counterparty has an incentive to deal with you on the side you want. There are of course potential pitfalls.

- If you shade too little the incentive may not be enough. If you want to be long or short a currency the chances are that the counterparty feels likewise.

- If you shade too aggressively you may give points away unnecessarily, or you may reveal that you are in a desperate situation.

Knowing your counterparty is essential. An FX deal with a corporate or institutional customer may simply reflect genuine business requirements, and is unlikely to be reversed in a short time. But a call from another market maker could mean that they are trying to read your thoughts, or plant ideas in your mind. As in poker, you must be able to bluff.

Summary

In this chapter, we have looked at a fundamental dealing skill: quoting market rates. Although the main factor is always the current market price, dealers need to identify relevant indicators so as to set their individual rate. We then examined two techniques, the spread and shading the rate, which are used to do this. However, since FX dealing is not a precise science, successful market makers always need a combination of information, experience and, of course, the ability to bluff.

Keywords

Before moving on, please be sure that you are familiar with the following concepts and their use in the market place:

- bid–offer spread
- choice prices
- shading the rate.

The exercises in Chapter 8 will give you important practice in quoting FX prices.

8

Exercise: Quoting Spot FX Rates

This is an exercise in "shading" spot FX quotations to encourage either buyers or sellers to deal with you rather than with the other dealers in the market.

Example:
The USD/DEM market is relatively quiet and you are long of US$5 million at a rate of 1.4539. Other dealers in the market are currently quoting:

USD/DEM
Dealer A	1.4539/44
Dealer B	1.4540/45
Dealer C	1.4538/46
Dealer D	1.4541/46
Dealer E	1.4542/47
Dealer F	1.4543/48

You want to square your position before going to lunch. Which of the following rates of exchange would you quote to encourage a buyer of US dollars to deal with you rather than any of the above dealers?

(i)   44/49
(ii)   38/43
(iii)   43/48
(iv)   39/45

Answer: (ii) 38/43

1. Cable looks weak as a result of the following news item: "Britain's trade deficit jumped to 2.3 billion sterling last month, against a market expectation of 1.5 billion." Your position is square but you receive a request for spot cable. Other dealers in the market are currently quoting:

   GBP/USD

Dealer A	Dealer B	Dealer C	Dealer D	Dealer E	Dealer F
1.9505/15	1.9507/17	1.9500/10	1.9502/12	1.9503/13	1.9506/16

   Which rate would you quote in response to the request?

   (i)   1.9508/18
   (ii) 1.9506/15
   (iii) 1.9501/11
   (iv) 1.9500/05

   *Answer:*_____

2. The mark is relatively quiet and you are short of US$5 million at a rate of 1.4580. The following news is received from New York: "The Fed has made a surprise intervention to boost the dollar. The amount bought appears to be very large." Other dealers in the market are currently quoting:

   USD/DEM

Dealer A	Dealer B	Dealer C	Dealer D	Dealer E	Dealer F
1.4599/04	1.4600/05	1.4601/06	1.4601/06	1.4602/07	1.4603/08

   You want to minimize your loss, but at the same time you receive a request for spot USD/DEM. You have to quote a rate of exchange that will encourage a seller of US dollars to deal with you rather than any of the above dealers. Which of the following would you quote?

   (i)   1.4604/09
   (ii) 1.4603/09
   (iii) 1.4597/02
   (iv) 1.4600/05

   *Answer:*_____

3. Other dealers in the market are currently quoting:

USD/DEM

Dealer A	Dealer B	Dealer C	Dealer D	Dealer E	Dealer F
1.4599/04	1.4600/05	1.4601/06	1.4601/06	1.4602/07	1.4603/08

You have just received information from a colleague in New York that there is a "a big order" in the market: a major corporate is buying DM550 million. Which the following rates of exchange would you quote to the market?

(i)   1.4599/05
(ii)   1.4598/08
(iii) 1.4604/09
(iv)   1.4601/05

*Answer:*_____

4. You have received a request for spot cable from a major corporate in "twenty pounds". You are already long in sterling to the extent of GB£30 million. Other dealers in the market are currently quoting:

GBP/USD

Dealer A	Dealer B	Dealer C	Dealer D	Dealer E	Dealer F
1.9925/35	1.9922/32	1.9926/36	1.9924/36	1.9920/30	1.9921/29

You would like to reduce your long position in sterling. Which rate of exchange would you quote in response to the request?

(i)   1.9918/28
(ii)   1.9926/36
(iii) 1.9920/30
(iv)   1.9927/35

*Answer:*_____

■ ■ ■

"You can construct any cross-currency rates from US dollar rates."

Cross-Currency Trading

9

About 90% of FX transactions involve the US dollar as one of the currencies. However, this proportion has declined over the years as the dollar's role as an international reserve currency continues to diminish. Here we will look at some FX transactions which do not involve it.

Definition: A cross-currency deal is one which involves the exchange of two non-dollar currencies.

Calculating Rates

You can construct any cross-currency rates from US dollar rates. The following (highly simplified) examples show how this works.

Case A *A customer asks its bank for a sterling–mark exchange rate. Rates against the dollar at the time are:*

GBP 2.0000–3.0000
DEM 3.0000–4.0000

The bank buys sterling and sells US dollars at US$2. It sells sterling and buys US dollars at US$3.

The customer would have to sell £1 to buy $2. The customer could then sell the $2 back to the bank and for each dollar it would receive DM3. In other words, if the customer wished to sell sterling and buy marks, the bank would multiply the dollar–mark and cable bid rates.

It follows that the bank's rate of exchange when buying sterling and selling marks is GBP/DEM 6 (GBP 1 = USD 2 and USD 1 = DEM 3).

If the customer wished to buy sterling and sell marks, the offer side of the rates would be applied: that is to say, USD/DEM 3 and GBP/USD 4. The bank's rate for selling pounds against marks would therefore be GBP/DEM 12.

However, there is clearly a difference when the currencies involved in the cross are both quoted against the same unit currency. This is the case with a DEM/FRF cross since these currencies will be quoted USD/DEM and USD/FRF. In this case, you must divide one currency's bid by another's offer. The following (again simplified) example shows how this works.

A customer asks its bank for a DEM/FRF rate of exchange. The **Case B**
rates against the dollar at the time are:

    DEM   3.0000–4.0000
    FRF   8.0000–9.0000

The bank buys US dollars and sells D-marks at DEM3. It sells US dollars and buys D-marks at 4.

The customer would have to sell DM4 to buy $1. It could then sell the $1 back to the bank and buy FrF8.

So the bank's rate of exchange when buying marks is FRF 2 to the D-mark (FRF 8 = USD 1 and USD 1 = DEM 4).

If the customer wished to buy marks, the bank would sell DEM3 for each dollar and would sell that dollar back to the customer and receive FRF 9. The bank's rate for selling marks is FRF 3 (FRF 9 = USD 1 and USD 1 = DEM 3).

Why is the cross-rate calculated differently in each case? Because sterling is quoted "upside down." The bank buys pounds and sells dollars at the left-hand rate. It also buys dollars and sells marks at the left-hand rate. So we have to multiply the two bid rates to get the rate at which the bank buys pounds against marks.

However with a DEM/FRF cross both currencies are quoted against the dollar. So we must divide one currency's bid by the other's offer.

Summary

In this chapter, we have defined cross-currency FX transactions. In particular, we have looked at how to calculate rates from US dollar rates, and at crosses where the base currency is different.

In each case, the procedure is as follows:

Either:

The unit currency between two pairs differs. In which case: you "multiply down" (bid × bid, offer × offer)

Example

GBP/USD	1.9720–1.9730
USD/DEM	1.5110–1.5115
GBP:DEM =	2.9797–2.98822

Or:

The unit currency between two pairs is the same. In which case: you "divide across" (bid/offer, offer/bid):

Example

USD/DEM	1.5110–1.5115
USD/FRF	5.7050–5.7065
DEM/FRF =	3.7744–3.7766 or
FRF/DEM =	0.2648–0.2649

The above examples show how a bank would construct its theoretical crosses. The actual prices quoted will of course depend on the bank's position at the time and its market view.

Keywords   Please make sure you are familiar with the following terms before turning to the Cross-Rates Calculations which form Chapter 10.

- unit or base currency
- cross rates.

10

Exercise: Cross-Rate Calculations

In this exercise, you have to identify the best rates against the US dollar at which you would perform certain transactions, and then derive the effective cross-rate achieved.

Example:
The following banks are quoting rates for GBP/USD and for USD/DEM. You wish to sell sterling to buy marks "going through the dollar."

	GBP/USD	USD/DEM
Bank A	1.6353 – 1.6363	1.8158 – 1.8168
Bank B	1.6355 – 1.6365	1.8159 – 1.8169
Bank C	1.6352 – 1.6364	1.8160 – 1.8170
Bank D	1.6356 – 1.6366	1.8157 – 1.8167
Bank E	1.6354 – 1.6368	1.8156 – 1.8166

(i)   Which bank would you sell sterling to and buy dollars from? What is the exchange rate?

(ii) Which bank would you sell the dollars to and buy marks from? At what rate?

(iii) What is the cross-rate GBP/DEM?

Answers:

(i)   Bank D at a rate of 1.6356

(ii) Bank C at a rate of 1. 8160

(iii) The cross-rate is 2.97025 (=1.6356 × 1.8160)

1. You wish to sell Swiss francs to buy Japanese yen.

	USD/CHF	USD/JPY
Bank A	1.4947 – 1.4957	141.75 – 142.05
Bank B	1.4946 – 1.4958	141.75 – 141.95
Bank C	1.4945 – 1.4956	141.70 – 141.90
Bank D	1.4948 – 1.4959	141.73 – 141.93
Bank E	1.4949 – 1.4960	141.75 – 141.85

(i) Which bank would you sell Swiss francs to and buy dollars from? What is the exchange rate?

(ii) Which bank would you sell the dollars to and buy yen? At what rate?

(iii) What is the cross-rate CHF/JP?

Answers:

(i) Bank _____ at a rate of _____

(ii) Bank _____ at a rate of _____

(iii) The CHF/JPY cross-rate is _____

2. You wish to sell Belgian francs to buy pounds.

	GBP/USD	USD/BEF
Bank A	1.6295 – 1.6305	37.65 – 37.75
Bank B	1.6290 – 1.6300	37.59 – 37.69
Bank C	1.6293 – 1.6303	37.63 – 37.73
Bank D	1.6294 – 1.6301	37.64 – 37.76
Bank E	1.6292 – 1.6304	37.66 – 37.76

(i) Which bank would you sell Belgian francs to and buy dollars from? What is the exchange rate?

(ii) Which bank would you sell the dollars to and buy sterling? At what rate?

(iii) What is the cross-rate in GBP per BEF100?

Answers:

(i) Bank _____ at a rate of _____

(ii) Bank _____ at a rate of _____

(iii) The cross-rate BEF 100/GBP is _____

3. You wish to sell Italian lire to buy Danish krone ("Copey").

	USD/ITL	USD/DKK
Bank A	1373.62 – 1374.62	6.9750 – 6.9800
Bank B	1373.50 – 1374.50	6.9762 – 6.9812
Bank C	1373.75 – 1374.75	6.9762 – 6.9815
Bank D	1373.25 – 1374.25	6.9770 – 6.9810
Bank E	1373.37 – 1374.37	6.9775 – 6.9805

(i) Which bank would you sell Italian lire to and buy dollars from? What is the exchange rate?

(ii) Which bank would you sell the dollars to and buy Danish krone from? At what rate?

(iii) What is the cross-rate in krone per ITL 1000?

Answers:

(i) Bank _____ at a rate of _____

(ii) Bank _____ at a rate of _____

(iii) The cross-rate ITL (1000)/DKK _____

4. You wish to sell Australian dollars ("Ozzie") to buy Hong Kong dollars.

	AUD/USD	USD/HKD
Bank A	0.7117 – 0.7125	7.8070 – 7.8080
Bank B	0.7115 – 0.7124	7.8069 – 7.8079
Bank C	0.7118 – 0.7126	7.8071 – 7.8081
Bank D	0.7119 – 0.7125	7.8072 – 7.8080
Bank E	0.7116 – 0.7127	7.8071 – 7.8078

(i) Which bank would you sell Australian dollars to and buy US dollars from? What is the exchange rate?

(ii) Which bank would you sell the US dollars to and buy Hong Kong dollars from? At what rate?

(iii) What is the cross-rate AUD/HKD?

Answers:

(i) Bank _____ at a rate of _____

(ii) Bank _____ at a rate of _____

(iii) The cross-rate AUD/HKD is _____

■ ■ ■

"An FX dealer must be able to calculate precisely the profit (or loss) on his or her deals."

Position Keeping

Establishing profit

The average rate

Summary

Overview In this chapter we will look at how FX traders work out the implications of their deals; a practice known as position keeping.

Establishing Profit

An FX dealer must be able to calculate precisely the profit (or loss) on his or her deals. The following example illustrates how this is done for a straightforward pair of spot transactions.

Example

This example follows the dealer conversation introduced in Chapter 3. You are Bank B, and at 10:00 hours you bought US$5 million from Bank A at 1.4145.

By 12:00 the rate has firmed and you sell the US$5 million at 1.4178 to Bank C to square your position.

$$\begin{aligned} \text{Profit} &= -\text{DM5m} \times 1.4145 \ +\text{DM5m} \times 1.4178 \\ &= -\text{DM7,072,500.00} +\text{DM7,089,000.00} \\ &= \ \text{DM16,500.00} \end{aligned}$$

In dollars: USD/DEM 16,500/1.4178
= US$11,637.75

In the first half of the calculation, you work out how many marks you need to pay Bank A, against those you will receive from Bank B. The net figure is your profit, since the dollar amounts balance out.

The profit or loss on a spot position is the net cash balance left over when all the deals have been settled.

The profit is "locked in" and in accounting terms it accrues today. However in cash terms it will not be realized until the value date, when your DEM nostro account (the one used for settlements) will increase by 16,500. If your profit and loss accounts are kept in marks, then this would be the end of the calculation. However, if they are dollar-based you must divide the DM16,500 profit by the current spot rate. This gives a profit of US$11,637.75.

The Average Rate

In a small dealing room, transacting a few deals each day, the profit calculation shown in the example is sufficient. Offsetting deals can be matched, and the profit or loss on each pair chalked up against a running total. But on a busy currency desk, with a high volume of customer and interbank deals, such an approach is impractical.

In this case, the average rate on the position is calculated and then compared with the current market rate to determine whether or not the position is making money. The first step – using either approach – must be to post all deals on to a "deal blotter" or Daily Position Sheet.

The table in Figure 11.1 shows all the deals made in the first 10 minutes of a trading day. By the end of this dealing activity, we need to know whether we are long or short dollars, and by how much. We also need to know the average rate at which this position was created.

To calculate the average rate, draw a line under the list, and add up the net D-mark balance. Then divide it into the net US dollar balance.

Sample deal blotter

Fig 11.1

BANK B. LONDON DAILY POSITION SHEET DEALER: Nikki K.

Date: 10 JULY 19XX
Currency: US $ - DEM

Opening Position:

Ref	CCY Bought (+)/ Sold(−)	Rate	$ Sold (−)/ Bought(+)	Net
001	−7,072,500	1.4145	+ 5	+ 5
002	−14,170,000	1.4170	+ 10	+ 15
003	+7,089,000	1.4178	− 5	+ 10
004	+1,416,500	1.4165	− 1	+ 9
Closing Position: Closing Rate:	−12,737,000	1.41522 1.4160	+ 9	
Profit: $4,940.01				

Average rate = 12,737,000/9,000,000 = 1.41522

Effectively we are "long $9 at 1.4152". If we had done just one deal, buying US$9 million at 1.4152, we would have arrived at the same position.

Suppose the market is now 1.4160/70. To square this position we would need to sell US$9 million at 1.4160. Our profit since the start of the day would be:

– DM9 million × 1.41522	+ DM9 million × 1.4160
= – DM12,737,000.00	+ DM12,744,000.00
= + DM7,000.00	

In US dollars:

= US$7,000.00/1.4170
= US$4,940.01

The dealer (or the position clerk, or a computer system) will perform this calculation many times during a busy day. Certainly all FX positions must be revalued at the end of each day, whether or not they have been squared. This information is vital for dealing room managers.

This does not mean that, to determine profit or loss, the dealer actually has to square out his position. All we are doing is to revalue or "mark to market" the net position at current rates of exchange. This tells us whether the position is worth keeping or not. The average rate provides a useful target or break-even rate for the dealer to aim for.

Summary

In this chapter, we examined the importance and practice of position keeping. We then examined how positions, updated many times on a given day, will be compared with averages so as to determine targets, profit (and loss).

Please be sure that you are familiar with the following terms **Keywords** before moving on:

- deal blotter
- average rate
- marking to market
- squaring positions.

In addition, the exercise in Chapter 12 provides practice in spot position keeping.

Exercise:
Spot Position Keeping

Complete this deal blotter by filling in the missing elements. Then, add up the closing balances, calculate the average position rate and also your revaluation profit/loss.

DAILY POSITION SHEET

Currency: USD/DEM

Time	Currency Bought (+) Currency Sold (−)	Rate	US$ Sold (−) US$ Bought (+)
08:00	_____	1.4525	+5,000,000
09:00	_____	1.4500	+3,000,000
09:05	_____	1.4490	+3,000,000
09:15	_____	1.4485	+3,000,000
10:00	−17,000,000	1.4450	_____
10:05	_____	1.4445	+3,000,000
10:25	−34,250,000	1.4440	_____
11:00	−20,000,000	1.4445	_____
11:15	_____	1.4450	+3,000,000
12:00	_____	1.4425	+5,000,000
13:00	−8,500,000	1.4420	_____
14:30	+15,000,000	1.4430	_____
15:15	+15,000,000	1.4435	_____
16:00	_____	1.4440	+3,000,000

CLOSING BALANCES:

	DM NET	AV. RATE	US$ NET
	_____	_____	_____

CLOSING RATE: 1.4445

NET PROFIT/LOSS _____

Spot FX Practice

The following is a set of questions of the type you might see in the ACI *Introduction to FX and Money Markets* examination.

In exam conditions, each question receives 1 mark for a correct answer, zero for no answer and minus 1/4 mark for a wrong answer.

We suggest you attempt as many questions as you can in half an hour. After this you can go over the remaining questions in your own time. Model answers are given in Appendix 3.

1. The current spot rates are:

   GBP/USD 1.6250/60
   USD/FRF 5.5550/60

   At what rate could you sell French francs against sterling?

   a) 3.4164

   b) 9.0269

   c) 9.0341

   d) 3.4191

2. Using the same rates as in the previous question and the following Italian lire rates:

   USD/ITL   1100.50/1101.50

   At what rate could you buy Italian lire against sterling?

   a) 1788.31

   b) 1101.50

   c) 1791.04

   d) 677.85

3. Using the same rates as in the previous questions, at what rate could you sell Italian lire against French francs?

   a) 198.07

   b) 1100.50

   c) 198.29

   d) 0.0051

4. Using the rates in the previous questions, how many French francs would you receive if you sold Italian lire 3,750,000,000?

   a) FrF 3,407,542.03

   b) FrF 743,587,500.00

   c) FrF 18,911,694.99

   d) FrF 8,932,700.56

5. In GBP/FRF you are quoted the following prices by four different banks, you are a buyer of French francs. Which rate is the best for you?

   a) 8.4790/00

   b) 8.4793/98

   c) 8.4792/95

   d) 8.4789/94

6. Four banks provide you with quotes in DEM/CHF. Which is the best price for you to deal at as a buyer of Swiss francs?

   a) .8702 – 04

   b) .8692 – 94

   c) .8699 – 03

   d) .8703 – 05

7. The mid-rate for USD/DEM is 1.5770 and the mid-rate for AUD/USD is 0.7060. What is the mid-rate for DEM/AUD?

   a) 0.4477

   b) 1.1134

   c) 2.2337

   d) 0.8981

8. The current spot rates are:

   USD/DEM 1.5660/65
   USD/FRF 5.4430/35

   What rate could you quote to a customer who wishes to buy French francs against D-marks?

   a) 3.4746

   b) 1.5660

   c) 8.5272

   d) 3.4761

9. Using the same USD/DEM rates and the following Italian lire rates:

USD/ITL   1150.50/00

At what rate could you sell Italian lire to your customer against D-marks?

a) 734.44

b) 1150.00

c) 1803.04

d) None of the above

10. Using the same rates, at what rate could you buy Italian lire from your customer against French francs?

a) 211.26

b) 1150.00

c) 211.35

d) 211.46

11. If you sold DM 2 million at 1.4510; DM 8 million at 1.4530 and DM 3 million at 1.4522, what is the average rate of your position?

a) 1.4530

b) 1.4521

c) 0.5008

d) 1.4525

12. In the example in the previous question, above, if the USD/DEM is now quoted at 1.4685/90, and if you deal at that rate, what profit or loss would you make?

a) NIL

b) Profit of US$ 97,470.22

c) Profit of US$ 100,528.54

d) Loss of US$ 99,980.83

13. You have quoted a bank spot USD/FRF as 4.9890/00. They say, "I take 5." What do they mean?

    a) They want to take a short break to think about it

    b) They buy US$ 5 million at 4.9890

    c) They buy FrF5 million at 4.9800

    d) They buy US$ 5 million at 4.99

14. GBP/USD is 1.61 20/25 and you have some dollars that you want to sell now. Which of the following rates would you quote?

    a) 18/23

    b) 22/27

    c) 25/your choice

    d) 18/27

15. When a broker says, "Pay 5 for 10, offer 15 at 20," he means:

    a) You can buy $5 million for the price of $10 million, and sell $15 million for the price of $20 million

    b) The market is 5/15 and there are $10 million behind the bid and $20 million on the offer.

    c) You can pay 10 for $5 million and take 20 for $15 million

    d) You can sell $10 million at 5 and buy $15 million at 20

■ ■ ■

"One of the key skills in spot trading is the ability to 'job' the market by opening and closing positions at a profit throughout the day."

Simulated Dealing – First Session

Objectives

This chapter uses the Spot Dealing Module provided with the book. The purpose of the session is to give you practical experience of buying and selling currency in the fast-moving interbank market.

In this particular scenario you will be dealing spot USD/DEM from quotations made to you by a number of market makers and you will be making a market (quoting prices) yourself. News items will flash up on the screen giving you an indication of the direction of the market. Success in this simulated dealing session will depend on your ability to determine the following:

- Based on how the market is moving, should you be long or short dollars (short or long marks)?

- When should you open, increase, decrease or square out your position?

- When you receive a quotation, should you deal at that price, or should you ask for another quotation from a different market maker?

- How should you shade your rates – and how wide should your spread be – bearing in mind your position and your view about the market direction?

The Scenario

Your base currency in the simulation is US dollars. This means that when you want to buy D-marks you must sell US dollars, and when you want to sell D-marks you must buy US dollars.

You will trade over approximately 15 hours in simulated time (in real time this will last about 20 minutes). At the end of the session you should close out any open positions; it is **very important** that you do this as the system will shut down automatically after 20 minutes.

At the end of your dealing session, the system will calculate a range of statistics on your dealing performance which can be compared with benchmarks set out at the end of this chapter.

It is important to tackle this task in the prescribed way. As a spot dealer you are not in the business of building up and running huge positions for the sake of it.

One of the key skills in spot trading is the ability to "job" the market by opening and closing positions at a profit throughout the day. You should be trying to achieve:

- a fast response to your counterparties;
- an accurate response to quotes (are you hitting the right price?);
- a good understanding of your position (are you long or short over-all, and what position should you have in the current market?).

Starting the Session

Follow the instructions for installing the software on to the hard disk of your PC as set out in Appendix 4 of this book.

We shall assume here the software has already been installed on your PC.

From the *Risk Manager* Program Group, select the Simulation icon and double click on it.

This takes you into the simulation Start-up screen, which looks like Figure 14.1 below.

The start-up screen

Fig 14.1

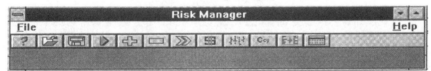

There is a menu at the top of the screen with a tool bar below it. The screen is quite empty at this stage and most of the controls are disabled.

If you click the mouse cursor on any of the available menu items, drop-down menus will appear. The simulation is controlled through these drop-down menu items.

To select a menu item either click on the keyword using the left mouse button, or press the **Alt** key + the relevant underlined letter on the keyword.

You can press the Help button in the Tool Bar or click on the Help menu option at any time to obtain context-sensitive on-line Help.

To load the first dealing session press the ⌹ button and select SPOT1.WLD from the list of files, or you can do this by selecting **Open** from the **File** drop-down menu. When the file has finished loading the display will change to something like Figure 14.2.

Before you start the simulation select **Markets** from the **Reports** drop-down menu. This allows you to read a brief economic summary of the trading scenario you are about to start.

When you have read the text, close the **Market** window.

Pressing the ▷ button will start the simulation.

If you have already started the simulation hit the ❚❚ button to pause it until you have read the instructions below. Then click ▷ when you are ready to start trading.

The Main Windows

The main windows created in this session are shown in Figure 14.2.

Fig 14.2

The main FX screen

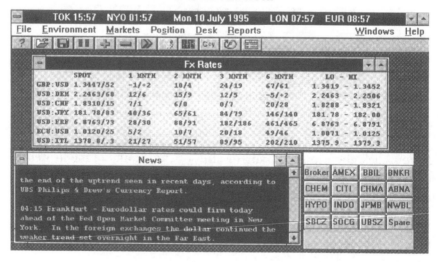

The Clocks

The clocks on the bar at the top of the screen show the time in Tokyo, New York, London and Continental Europe. The simulation date is shown in the middle of the bar.

When the simulation is running the clocks pulsate. Each financial centre is open from 08:00 to 17:00 local time.

You can deal round the clock but the date will change at midnight, London time (GMT).

The clocks provide useful information about the state of the world-wide currency market – market depth depends on the number of buyers and sellers active at any one time. The market is deepest at around 15:00 when London and New York are both open. Depending on the depth of the market, a large currency transaction can cause market prices to move against you.

FX Rates

The **FX Rates** window consists of a table with currency codes down the left-hand side. The table shows exchange rates for spot and standard, or *fixed*, forward dates. In this dealing session we are concerned only with the spot prices.

This is a typical "composite" page which shows the latest indication rates contributed by a number of banks. Like most such services, there can be a disparity between the firm rates you are actually quoted by a named counterparty and the indication rates quoted on this window.

Most currencies are priced in terms of units of currency per US dollar, with the notable exceptions of sterling and the ECU, which are shown in terms of dollars to the pound, and dollars per ECU.

Display Formats

When you enter the program you will see two-way prices, with the numerically smaller of the two spot rates (the bid) in full, and only the "small figures" shown on the other rate (the offered).

By pressing the [image] button in the toolbar when this window is active (i.e., when the FX Rates window has a blue surround) you can toggle the display to show only the bid rates in full, then the ask rates in full and then back to the two-way price format.

Alternatively, you may click the right mouse button anywhere on the window to the left of the six-month column.

Days Hi–Low and Trade-Weighted Index

Press the right-hand mouse button on the window to the right of the **6 MNTH** column to toggle the display to show either the daily low and high for the spot currencies, or the currencies trade-weighted indices. The trade-weighted index relates a currencys spot exchange rate to a group of other currencies, in proportion to the volume of trade between that country and each of the others.

All indices are scaled starting at 100 at some convenient date. For example, if the GBP index is at 80.0, this means that sterling is now worth 80% of the value it had when the index was last re-based.

News

Messages come into the **News** window at various times. Only the latest news item is displayed. If you miss any news item, or you want to go back over earlier news, click up or down on the vertical scroll bar to the right of the window, or PgUp or PgDn on the scroll bar.

Charts

Selecting the option **Charts** from the **Desk** menu opens a window where you can look at the yield curve, spot FX rates, benchmark bond prices or the Eurocurrency futures prices for each currency.

Press the [image] button to display a different currency on the Charts window

Press the [image] button to change the price series displayed

From the toolbar inside the charts window use the Daily or Tick buttons to view either daily or tick price charts. You also have two buttons to compress or expand the chart horizontally.

Dealing – Market User

To ask for a quotation select **Deal** from the **Desk** menu (**Alt+d** followed by **d**). A window will open up listing the names of the counterparties you can deal with, with their four-letter dealing code, the size of their limits and how much of their limits you have already used. Alternatively, click on a button in the phone pad.

Deal slip

Fig 14.3

Deal Fx		
To: CHEM ◆ Outright ◇ Swap ◇ FXA ◇ ERA	From: CHEM Limit: 60,000 Used: 0	✔ OK
Value date ■ Currency		✘ Cancel
Deal type Amount	Deal rate Counter	? Help

The left of the deal slip is where you enter the details of the deal you wish to make. To the right of the deal slip is where the simulated counterparty will respond.

- In this session we focus on the spot market, so only the **Outright** field is enabled.
- To enter the **Value date**, either point the mouse cursor next to the **Value date** (or type **Alt + v**) and a light grey box will flash. Type s (for **spot**) and press **Enter** or click **OK**.
- To enter the **Currency**, type the quoted currency code (in this session it will be **DEM**) and press Enter.

The counterparty will now respond with a firm two-way price, just as if you had asked for a quote on the telephone, and the maximum amount for which this quote is good for.

The market maker will not hold his rates indefinitely, so you must decide fairly quickly. The rates quoted may not be the same as those shown on the **FX Rates** window. They may be higher or lower, depending on which way the counterparty wants to trade, so make sure you compare them with the current market prices.

If you do not like the rates, click on the Cancel button or hit the Esc key.

Sometimes the counterparty may revise his rates if the market moves before the deal has been completed: the word "Change!" will appear against the rate quoted.

- To enter the **Deal type** press b **(buy)** or s **(sell)**. You can also "hit the rate" – e.g., if you are quoted 1.9250/60 and you enter 50 against this heading, this means that you sold dollars.

You cannot cancel a deal once you have agreed to buy or sell, or you have hit a rate.

> **Unless otherwise specified, the system will assume that you are buying or selling base currency amounts (US dollars in this session).**

- Against the **Amount** heading enter the amount you wish to deal, in thousands, or follow the figure you enter with an **m** to indicate millions – for example **5m** if you are dealing in 5 million. If the amount you enter is very large or very small, a message may tell you that the rates are only good for amounts in a certain range.

Sometimes you may need to trade counter-currency amounts (e.g., to mop up small currency positions). To do this, type the currency code before the amount – for example **DEM 1.2M**.

Deal Rate and Counter-Amount

As soon as you have entered the deal type and amount, the counterparty will confirm the rate deal, and the deal will be automatically logged into your position. The value of the deal in units of the counter-currency is also shown.

Your dealing limit utilization with this counterparty will also be updated. This is shown on the field at the top right of the deal slip.

Dealing – Market Maker

While the simulation is running, you will hear a double ringing sound from time to time and one of the "lines" on the phone pad will be highlighted. This tells you there is a specific incoming call from a counterparty, asking for a quotation. To pick up the call click the mouse on the highlighted button, and a message like this will appear:

Message

Fig 14.4

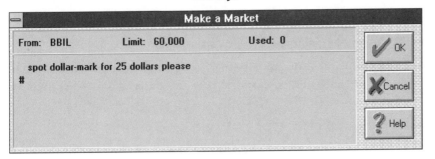

Underneath the message is where you enter your quote. You must enter two rates separated by a space or a "/". You can enter the figures in full, or just the small figures. If a figure has a decimal point the computer will interpret the figure as a full rate, otherwise as a small figure.

You can qualify the maximum amount you are prepared to deal in by adding (for example) **in 10m** after your two-way quotation.

Once you have entered a rate (and an amount if you so desire) the caller will decide whether they wish to deal. If a deal is made, a new message will appear stating the amount and whether they have bought or sold dollars. The limit utilization information will be updated and you should then click the OK button to clear the deal slip.

Remember: the counterparties will reciprocate. If you quote wide spreads, they will quote wide spreads to you.

The Position Keeper

The simulation comes with a full electronic position keeper. Select **Position (Alt+p)** from the drop-down menus.

Deal Blotter

This window shows the list of deals that have been already executed and are awaiting settlement or maturity. *Risk Manager* automatically settles all deals from the list when they reach maturity and effects all the required balance sheet adjustments.

Each entry has the following information:

- the time and the date of the trade;
- the currency or reference code of the deal;
- the amount (in thousands) – if you are long the amount is shown as +ve in that currency; and if you are short it will be shown as –ve;
- the settlement date;
- THRU: the counterparty dealing code – if you have dealt on your prices, by answering an incoming call, a **t** will be appended to the code;
- the RATE at which you dealt;

The Ladders

If you select **Ladders** from the list a window will appear that looks like Figure 14.5.

The ladder summarizes for each currency your dealing limits and net position for settlement or maturity on various dates, or date bands.

> Press the [Ccy] button to toggle the display to a different currency ladder.

The ladder starts with your **CASH** (or bank) position and ranges all your deals into various maturity bands. **TOM** shows the net amount of all the deals maturing tomorrow, and **SPOT** shows

Fig 14.5

Exposure ladder

		USD Exposure					
MAT	SHORT	LONG	LIMIT	NET	YLD	VAL 1%	CUMUL
CASH			5,000	0		0	0
TOM			75,000	0	6.18	0	0
SPOT			150,000	10,000	6.16	0	10,000
– 1 MTH			100,000	0	5.89	0	10,000
– 2 MTH			100,000	0	5.70	0	10,000
– 3 MTH			100,000	0	5.50	0	10,000
– 6 MTH			100,000	0	5.33	0	10,000
– 1 YR			100,000	0	5.16	0	10,000
– 2 YRS			100,000	0	5.00	0	10,000
– 3 YRS			0	0	4.86	0	10,000
– 5 YRS			0	0	4.72	0	10,000
–10 YRS			0	0	4.62	0	10,000
>10 YRS			0	0	4.59	0	10,000
NET			500,000	10,000		0	

amounts for value spot. The other dates are for forward values, which do not apply in this session.

The dots under **SHORT** and **LONG** represent your dealing limits, and the squares, if any, represent your net position in each maturity band. This display gives you an idea of your position at a glance. If you have exceeded your limits, ! marks will appear under these columns.

The **NET** and **LIMIT** columns show in figures (000s) what the **SHORT** and **LONG** columns represent graphically. The **CUMUL** column shows what your cash position would be at the end of each maturity period given your present portfolio. This is sometimes called a liquidity run.

> Press the button or click on the right mouse button inside the window to toggle the analysis between Liquidity, Exposure and Present Value.

- The **Liquidity** run includes all payables/receivables on various future dates, including principal amounts, interest and options premiums;
- The **Exposure** analysis looks only at your net trading position (no interest or premiums) and helps you identify quickly where your main exposures lie;
- The **Present Value** analysis looks at the present value of all the forward cash flows identified in the **Liquidity** run, discounted at the corresponding zero-coupon swap rate shown under **YLD**. The total of these present values, shown against **NET** at the bottom of the table, give you an indication of the net liquidation value of your book.

The different ways of expressing the ladder are especially useful when dealing in the fixed-interest markets. In the context of spot FX dealing this is not so relevant and we suggest you work with the **Exposure** analysis, which is the default in SPOT1.

Fx Book

When you select FX from the Position menu, a window will open showing your net open FX position in any currency against the USD (your home currency). Each line of analysis shows:

- The counter-currency (**CCY**) code;
- The net **AMOUNT** in 000s foreign currency units;
- The **VALUE** date;
- The average **RATE** implied in the position;
- The net base currency amount (**BCY**);
- The market rate used to revalue the open position;
- The mark-to-market profits or losses on the open position, in local currency or USD equivalent – press the Ccy button to toggle between the two.

Risk Manager adopts a liquidation approach to revaluing all positions: it calculates the profit or loss that would be incurred if you were to cover your position with offsetting deals at current market prices.

Dealing Performance Assessment

When you have reached the end of the session make sure you have squared out your positions. You will get a warning to square positions at 22.00 London time anyway, before the system moves on to the next date.

Select **Reports** from the main menu, and go into the **Dealing** option. A window like the one shown in Figure 14.6 will appear.

Below are some benchmarks against which you can compare your own performance. These are based on the performances of the many dealers who have completed our spot FX dealing simulation. Our experience shows that they establish a "profile" of the kind of person who tends to be successful in spot dealing.

Benchmarks

You are, of course, aiming to make a profit in the simulated dealing session. The following figures give an overall indication of how well you have done.

Dealing performance report

Fig 14.6

Dealing Report					
TRADING DAYS [Real-time]		**PROFIT $'000**		**TURNOVER**	
1	[00:37]		245		510,052
				SPREAD/MARKET [s.devn]	
DEALS	**[calls]**	**AV. SPEED [s.devn]**		---- Bid ----	---- Ask ----
Out	45		00:05 (00:05)		
In	25	[55]	00:11 (00:04)	3.4 (1.4)	-3.5 (3.4)
Network	0		00:00 (00:00)		
Corps	0				
Total	65		00:06 (00:05)		

SYSTEM USAGE		EXPOSURE		LIMITS BROKEN	
Pause	2	Matched Profits	88	Currency	0
Typos	2	Max Fx	55m	Total Net	0
		Max VAL1%	0	Structure	0
				Gearing ratio	0
				Cash ratio	0
				Counterparty	0

[✔ OK]   [Clear]   [Print]   [? Help]

Profit (US$ 000s)

251–300	Excellent
151–250	Very good
101–150	Good
25–100	Fair
Less than 25	Further practice required

However, from a learning point of view, it is equally important that you should understand exactly *how* you achieved the result you did, and draw some lessons for the future. If you made a loss, then think carefully about where you went wrong. If you made a profit, ask yourself honestly whether this was the result of good luck or good judgement.

Deals

Out tells you how many deals you made with simulated counterparties as a market user – i.e., you called them and dealt on their prices.

In deals are transactions where you have quoted rates in response to counterparties' requests for rates. The figure in parentheses indicates the number of calls that were made to you, whether you answered the phone or not. From this figure you can establish how many calls you have "dropped" and therefore how active you were as a market maker.

Each incoming call in which you quoted rates counts as a call even if the counterparty did not in fact deal.

Network deals are deals done with named counterparties in an Interactive trading session. This item is not relevant in this version of *Risk Manager*.

Corp deals are trades made by your simulated corporate dealers – not relevant in this version of *Risk Manager*.

We would be looking for you to complete an average two or three deals per simulated hour's trading.

Spread/Market

These statistics show how close your quotations were, on average, to the prevailing market rates.

A positive number under the **Bid** column indicates that you quoted, on average, outside the market bid; a negative number indicates that you quoted inside it.

A positive number under the **Offer** indicates that you have quoted outside the market offer, on average; a negative number means that you have quoted inside it.

A positive number under both the **Bid** and the **Offer** columns therefore indicates that your spreads were, on average, wider than the market's. If your spread was significantly wider than the market, this indicates a lack of comfort with the market-making role.

The figures in brackets show the dispersion of your quotes from prevailing market rates – in technical terms, the standard deviation of the average spreads.

Average Speed

This shows the average time (in seconds) you took to execute a trade, as a market user (**Out**) or market maker (**In**). The time is measured from the moment you press the phone line button to the moment the trade is confirmed or cancelled. But speed alone is not the vital factor – it is of course possible to react very quickly but wrongly.

We recommend that you deal at a "safe speed," one in which you have control – you know what you are doing and what the results of your actions will be. A reasonable average response time to aim for is 15 seconds per deal.

System Usage

Pause: Hitting the button is recorded on each occasion. If it is pressed more than a couple of times during the session we take this as a sign you may be feeling the stress of the market and are not perhaps as comfortable as you might be with interpreting the information presented to you.

Typos: the number of typing errors that are made when entering a deal, giving rise to an error message like "I don't understand what you have entered" from Risk Manager. This is a useful measure of the propensity of the user to make clerical errors. A high figure here suggests that the user must improve his/her accuracy, as keyboard errors can be a costly source of problems in deal execution and settlement.

Exposure

% Matched Profits: shows the % of deals matched at profit. For example, if you bought US$10 million at 45 and closed this position with two deals – one for 4 million at 55 and one for 6 million at 20 – the figure reported would be 50% since only one of the two closing deals was profitable.

This statistic does not attempt to weight profitable trades either by size or price. It is a simple measure designed to capture the trainee's jobbing skill. Looked at alongside the total number of deals done, it shows the extent to which the user has been able to turn positions around profitably.

Max Fx($): shows the maximum net FX exposure attained during the trading session, in US dollars equivalent.

Max VAL 1%: shows the maximum interest rate exposures (market risk) taken during a trading session. It is measured in cash terms as the profit/loss that would result from a 1% parallel shift in the yield curve. (This statistic applies only to forward or fixed-interest dealing sessions.)

Trading Lessons

There are a number of basic trading rules which have been learned by FX dealers over the years through trial and error. Here are some of the main ones. Think about your performance in the first simulated dealing session and consider what areas you believe need improvement.

Never break a limit (it may cost you your job)

Dealing limits are there to control risk. Exposing your organization beyond those limits may put at risk the performance and standing of the whole institution, not just yourself. There should not be too many problems if you go over a limit by a few thousand dollars in the heat of the moment. But if you must exceed a limit by a significant amount, ask your Chief Dealer first.

Which currency am I trading?

In the simulated dealing session just completed, you may have had problems remembering which currency you are buying or selling. The convention is that by default you buy or sell base currency (in this session dollars) unless the amount is preceded by the currency name.

If the mark is strengthening, for example, the obvious reaction is to buy marks. If you enter **b** for buy into the deal slip, however, you **must** remember to put **DEM** before the amount. Alternatively, you should enter **s** for sell and then enter a dollar amount – if you are buying marks, you are also selling dollars.

Suppose that you have filled in a deal slip with the data shown in Figure 14.7.

You have asked CITI for a quote in "spot dollar-mark" (quoted currency is D-marks).

• The market maker has quoted you 2.2550/55 in amounts of up to $5 million. That means that they will buy US dollars and sell

Fig 14.7

Deal slip for DEM amount

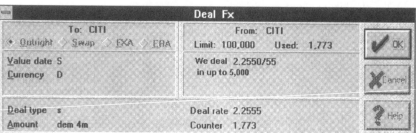

D-marks at 2.2550, and sell US dollars and buy D-marks at 2.2555.

- You then sold DM4 million at 2.2555, so you bought US$1.773 million.

If you trade an amount which is less than US$1 million, the market maker will consider that the amount is less than a normal market amount and re-quote the rates by widening the spread.

Suppose the dollar now weakens to a *big figure* of around 2.24. You could take your profit by completing the following deal:

Deal slip for a USD amount

Fig 14.8

Deal Fx		
To: CHMA	From: CHMA	
◆ Outright ◇ Swap ◇ FXA ◇ FRA	Limit: 100,000 Used: -1,773	✔ OK
Value date S	We show 2.2463/68	
Currency D	Good for 1773	✖ Cancel
Deal type s	Deal rate 2.2463	? Help
Amount 1773	Counter 3,983	

In this example you have entered a dollar amount – the computer interprets the number 1773 as thousands of dollars, so the amount is US$1,773,000. Note that the counter-amount incorporates your loss of DM17,000. In the first deal you sold DM4 million and in the second deal you will receive only DM3.983 million.

The lesson is: make sure you know which currency you are dealing in, and make sure that you complete the deal slip correctly.

K.I.S.S (stands for "keep it simple, stupid!")

A good dealer concentrates on one or a small group of currencies. He or she will formulate a strategy and close the position before starting a new one. A dealer may "test the water" first with smaller deals and only then build up into a position in stages.

If the trend starts to change, the dealer will start to unwind his/her position, gradually if the change is uncertain, more aggressively if it is confirmed. Large deals tend to be more difficult to execute, especially when the market is moving quickly – and they may move the market against you.

Know your position

A good dealer does not need to consult the electronic position keeper on the system to know whether he is long or short a currency, or whether he is in profit. The net position can be kept in your head or jotted down (the latter is more reliable).

At all times you need to know whether you are on the right side of the market or not and by how much. Then you need to have at least a broad idea of the average rate at which you are in. Most dealers think in terms of "pips made" or "pips down." Time spent on the details shown on the position keeper is time away from the market.

What to do with overnight positions

If you have a position when the date changes, effectively you will have carried an overnight position. Having moved one day forward, this position cannot now be squared by means of a spot deal since it settles tomorrow. To square a position for value tomorrow you should buy or sell the currency (as required) by entering **tom** against VALUE DATE in the deal slip.

In the real world, this position would normally be "rolled over" so that its value date is once again spot. This allows you to continue managing the position in the spot market, which has the greater depth and the narrower spreads. However, you do not have rollover facilities in the Spot Dealing Module.

Thus if you are long 10 million dollars for value spot but short 10 million for value tomorrow, effectively you do not have an FX exposure – although you do have a one-day funding gap.

Cut your losses early

It is easy to get obsessed with the prospect of hitting the jackpot and to forget to cut losses before they get worse. Also resist taking a profit before a change in the market trend has been confirmed. Statistically, a dealer who cuts losses quickly and holds on to profitable positions for as long as possible cannot help but make profits over the longer run, even if he reads the market right only 50% of the time. Nobody should be too concerned with the occasional "bad day." If you are not allowed to make losses you cannot trade for profit. What matters is the dealer's performance over the course of a few months to a year.

See also *Stay active* and *Shading your rates* on page 249.

Part 3

The Money Markets

■ ■ ■

"... it becomes increasingly possible to speak of 'the money market,' rather than a collection of sometimes totally independent domestic markets."

Market Overview

Definition

The money markets are wholesale financial markets in which sovereign states, banks and major corporations raise funds through certain types of loans, or by issuing debt securities.

Many of the securities issued are negotiable and actively traded in a secondary market by investors and intermediaries worldwide. The market includes various types of discount bills, promissory notes, certificates of deposit and bonds. It also includes certain types of short-term deposits which, although strictly speaking they are non-negotiable, can be "bought" and "sold" as if they were.

As exchange controls and other barriers to the movement of international capital continue to be dismantled across Europe and elsewhere, it becomes increasingly possible to speak of "*the* money market," rather than a collection of sometimes totally independent domestic markets.

Except for some markets in "derivative products," which are traded in organized exchanges, there are no physical trading floors for money market instruments. As in the foreign exchange market, trading takes place over the phone, telex or fax, and the market keeps in touch via the electronic news and price information networks supplied by Reuters, Telerate or by the individual brokers.

Participants in this market are scattered around the world. Instant 24-hour communication between them makes it virtually impossible nowadays to exploit wide discrepancies between the cost of money (net of exchange cover) in different financial centres. Large institutional investors monitor the returns available in each market and can switch funds virtually instantaneously into higher yielding assets. At the same time, borrowers constantly search for the cheapest ways to raise money.

New York is far and away the largest money centre, servicing the richest economic nation in the world. Its size is difficult to quantify, as it is to a large extent a matter of definition. However, we are talking of a total amount of national and international debt outstanding of the order of $2–3,000 billion, with a daily turnover in the secondary market of at least $500 billion. Because of its colossal size and openness, developments in the US money markets have immediate repercussions in the rest of the world.

The next two major money centres, by size, are Tokyo and London, although in terms of influence, London is far more significant, being the principal base for Eurocurrency operations.

Traditionally a distinction is made between the money markets, which cover debt instruments with maturities of up to 12 months, and the capital markets which deal with longer-dated securities.

The 12-month barrier exists because in the wholesale market interest on loans maturing inside a year is typically paid in "bullet" form – that is, in one chunk at maturity of the loan – whereas interest on longer debt tends to be paid in installments, or "coupons," throughout the life of the loan. Not many investors are prepared to take a risk on all the interest as well as the principal for a number of years.

How the interest is paid makes a big difference to the way debt securities are valued, as we shall see. However, nowadays the distinction between these two "markets" is blurred.

Obviously, as medium-term securities approach maturity they become comparable to money market investments, and indeed they are traded as such.

Various markets in derivative products straddle the 12-month barrier. For example, interest rate futures contracts are now traded out to seven years in some exchanges.

Derivative products are synthetic instruments whose market prices are derived from underlying "cash" securities; we shall look at some of these later in the book.

Some short-dated securities pay interest before maturity while other long-term instruments, such as zero-coupon bonds, pay no interest at all but are purchased at a price less than their face value.

Money market traders eventually become to a greater or lesser extent specialists in one or a set of related instruments, but it is no longer possible to be completely insulated from the long end of the market.

Market Participants

Borrowers include corporations, banks, governments and supranational entities. The major investors are pension funds, insurance companies, mutual funds and also corporate treasurers who manage their firms' liquid assets.

End-users (borrowers and investors) are brought together by professional dealers working for investment banks or securities houses. These firms specialize in bringing new issues to the market and providing liquidity to the secondary market. They include legendary names like Salomon Brothers, Nomura, J.P. Morgan, Credit Suisse First Boston, and hundreds more besides.

Dealers make markets in deposits and negotiable paper by quoting bid and offer (ask) prices to other dealers, brokers and investors.

One major source of revenue, for dealers with strong distribution networks, is in the bid–offer spreads they make to retail customers. However, most dealers will also take positions in securities, for their own account, looking to make profits from movements in interest rates.

Other key players are the brokers and the central banks. We shall briefly examine the role of brokers next.

Brokers

Brokers link buyers and sellers of money market instruments (borrowers and lenders of funds).

Dealers have direct lines to inter-dealer brokers through which they feed their bid and offered prices. The brokers take the highest bid and the lowest offered prices and broadcast these back to all their clients by phone or, increasingly, through electronic price screens. Any dealer can call the broker and within seconds deal at the broadcast prices.

Brokers are a valuable source of general information on market conditions although they are always careful not to divulge who, specifically, is in the market.

Buying or selling through a broker gives the benefit of anonymity. Only when a price has been struck is the name of the counterparty revealed to each side, for settlement purposes, although the preservation of anonymity is so crucial in some markets that some brokers will work on a "no-name basis."

Brokers do not themselves take "long" or "short" positions in securities, but make their profits by charging commission for the deals they help to arrange, as agents.

On US treasury notes and bonds typical brokerage would be **Examples** 1/128% of the principal amount. So a trader dealing in $1 million bonds would pay:

(1/128) / 100 × 1,000,000
= $78.12

In most short-term markets brokerage is calculated not as a flat percentage, as above, but on a percentage *per annum* of the amount traded.

In New York brokerage of 0.005% ("1/2 of an 01") per annum of the amount dealt would be paid on six-month treasury bills by the side initiating the trade. So for a $1-million deal the trader would pay:

0.005/100 × 1,000,000 × 6/12 = $25

These are high-volume markets where broker competition is fierce. In less liquid markets brokerage can be significantly more expensive. For example, on a three-month Euro-time deposit brokerage in London, at "2 basis points," would work out at about $50 per million and would be payable by both parties.

The more tiered the market, the more counter parties prefer to deal directly rather than through a broker.

Brokers tend to be very strong in markets such as those for government securities, where the products are fairly homogeneous in terms of credit risk. In such markets dealers save a lot of "shopping" time by dealing through brokers, rather than directly with each other.

However, in markets where the quality of the borrower is important – for example in bank certificates of deposit, where a CD issued by Morgan is not the same thing as a CD issued by Chase – the concept of a market price, which can be broadcast by the broker, is less meaningful. In such markets dealers prefer to trade direct.

Broking nowadays is dominated by a small number of large firms. Clients want their broker to supply them instantly with prices and speedy execution on a whole range of related instruments for wafer-thin fees.

How Interest Rates Move

The cost of borrowing money (its "time value") is measured by the rate of interest. There is not one but a whole range of interest rates, each applicable to a different class of borrower and for a different term. Thus, the cost of 12-month money will be different from the cost of one-month or five-year money. The lender will require a different price for locking his money into investments of different maturities. Three key factors come into play:

- **Credit risk.** The longer the term of the loan the higher the risk that the borrower, through a change in circumstances, may not be able to repay the principal.

- **Liquidity Risk.** Some types of money market paper are less easy to liquidate in a hurry than others, because the market may not be deep enough, dealers may quote very wide spreads, the securities may not be in bearer form, etc.

- **Market risk.** The risk of making a loss on a portfolio, after having locked into a given rate, as a result of changes in general market conditions rather than in the quality of a specific investment.

Market risk is often put forward as a reason why long-term rates should be higher than short-term rates. By going into short-maturing investments, lenders can "keep their options open" and therefore take advantage of favorable market developments; whereas long-term investors, by being locked into a fixed rate, clearly cannot.

As we shall see later, short-term investments are actually riskier to long-term investors such as pension funds and insurance companies, who need fixed income in order to service their long-term liabilities. One investor's poison is another's medicine.

We shall explore the time dimension first, which relates to market risk, leaving credit risk to a later section (see pages 135–137).

The Yield Curve

We can separate credit risk from market risk by looking at the term structure of interest rates on government securities, which in most developed markets is assumed to be credit risk-free.

The yield curve displays graphically the relationship between interest rates for different maturities – the term structure of interest rates.

Analysis of the yield curve is central to money market trading and investment, as we shall see throughout this section of the book.

Yield curve for UK Government securities

Fig 15.1

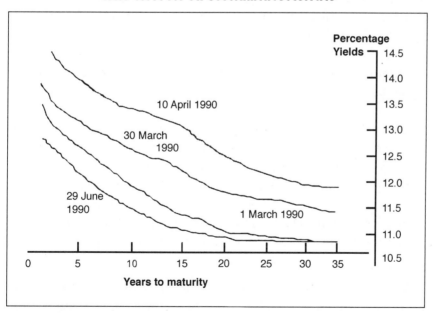

Percentage yields are plotted along the vertical axis and term to maturity along the horizontal one.

The yield curve reflects expectations about future interest rates. An upward slope means that short-term rates are expected to rise; an inverted curve means that the market thinks they will fall.

If the investor expects interest rates to rise within the next 12 months he will demand a higher rate to lock into two- or three-year loans because by committing his funds for a long period he forgoes the opportunity of benefiting from higher rates in the near future. Conversely, if the investor expects future rates to fall, he can afford to lock into long-term lending at a lower rate.

Central banks can influence short-term interest rates directly by adding funds to, or soaking up funds from, the money markets. When the central bank sells government securities to the private sector, funds flow out of the money market and less is available for other lending, so interest rates rise. Conversely, when the central bank buys paper from the market the money supply is increased and interest rates fall.

If a credit squeeze engineered by the central bank is believed to be a temporary phenomenon (in support of a weak currency or to stem excess demand), the yield curve will invert: short-term rates go higher than long-term rates. Borrowers become reluctant to commit themselves to high funding costs for long periods because they believe rates will come down again.

Interest rates seldom move up or down by the same amount across the board.

Shifts at the long end of the yield curve are less dramatic but also less predictable. The long end is more strongly affected by inflationary expectations. Investors adjust market rates to maintain the perceived time value of their investments in real terms. Just about every economic statistic has some effect on market sentiment: the current trade balance, consumer borrowing and spending trends, the level of business inventories, the money supply growth, and so on.

The role of the money market economist working in the dealing room is to monitor these statistics and consider their implication for future inflation and interest rates.

Market rates move whenever the published figures differ significantly from what the market had anticipated.

Most of the time yield curves slope upwards. Many trading strategies in the money markets rely on the yield curve not being flat, as we shall see.

Credit Risk

One key factor affecting the value of a debt security is the perceived risk of the issuer not being able to meet its obligations.

In bank lending the bank determines the credit risk of the borrower and adjusts its rates accordingly. When borrowings are made directly from investors through the issue of debt securities, the investors themselves must have access to information on the creditworthiness of the issuers.

This is achieved through the services of credit ratings agencies, of which the two most important ones are Standard & Poor's and Moody's Investor Service. A borrower must have a credit rating to attract investors, and pays the agencies to carry out their investigations. However the agencies remain fully independent.

The Ratings

The two main agencies use different rating systems, although they are directly comparable. Figure 15.2 shows the equivalent ratings for long-term paper.

Credit ratings – long-term paper

Fig 15.2

	S&P	Moody's
Best-quality grade	AAA	Aaa
	AA+	Aa1
High-quality grade	AA	Aa2
	AA−	Aa3
	A+	A1
Upper-medium grade	A	A2
	A−	A3
	BBB+	Baa1
Medium grade	BBB	Baa2
	BBB−	Baa3

Ratings go down to single C, but anything below BBB– and Baa3 is classified as speculative to low grade, which is not considered suitable for institutional investment. Most "junk bonds" fall within such categories.

Most of the world's strongest banks are rated AA+ to AA– (Aa1 to Aa3). Very few nowadays are still AAA, which is a highly prized rating.

The agencies rate specific issues of long-term securities and not the borrower itself. In practice, the main differences arise between a borrower's senior debt and its subordinated debt, which ranks below the senior debt for payment of interest and principal, in the event of liquidation.

While the rating scales are equivalent, both S&P and Moody's do their own independent risk evaluations. It is quite common to see a security with different ratings from the two agencies, although a difference of more than one level would be unusual.

Short-term paper ratings are usually applicable to all the short-term debt securities issued by a particular borrower. In other words they reflect an assessment of the asset backing and liquidity of the borrower. These ratings are shown in Figure 15.3.

Fig 15.3

Credit ratings – short-term paper

S&P	Moody's
A1+	P1
A1	
A2	P2
A3	P3

Moody's P1 is intended to cover S&P's A1+ and A1. In practice the cut-off between P1 and P2 is a little higher than that between A1 and A2. Thus it is quite common to see ratings of A1/P2 or A2/P3, but A2/P1 or A3/P2 would be most unusual. There are no ratings below A3 and P3: paper in this category would be regarded as below investment grade and therefore unrated.

Event risk refers to the risk that the credit rating of the borrower or issuer might be downgraded.

Before a rating agency changes the credit rating of a name, they will normally put the name or the paper on "credit watch with positive/negative implications." However, where an event happens overnight – such as a take-over bid – the agencies may alter the ratings immediately.

A borrower's credit rating affects the level of interest it has to pay to sell its securities to investors. The difference in the cost of capital between an A1-P1 and an A2-P2 borrower can be anything from 1/4% to 2% per annum, depending on general market conditions.

To distinguish clearly between credit risk and market risk, the return on corporate paper is expressed as a percentage margin or spread over the current yield on government paper for the same maturity. For example, three-month US commercial paper typically trades between 1/4% and 1.1/2% above the three-month US treasury bill, to which it is identical in every respect, except in the credit quality of the borrower.

An alternative benchmark in the money markets is to price corporate debt as a margin over the banks' cost of funding. One of the most widely used reference rates is LIBOR, the London Interbank Offered Rate, which is the rate at which top-name banks can borrow Eurodollars or other Eurocurrencies to fund their loan books.

Summary

In this chapter we have introduced, defined and examined the money markets. We distinguished between the capital and money markets and identified key players such as brokers. We then studied the main factors which cause interest rate fluctuation, and introduced the yield curve as an important analytical tool in money market trading. Finally, we took a close look at credit risk, and the systems of ratings which partially determine how it is perceived.

Keywords

Before moving on to the next chapter, please make sure that you are familiar with the following terms and their definitions:

- bullet investments
- derivatives
- credit risk
- liquidity risk
- yield curve
- credit ratings
- event risk
- market risk.

■ ■ ■

"The Eurodeposit market is a huge, round-the-clock business spanning Singapore and Hong Kong, Bahrain, Frankfurt, Paris, London and New York."

Eurodeposits

Overview The Eurodeposit market is a huge, round-the-clock business spanning Singapore and Hong Kong, Bahrain, Frankfurt, Paris, London and New York. In this chapter we will cover the major features of this market.

Fundamentals

While the Eurodeposits market is 24-hour, it is deepest when London opens. London interbank money market rates are the finest rates at which top-name banks will lend to or borrow from each other.

The bulk of Eurodeposit deals are in the three- to six-month maturity. This is because most of these deposits are used to fund medium-term bank credits with similar rollover periods. However, fixed-deposit deals for up to five years do sometimes occur. The pricing and interest rate calculations on such deals resemble those used in the bond markets and we shall not use them in this book.

Money market dealers quote two-way rates:

- **London Interbank Offered Rate (LIBOR):** the rate they charge for lending money (they offer funds).
- **London Interbank Bid Rate (LIBID):** The rate they pay for taking a deposit (they bid for funds).

LIBOR is of special importance. Most Eurocurrency loans are based on a three- or six-month LIBOR plus a margin which reflects the perceived credit risk of the borrower. The riskier the borrower, the higher the margin over LIBOR. Triple-A corporates are able to extract sub-LIBOR funding from their bankers.

LIBOR is also used to "fix" payments in a variety of derivative contracts. The British Bankers Association (BBA) publishes daily official LIBORs used in the calculation of settlement amounts on derivative contracts such as Forward Rate Agreements ("FRABBA rates") and interest rate swaps ("BBAIRS rates"). Such rates are calculated as an average of the rates actually quoted by half a dozen or so representative market makers at a specific time of the day.

Figure 16.1 shows a Dow Jones Telerate information page for Eurodollar rates.

Typical Eurodollar rates prices screen (FRAs and swaps also shown)

Fig 16.1

```
                        [M.W. MARSHALL & CO LTD]
  13/09  13:27 GMT       [ USD MONEYMARKETS ]        13/09/96 13:27  4845
      USD EURODEPOSITS         USD FRA        SHORT SWAPS          MEDIUM SWAPS
 O/N| 5  1/4 - 5  1/8 |1X4  5.71-67  SEP/SEP| 6.04-00  2Y| 6.33-29
 T/N| 5  3/8 - 5  1/4 |2X5  5.79-75  DEC/DEC| 6.23-19  3Y| 6.52-48
 S/N| 5  3/8 - 5  1/4 |3X6  5.87-83  MAR/MAR| 6.38-34  4Y| 6.66-62
 1WK| 5  3/8 - 5  1/4 |4X7  5.87-83  JUN/JUN| 6.52-48  5Y| 6.79-75
 2WK| 5  7/16- 5  5/16|5X8  5.94-90  12M V 3| 6.04-01  7Y| 7.96-92
 3WK| 5 15/32- 5 11/32|6X9  5.99-95  18M V 3| 6.17-13  10Y| 7.13-09
 1MO| 5  7/16- 5  5/16|9X12 6.16-12  24M V 3| 6.33-29      UPDATED NY TIME
 2MO| 5  1/2 - 5  3/8                               ONLY QUOTES PLS
 3MO| 5  9/16- 5  7/16|1X7  5.84-80                 CALL NO. BELOW
 4MO| 5 11/16- 5  9/16|2X8  5.91-87  FOR ASIA TIME UPDATES & QUOTES PLS CALL
 5MO| 5 23/32- 5 19/32|3X9  5.98-94  MARSHALLS CMTS HK 2868-0566
 6MO| 5  3/4 - 5  5/8 |4X10 6.01-97  ODD RUN:
 9MO| 5 29/32- 5 25/32|5X11 6.07-03
 1YR| 6  1/32- 5 29/32|6X12 6.12-08  [FOR NY QUOTES SEE PAGE 4834        ]
```

Source: Dow Jones Telerate

In London the offered rate is quoted first, followed by the bid rate. In other financial centres the bid rate is quoted first, then the offer. If you are quoted two rates by a money market dealer, you will have to pay the higher rate for a loan but receive the lower rate for a deposit.

Eurocurrency rates are always quoted on a percentage per annum basis. Eurodollar rates are quoted to the nearest 1/16 (0.0625) or even 1/32 (0.03125) of a percent. Bid–offer spreads are typically 1/16% to 1/8%. Sometimes they widen to 1/4%, or they can be as fine as 1/32%.

A quote to the nearest 1/16% means that the minimum interest rate movement is 6.25 "basis points" (100bp = 1%). Eurosterling is also quoted in 16ths or 32nds.

Most other Eurocurrency rates are quoted in percentage decimals, to two decimal places. For example, a London dealer's offer and bid prices for Euromarks might be 8.45–40%. He will pay 8.40% for inward deposits, and will expect 8.45% for outward deposits of D-marks. The minimum interest rate movement here is 1 basis point.

Fixed Date Conventions

The market quotes prices for various "fixed dates." The short dates are shown in Figure 16.2.

The longer dates range from spot–one month (1M) all the way up to spot–12 months. The delivery or value date for funds is spot (two working days) unless specified otherwise.

Fig 16.2

Short dates

Overnight (O/N):	Starting today and maturing tomorrow.
"Tom-next" (T/N):	Starting tomorrow and maturing the next day (i.e., the spot date).
Spot-next (S/N):	Starting on the spot date and maturing the day after spot.
Spot-one week (S/W):	Starting spot and maturing seven days later.

Fixed money market dates coincide with forward FX value dates.

In the interbank market rates will of course be quoted for any irregular, "broken" or "cock" dates, on request. In normal market conditions rates of interest for broken dates are calculated by straight-line interpolation between the two adjacent fixed rates, although the bid–offer spreads for these may be a little wider.

The first step in identifying forward dates is to fix the spot date. A spot FX deal is normally settled two working days hence. So, if a spot trade is transacted on a Monday, it will be settled on the Wednesday.

If the settlement day should happen to fall on a weekend or a holiday, the settlement date will be "rolled over" to the next working day. Likewise, a deposit for value spot in a major foreign currency normally clears in two working days, although in quite a few money centres (e.g., London and New York), spot settlement in the local currency is nowadays normally for same-day value.

Once the spot date has been established, it is easy to find the forward fixed dates. If the spot date is 6 January, then the one-month forward date is 6 February, the two-month forward date is 6 March and so on.

If the forward date falls on a weekend or a holiday, it is rolled over to the next working day on which the relevant centre is open for business.

End/End Rule

If the spot date is a month-end, then all forward fixed dates will be month-end.

Month-End Roll Back

If the forward date lands on a month-end and that happens to be a weekend or a holiday, then it cannot be rolled forward to the next month. Settlement will be rolled back to the last working day of the same month.

Example

A two-month Eurodeposit booked in London on 26 February will be for value 28 February, the spot date. Since this is a month-end, the deposit will mature on 30 April. If 30 April is a Sunday, the deposit will mature on 28 April.

Interest Calculation

Interest on "depos" maturing within 12 months is paid at maturity only. It is paid at regular (typically half-yearly) intervals for longer-term contracts.

Normally the interest amount due on a Eurocurrency deposit or loan is calculated on the actual number of days elapsed, based on a 360-day year. With Eurosterling, the interest calculation is on a 365-day basis. These interest rate conventions are referred to as Actual/360 and Actual/365 respectively.

Example

On Monday, 17 September, a market maker quotes a six-month Eurodollar rate of 8.7/16–8.5/16% and takes US$20 million at 8.5/16%.

The funds will be for value (they will be made available) on Wednesday, 19 September. The deposit will mature on Tuesday, 19 March.

In this example, interest would be payable for a total of 183 days:

= 20,000,000 × 183/360 × 8.3125/100
= US$845,104.17

A 12-month (365-days) dollar deposit at 8.5/16% would pay $8.3125 per $100 for the first 360 days, plus an extra five days' interest at 8.5/16%.

This means that to convert an Actual/360 money market yield into a true annual yield we must multiply the quoted deposit rate by 365/360. Conversely, to represent a true yield in Eurodeposit terms we must multiply by 360/365.

Thus the true yield on a 12-month dollar deposit at 8.5/16% is 8.42795% and not 8.3125%: what you see on the screen is *not* what you get! The true rate is said to be "on a bond basis", because that rate is more directly comparable with bond yields. No adjustment is necessary in order to express a money market rate on a bond basis in the case of Actual/365 deposits, where the quoted rate is the true 365-day rate.

Fig 16.3 **Interest accrued and repayment amount on Eurocurrency deposits**

Accrued interest = $n/360^* \times r \times P$

where: n = number of days from value to maturity.

P = principal amount deposited or borrowed.

r = interest rate per year divided by 100.

Repayment amount = Principal   + Accrued interest

= P $+ n/360 \times r \times P$

= $P \times [1 + (n/360^* \times r)]$

*365 for Eurosterling

Typically, in debt instruments with maturities of 12 months or less, every day elapsed adds to the interest accrued, so the annual rate is pro-rated by the actual number of days elapsed. On the other hand, interest on deposits with maturities of 12 months or less is usually paid at maturity, so it is not necessary to allow the compounding of interest on interest.

Cancellation

The Eurodeposit is non-negotiable. Title to it is registered by the borrower, and cannot be assigned or transferred without the approval of both parties. Early cancellation by the lender or the borrower usually incurs an administration fee.

The easiest and most effective way for the lender to liquidate early is to borrow, from the same or another bank, using the first deposit as collateral. A borrower too can "cancel" his loan by placing the funds on deposit for an equivalent maturity. This can be done quickly in a market which is fairly liquid, although of course there may be brokerage costs and market rates may have moved against the trader.

The drawback is that deposits cancelled by offset increase the size of the trader's balance sheet and can put pressure on its capital adequacy ratios. In Chapter 18, we shall look at a negotiable version of the time deposit which gets around this problem – the certificate of deposit.

Summary

In this chapter, we have defined and examined the market in Eurodeposits, and listed the various fixed-date conventions used by the market. We then examined how interest on deposits is calculated, and looked at the terms and conditions which govern their use.

Before moving on, please be sure that you are familiar with the following terms and their definitions:

Keywords

- LIBID
- LIBOR
- BBA
- basis points
- fixed dates
- broken dates
- accrued interest.

The exercises in Chapter 17 provide practice in Eurodeposit dealing.

Exercise:
Deposit-Dealing

Listed below are various banks' Eurocurrency rates for various maturities, that is to say, the rates of interest that the banks would charge you for borrowing money and the rates that they would pay you for accepting a deposit with them.

1. Eurodollars   1 MONTH (31 days)
BANK A	8.11/16 – 8.1/2
BANK B	8.23/32 – 8.9/16
BANK C	8.21/32 – 8.17/32
BANK D	8. 5/8 – 8.15/32
BANK E	8.19/32 – 8.7/16

    (a) From which bank would you borrow dollars and what rate of interest would be applied?

    (b) What is the total interest payable to the lender at the maturity on your Eurodollar 10 million borrowing?

    (c) With which bank would you deposit money and at what rate of interest?

    (d) Quote a two-way rate, both for lending (offer) and borrowing (bid), that will encourage a "placer" of money to deal with you rather than with the other banks.

Answers

(a) Bank _____ lends dollars at _____

(b) Interest amount payable at maturity: _____

(c) Bank _____ borrows dollars at _____

(d) Your rates are _____ – _____

2. Eurosterling   3 MTHS (93 days)

BANK A	8.7187 – 8.90625
BANK B	8.75 – 8.9375
BANK C	8.6875 – 8.921875
BANK D	8.7812 – 8.96875
BANK E	8.8125 – 9.03125

(a) Which bank's bid would you hit and what rate would be applied?

(b) How much interest would you receive at maturity on a Eurosterling 7 million deposit?

(c) From which bank would you take sterling and what rate would be applied?

(d) Quote a two-way rate that will encourage a counterparty to "lift your offer" rather than the other banks'.

Answers

(a) Bank _____ borrows Eurosterling at _____

(b) Interest amount receivable at maturity:

£ _____

(c) Bank _____ lends Eurosterling at _____

(d) Your rates are _____

3. Euromarks   6 MTHS

BANK A	9.09 – 9.15
BANK B	9.11 – 9.17
BANK C	9.08 – 9.17
BANK D	9.09 – 9.13
BANK E	9.08 – 9.17

(a) From which bank would you borrow and at what rate?

(b) With which bank would you place and at what rate?

(c) Quote a rate that will encourage a lender to place with you, rather than with the other banks.

Answers

(a) Bank _____ lends D-marks at _____

(b) Bank _____ borrows D-marks at _____

(c) Your rates are _____ –_____

4. Eurodollars   2 MTHS

BANK A	8.5312 – 8.71875
BANK B	8.1/2 – 8.11/16
BANK C	8.4843 – 8.703125
BANK D	8.33/64 – 8.11/16
BANK E	8.17/32 – 8.23/32

(a) Which offer would you lift and at what rate?

(b) Which bid would you hit and at what rate?

(c) Quote a rate that will encourage a counterparty to hit your bid.

Answers

(a) Take bank _____ at _____

(b) Hit bank _____ at _____

(c) You "bid up" to: _____ – _____

5. Eurosterling   6 MTHS

BANK A	9.0781 – 9.265625
BANK B	9.00 – 9.3/16
BANK C	9.1/16 – 9.1/4
BANK D	9.0937 – 9.28125
BANK E	9.0468 – 9.265625

(a) Take bank _____ at _____

(b) Hit bank _____ at _____

(c) "Offer down" to: _____ – _____

■ ■ ■

*"The key concept
is the 'time value
of money.'"*

Fixed-Income Concepts

Overview   In this chapter we look at the valuation of future income flows arising from fixed-interest financial instruments. The key concept is the "time value of money."

Present Value and Future Value

A dollar today is worth more than a dollar in the future, because it can be invested and earn interest.

A dollar receivable in the future is worth less than a dollar receivable today, because an opportunity to earn interest has been lost.

The future value (FV) of $1 on a specific date in the future is the amount of money you would have if you invested $1 today for that period of time at a given rate of interest. FV is none other than the repayment amount, introduced previously. In a Eurodollar deposit FV was calculated as:

$$FV = \text{Principal} + \text{Accrued Interest}$$
$$= P \times [1 + (r \times n/360)]$$

where: P = Present value (the principal amount)
  n = Actual number of days elapsed
  r = Rate of interest / 100

Now, if $P today can generate $P \times (1+r \times n/360)$ in the future, it follows that $\dfrac{P}{[1+(r \times n/360)]}$ will generate $P in the future, where $\dfrac{P}{[1+(r \times n/360)]}$ P is the present value of P discounted at a rate of r%.

Example   You are to receive $10,000 in 182 days' time. What is the present value (PV) of this sum, given that current market interest rates are 10% per annum?

$$PV = \frac{\$10,000}{[1+(0.10 \times 182/360)]}$$
$$= \$9,518.77$$

In other words, $9,518.77 is the amount of money you would have to invest at an annual rate of 10.00% for this to grow into $10,000 after 182 days.

Figure 18.1 summarizes the relationships.

Present value and future value

Fig 18.1

Discount rate used = 10% per annum

TODAY   182 DAYS

PV = $9, 518.77   FV =
                                              $9, 518.77 ×
                                              [1+ (0.1 × 182/360)]
                                              = $10, 000

PV =   FV = $10, 000

$$\frac{\$10,000}{[1 + (0.1 \times 182/360)]}$$
= $9, 518.77

The Effect of Compounding

In the previous example we assumed the investment did not pay interest before maturity. Now let's see how the present value formula changes when we allow for interest payments during the life of the investment.

We place £10,000 on a two-year deposit which pays interest at a **Example** fixed rate of 10% per annum. The first interest amount, or coupon, will be paid on the anniversary of the deposit and the second coupon will be paid at maturity, one year later, together with the principal.

The *interest period* is one year and the rate for each period is assumed to be 10%. What is the future value of this investment?

The interest period (or coupon period) is the number of days between one interest (or coupon) payment and the next.

Interest on sterling deposits is calculated on a 365-day year basis, so we do not need to pro-rata the rate of interest (in fact, debt instruments with a maturity of more than one year do not use the Actual/360 money market day-count convention anyway).

At the end of the first year, the deposit will pay interest at 10% on 10,000. If the investment matured at this point the total repayment amount would be:

$$10,000 + (10,000 \times 0.10)$$
$$= 10,000 \times (1+0.10)$$
$$= 11,000$$

In fact, at the end of Year 1, we will be reinvesting a total of £11,000, at an assumed rate of 10%, for another year. This consists of the original £10,000, which is automatically rolled over, plus the first interest payment of £1,000 which has now been "capitalized".

Therefore, at the end of Year 2, the final repayment amount will be:

$$11,000 \qquad \qquad \times (1 + 0.10)$$
$$= [10,000 \times (1 + 0.10)] \times (1 + 0.10)$$
$$= 10,000 \times (1 + 0.10)^2$$
$$= 12,100$$

If all the interest had been paid at maturity of the loan and without "compounding" the first year's payment, then the final repayment amount would have been only £12,000 – the £10,000 of principal plus two years' worth of interest at 10%, or £2,000. The difference in income amounts to £100, which is the interest on £1,000 at a rate of 10%.

The stage-payment of interest has compounded our returns by allowing us to earn "interest on interest."

When you think about it, it is not so much that interest is physically paid out on the first anniversary that makes the difference, as the fact that it is compounded. Even if a loan paid no interest until maturity, but interest on it was compounded annually at 10%, its final repayment amount would be the same as in our example.

It follows that the present value of £10,000 payable in two years' time, when we assume that interest is compounded annually, will be less than the present value when we assume that it is not. Figure 18.2 shows the general formulae for present and future value, in the case where interest is compounded during the period to maturity. Spend a minute comparing these formulae with the ones shown earlier, where interest was not compounded.

Future value and present value – the compounding case

Fig 18.2

Future value (FV) = P x $(1 + r/t)^t$

Present value (PV) = $\dfrac{P}{(1 + r/t)^t}$

where: P = principal amount

t = number of interest periods the money is invested for

r = nominal interest rate or discount rate per year divided by 100.

Equivalent Returns

The compounding phenomenon is one of the factors which distinguishes short-term money market instruments, with maturities of 12 months or less, from medium-term capital market instruments. The main reason is that traditionally investors like to see the borrower paying something during the term of a medium-term loan, even if this is only interest. However, the compounding phenomenon is not unique to the capital markets.

Example

A money market investor is offered the opportunity of placing $10,000 either at 10% for a straight 12 months (assume 360 days) or at 9.80% for six months (180 days) with automatic rollover for another six months, also at 9.80%.

Which option should the investor chose?

At first sight it appears that he should chose the first option – the 12 months at 10%. However, if we work out the annual equivalent rate on the second option, we discover that, because of the compounding effect, it is actually a more interesting proposition. We do this as follows:

Return on two six-monthly depos = Annual equivalent rate

$10,000 \times (1 + 180/360 \times 0.098)^2 = 10,000 \times (1 + r_a)$

$(1 + 0.098/2^2)$ $= (1 + r_a)$

     $r_a = (1 + 0.098/2)^2 - 1$

        $= 0.1004$ or 10.04%

When the calculation proceeds from left to right, as in our example, we are effectively "decompounding" a semi-annual rate into an annual equivalent rate. You can also go the other way, from right to left, if you want to calculate the semi-annually compounded equivalent of an annual rate.

The compounding/decompounding relationship crops up in a wide variety of contexts, as we shall see.

Summary

In this chapter, we examined the "time value of money" in relation to its present and future value, and studied how these values are calculated. In particular, we examined the effect of compounding on an investment return, and introduced the relationship between simple and compound rates of return.

Keywords

Before turning to Chapter 19, please make sure you are familiar with the following terms and their definitions:

- present value and future value
- interest period
- capitalized interest payments
- compounding and decompounding.

■ ■ ■

"When interest rates rise, the market value of fixed income securities will fall, and vice versa."

Coupon Securities

In this and the next chapter we shall turn to the main negotiable money market securities – certificates of deposit,
treasury bills, bankers' acceptances and commercial paper.

Definition

These instruments have a number of common features:

- They are issued with a fixed "face value" or redemption amount.
- They mature at some specified future date, at which point the principal amount or face value is repaid to the holder of the paper.
- If they pay fixed amounts of interest, either during their life or at
  maturity, the "coupon" rate is established at the time of issue.
- Their market value can differ from their face value, and depends
  upon whether interest is payable, and how the interest payable
  compares with current market rates.

**A fixed-income security is any money market instrument
whose future cash flows have been contractually defined
and can be determined in advance.**

Both Eurocurrency deposits and fixed-coupon bonds fall clearly
into this category, as the income streams on both these securities
can be calculated precisely in advance. They are fixed for the term
of the contract and do not vary with changes in market conditions.

Company stocks, on the other hand, are not fixed-income securities
because they don't mature, and their future income streams cannot
be precisely determined – they can only be assumed or forecast.

The term is used rather loosely nowadays, as many so-called fixed-
income securities contain embedded options or other conditional
clauses which make their future cash flows anything but fixed.
However, it highlights two important characteristics which all these
types of assets have in common:

- Any financial asset which gives its owner title to a known future
  income stream (no matter how irregular) can be priced by
  discounting all the future cash flows back to a present value.

- Since the future income streams are fixed, the higher the discount rate applied, the lower their present value (hence market price).

When interest rates rise, the market value of bonds, bills, commercial paper, certificates of deposit and a myriad other fixed-income securities will fall, and vice versa.

Certificates of Deposit

A CD is a receipt for funds deposited at a bank or other financial institutions for a specified time period and at a specified interest rate.

CDs are bank IOUs issued in bearer form: title to the funds, as evidenced by the certificate, is conferred upon its holder. For investors, there is an obvious advantage over the time deposit, since CDs can be easily negotiated in the secondary market in the event of an unexpected cash requirement. Obviously, the certificates must be kept in safe custody.

Fig 19.1

Sample fixed-rate certificate of deposit

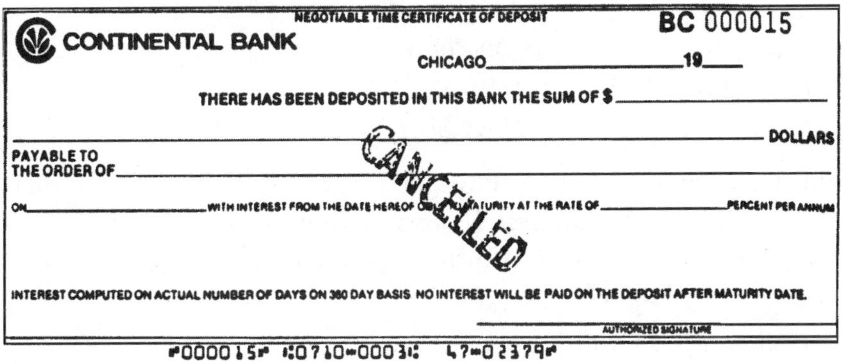
CONTINENTAL BANK
NEGOTIABLE TIME CERTIFICATE OF DEPOSIT
BC 000015
CHICAGO ______ 19__
THERE HAS BEEN DEPOSITED IN THIS BANK THE SUM OF $ ______
______ DOLLARS
PAYABLE TO THE ORDER OF ______
ON ______ WITH INTEREST FROM THE DATE HEREOF ON MATURITY AT THE RATE OF ______ PERCENT PER ANNUM
CANCELLED
INTEREST COMPUTED ON ACTUAL NUMBER OF DAYS ON 360 DAY BASIS NO INTEREST WILL BE PAID ON THE DEPOSIT AFTER MATURITY DATE.
AUTHORIZED SIGNATURE
⑈000015⑈ ⑆0710⑉0003⑆ 47⑉02379⑈

The fine print on most CDs begins with a statement like "There has been deposited in this bank the sum of . . ."
Source: Stigum (1983)

For this convenience a top-name bank can secure funds by issuing CDs in the Eurocurrency market, and paying perhaps 10–15 basis points below the comparable LIBOR.

The interest on a CD, like interest on the time deposit it represents, is calculated on the actual number of days the instrument is outstanding. In most Eurocurrencies the calculation is based on a 360-day year, with the notable exception of sterling CDs which are based on a 365-day year.

For short-term CDs interest is usually payable at maturity, so they are "bullet" securities. However with CDs which are issued with maturities of more than one year, interest is typically paid semi-annually.

Fair Value

A CD is a title to a known future cash stream of principal plus interest. How can we calculate a fair market price for such an asset? The key concept again is that of present value.

Example

Issuer	Citicorp
Rating:	A1-P1
Issue date	1 January 1995
Maturity:	1 January 1996
Face value:	$1,000,000
Interest payable:	8.1/2% pa
Settlement date:	1 November 1995

This Citicorp 8.1/2% had an original maturity (or "tenor", as they say in London) of 365 days. What we know for certain is that whoever presents the certificate to the appointed Paying Agent at maturity collects a total of:

$$1,000,000 \times (1 + 0.085 \times 365/360)$$
$$= \$1,086,180.56$$

What we don't know is how much the paper is worth today.

There are now only 61 days left to maturity and the current two-month deposit rates are 9.3/4%. The fair price should be that amount of money, P, which when placed on deposit today at 9.3/4% for 61 days will also result in $1,086,180.56. This equates the return on the CD with the return currently available on a deposit for the same maturity. In other words:

$$P \times [1+(0.0975 \times 61/360)] = 1,086,180.56$$

$$P = \frac{+\ 1,086,180.56}{[1 + (0.0975 \times 61/360)]}$$

$$= \$1,068,527.63$$

This is the present value of the CD's future cash flow, 61 days from maturity, when discounted at 9.75%. It sets a theoretical price for the instrument – its actual market value will be somewhere around this price, depending on market liquidity and issuer-specific credit risk considerations, which we have ignored.

Calculating proceeds of secondary market CD

Fig 19.2

$$Proceeds = FV \times \left[\frac{(Coupon \times original\ life) + (B \times 100)}{(YTM \times days\ remaining) + (B \times 100)} \right]$$

Where:
FV = Face value
B = Day count basis (360 or 365)
YTM = Yield to maturity (in percent, i.e., 0.05 is 5%)

Yield

Of course you may or may not get a fair price for your CD in the market. Some measure is required to indicate how good or bad is the price you are offered. This is what the yield to maturity (YTM) – also known as the money market yield (MMY) – does.

YTM is the rate of return that you would achieve on a fixed-income security, if you bought it at a given price and held it to maturity.

The yield on a CD can be compared with the returns available on time deposits and other money market instruments.

Example You are offered the Citicorp 8 1/2% CD in the previous example at US$1,065,000.00. What yield does this represent?

We could use the present value formula above, except that now we know what P is. What we don't know is the rate of discount, r, to which this equates:

$$1,065,000.00 = \frac{1,086,180.56}{[1 + (r \times 61/360)]}$$

Rearranged, this formula tells us that:

$$r = \frac{360}{61} \times \frac{(1,086,180.56 - 1,065,000)}{1,065,000}$$

= 0.1174 or 11.74%.

At the price it is offered, therefore, the CD yields nearly 2% more than the comparable time deposit – an excellent deal!

Another way to arrive at the yield formula is to start from its definition and express the profit made on the deal in percentage per annum terms:

Profit to maturity on investment (in dollars):

$$= (1,086,180.56 - 1,065,000)$$

As a proportion of amount invested:

$$= \frac{(1,086,180.56 - 1,065,000)}{1,065,000}$$

Annualized:

$$= \frac{360}{61} \times \frac{(1,086,180.56 - 1,065,000)}{1,065,000}$$

= 11.74%, which is identical to the earlier equation.

Dealers and Brokers

As well as on-selling the CDs to retail, dealers make an "inside market" showing two-way prices to each other on demand. They create the secondary market by standing ready to quote bid and offer prices at all times to clients and to other dealers. The normal settlement date for domestic CDs is the following day, the same as domestic deposits.

The largest profits come not from the margin earned on retail distribution but from taking long or short positions in anticipation of changes in market interest rates. As we have seen, a fall in market (discount) rates will increase CD values on the secondary market. However, the risk is that if market rates rise, CD prices will fall and the relative illiquidity of such instruments, in comparison with government paper such as Treasury Bills, can make it difficult for dealers to get out of large positions. Consequently, not many dealers run very large positions in CDs.

As in other markets there are brokers who provide anonymity and speedy communication between dealers. Typical brokerage is 1 basis point per annum on the amount dealt ("an 01") which is paid by the party initiating the trade.

Price runs in the three–six month maturities are typically quoted. However, the market does not lend itself as easily to broking as the government securities market, where the product is homogeneous from the point of view of credit risk.

Market Pricing

In the previous example, the price quoted on that 8 1/2% Citicorp CD would have been 11.74%, rather than US$1,065,000.00 which is the settlement amount.

CDs are quoted on a discount-to-yield basis rather than in cash terms.

There is a very good reason for this. If you were quoted 11.80 – 11.74 for that 8 1/2% Citicorp paper, this means that the market maker is willing to buy it from you for a cash amount that will give him a yield of 11.80%, or he will sell it to you for a cash sum that will yield you 11.74%.

This method of quoting makes the true value of a CD very transparent and easy to compare against the rate of interest on fixed deposits. There are two implications:

- When trading CDs, the yield price is agreed first and then the two traders (usually their settlement departments) will work out the settlement amounts.
- The higher the quoted price, the lower is the settlement value of the asset. If you run a long position in CDs, you want the figures on the broker's screen to go down, not up.

Note that the price on CDs is a money market yield, as opposed to a true annual yield. We may still have to make a further adjustment if we want this yield on a "bond equivalent basis" as described in Chapter 18.

US Domestic CDs

In the US domestic market, most bank CDs are issued with maturities of one to six months (although CDs with maturities of up to seven years have been sold in the past). They are normally issued in US$1 million units (or "pieces") at par – i.e. for a settlement value equal to its face value – and the majority are payable at maturity in New York. To issue a CD a bank must have a good credit rating.

Most banks in the USA issuing CDs prefer to place as many as possible directly with customers. They feel that the less visible their borrowing, the better their credit will appear to be. Also, CDs issued through dealers may reappear on the market at the "wrong time," when the bank is seeking to launch a new issue.

Although corporate treasurers used to be large buyers of CDs, increasingly the bulk of demand has come from money market funds. These funds are required to maintain a short average maturity on their portfolios, and CDs are therefore highly attractive to them. Other investors in the USA include State and local governments and savings and loan associations (S&Ls).

Because of their higher credit risk and lower liquidity than treasury bills, CDs typically yield between 8 and 35 basis points more than T-bills of comparable maturities. The spread between CDs and US treasury bills is closely monitored by dealers. It tends to widen when money is in short supply and there is a "flight to quality."

Variable-Rate CDs

Variable-rate CDs appeared in the US in the late 1970s. The two most common types are six-month instruments with a 30-day "roll" and one-year paper with a three-month roll. (On each roll date accrued interest is paid and a new coupon is set.)

The coupon is first established on the issue of the CD and on each roll date, it is reset at a number of basis points above the average rate which banks are paying on new CDs with an original maturity equal to the length of the roll period.

The buyer has some protection against rising interest rates, but this is offset by the fact that variable-rate CDs tend to be less liquid than normal CDs. The major buyers are money market funds.

Euro-CDs

A Euro-CD is a receipt for a Eurocurrency fixed-term deposit typically with a London-based bank. They are mainly in bearer form, mostly dollar-denominated and issued in $1 million units.

Euro-CDs pay interest on an actual-over-360 day basis, with the exception of Eurosterling CDs, which have a 365-day basis.

The main issuers are branches of major US banks, British clearing banks, branches of banks from continental Europe, and Japanese banks. The first Eurodollar CD was issued in 1966 by Citibank. It was made at a time when domestic dollar CDs in New York were subject to Regulation Q, which set a ceiling on the interest which banks could pay on deposits. About $14 billion Euro-CDs were issued in London between 1966 and 1969, when Regulation Q was finally lifted on deposits of over $100,000.

There is a secondary market for Euro-CDs; however, as much as 50% of current issues are "lock-ups": they are bought and held to maturity, often in safe custody with the issuing banks.

In the secondary market normal settlement is two days (spot), although same-day and next-day settlement are also possible. As with all Eurodollar transactions, settlement of Eurodollar CDs is by payment of funds in New York, although the actual securities may be kept in London.

Summary

In this chapter, we introduced negotiable fixed-income securities, and examined their main features. In particular, we examined the Certificate of Deposit, and studied the calculation of its settlement value and yield. We then looked at how CDs are quoted (on a dis-count-to yield basis), and concluded with a note on some of the main sectors of this market.

Keywords Before finishing this chapter, please be sure that you are familiar with the following terms and their definitions:

- face value
- bearer security
- settlement amount
- market price
- yield to maturity (YTM)
- money market yield (MMY).

The exercise in Chapter 20 will enable you to practice pricing CDs.

Exercise: Pricing CDs

1. For a settlement on 9 February 1990 you purchase the following Eurodollar CD at a price of 8.38%.

   Issuer: National Westminster Bank
   Date of Issue: 4 November 1989
   Maturity: 4 November 1990
   Principal Amount $100,000.00
   Coupon   9.3/4%

   (a) What is its purchase cost, in dollars? _____

   (b) Why does the CD pay more than $9,750 in interest (i.e., 9.75% of $100,000) at maturity?

   _____ _____

   (c) On 19 February 1990 the CD is sold at 8.50%. How much profit or loss has been made and what is the return achieved?

   Profit/loss _____

   Return (%) _____

2. Calculate the settlement amounts, in dollars, on the following CDs.

    Remember that the interest on a Eurodollar CD is calculated on the basis of the actual number of days elapsed in a 360-day year.

    (a) Issuer: ABN Bank
        Date of issue: 19 December 1989
        Maturing: 19 December 1990
        Face value: $1,000,000
        Coupon: 9.00%

        Settlement date: 25 July 1990
        Purchase price: 8.40%

        Settlement amount _____

    (b) Issuer: Morgan Bank
        Date of issue: 23 January 1990
        Face value: $1,000,000
        Coupon: 9.00%

        Settlement date: 25 July 1990
        Purchase price: 8.40%

        Settlement amount _____

3. What is the profit made if the CDs you purchased in the previous exercise were both sold at a price of 7.80% on 25 August 1990?

    (a) Profit in dollars _____
        Return _____
    (b) Profit in dollars _____
        Return _____

■ ■ ■

"Discount securities are issued and traded on a 'discount to par' basis."

Discount Securities

Overview

There is a class of money market instruments which do not pay interest, at least not explicitly. Instead they are issued and traded at a "discount to par" or face value. The "interest" paid by the borrower is implicit in the difference between their price before maturity and their value at maturity.

This chapter explains the characteristics of three main discount securities:

- treasury bills
- bankers' acceptances
- commercial paper.

Although each of these markets has its own specialist traders, their comparable maturities makes them suitable for spread trading – creating partially offsetting positions straddling two or more markets.

Treasury Bills

Treasury bills are short-term negotiable instruments issued by the government to help finance its debt. They are fully guaranteed government obligations.

In the USA, the Federal Reserve typically auctions 13- and 26-week T-bills on behalf of the US government every Monday, for delivery on Thursday. It also auctions 52-week bills every month.

Money centre banks and large institutional investors as well as primary dealers are allowed to submit bids, or "tenders", at the auctions.

Between the auction and the settlement of the new issues the primary dealers make a market in "when issued" (or "wi") bills. This market is especially attractive for dealers who want to run positions, as there is no immediate delivery and therefore no carry costs involved. In contrast, settlement in the secondary market is for the following business day at the latest (i.e., trade date plus one day or "T + 1" delivery).

Bills are traditionally traded in minimum round lots of $5 million. The market is extremely liquid with a daily turnover of around $150 billion which is roughly half the total turnover in US government securities. It is not uncommon to see trades for $100 million or more being executed in just a few seconds.

The fact that T-bills carry no risk of default has two important implications:

- Yields on T-bills are lower than those available on CDs and other short-term paper. Indeed the yield on T-bills is used as the benchmark for assessing credit "yield spreads" in the money markets.
- It is easy for brokers to quote price runs for different maturities, since all bills maturing on the same date should have the same price, irrespective of how long ago they were issued.

Virtually all secondary T-bill trading in the USA is done through brokers. The 30 or so primary dealers transact with each other through the brokers on a no-names basis; that is, they settle their trades with the broker rather than directly with each other. This makes it more difficult for any dealer to determine who is in the market in size at any one time.

> **Thanks to the liquidity of this market and the easy availability of repo (sale-and-repurchase) facilities to finance stock holdings, dealers often build up huge long or short positions in T-bills, running into many hundred millions.**

In the UK, treasury bills (typically 91- and 182-day bills) are also issued by auction. The main holders are the discount houses which intermediate between the Bank of England and the commercial banks. Discount houses' holdings of bills and other securities are mainly financed with call loans from the banks.

In both the USA and the UK, ownership of T-bills is recorded on a centralized computer system, so there are no physical certificates being shuffled around the market. The "book entry" system makes trading in T-bills very fast and efficient.

Market Pricing

T-bills are quoted in the market on the basis of a percentage discount from par. This is a matter of tradition dating back to the way commercial bills used to be (and still are) discounted by the merchant banks.

Example An exporter in London holding a bill of exchange for £100 payable one year hence could raise working capital against it from its bankers. If the bank were to advance the trader £100, then the bank would be taking on two credit risks:

- A risk on the trader's customer not being able to pay the £100.
- A risk on the trader not being able to pay the interest on £100.

To eliminate the second of these risks the bank would take the interest from the trader up-front by purchasing the bill at a discount of, say, 10% paying the trader £90.

This was all well and good. But if the exporter thought he was being charged 10% interest, he was in for a big surprise.

> **The discount rate quoted (known as a bank discount rate) is different from the yield on the bill, or the effective rate of interest paid by the borrower.**

If the trader placed the £90 advanced on deposit for a year at 10%, he would only recover a total of £99, not £100; so the effective rate of interest charged on the advance must have been more than 10%.

> **The discount rate understates the money market yield on the paper.**

As we will see, it is quite simple to convert from a bank discount basis to a yield. But the tradition has remained to quote T-bills and other discount paper on this basis.

Example The quoted rate on a US T-bill with 50 days to maturity is 8.12% (bank discount basis). How much would you have to pay for the bill, for a $100 deal?

The quoted discount rate is on a percentage per annum basis, so the actual discount must be pro-rated down to 50 days in a 360-day year (365 for UK bills), as follows:

$100 - (50/360 \times 0.0812 \times 100)$

$= 100 \times [1 - (50/360 \times 0.0812)]$

$= 98.8722 \ldots$ or \$98.87

As in the CD market, once a price has been agreed, the dealers (or their settlement departments) will work out the amounts payable.

In the secondary market traders deal with each other on the basis of quoted bid and offer discount rates.

As in all fast-moving markets, the dealer's conversation is pared to a minimum. A broker's price run might be: "three-month 50–49, 2 by 5; six-month 70–69+, 10 by 12; one year 96–95, 1 by 10."

Points to note

- "50–49" means the dealer bids three-month bills at a discount of, say, 8.50% and offers at 8.49%. In other words, you pay more to purchase the bills than the market maker pays you for selling them to him.

- The big figure of 8%, called "the handle," is never quoted: only the basis points.

- "69+" means 69.5 basis points.

- "2 by 5" means there are \$2 million available on the bid side, \$5 million on the offer.

Discount-to-Yield Conversion

You can see from the first formula shown in Figure 21.1 that if the discount rate stays the same, the cash proceeds of a bill must rise and converge to its face value as it approaches maturity (as n approaches zero). For example, at a discount rate of 9%, a six-month (182 days) US T-bill must cost \$95.45 per \$100. Three months later, for the same rate of 9% it would have to increase to \$97.72 per \$100.

However it is unlikely that the discount rate on a bill would stay the same over a three-month period. This is because of changes in the general level of market interest rates.

Figure 21.1 also gives the general formula for calculating the money market equivalent yield (MMY) on a quoted T-bill rate. It is

Fig 21.1 **Calculating proceeds from straight discounts**

$$\text{Proceeds} = FV - \left[FV \times \left[\frac{T \times DR}{B \times 100} \right] \right]$$

Where

FV = Face value
T = Tenor (number of days)
B = Daily basis (360 or 365)
DR = Discount rate (as a percentage,
    i.e., 0.105 is 10.5)

By rearranging the above formula you can see that:

$$DR = \frac{(FV - \text{Proceeds})}{FV} \times \frac{B \times 100}{T}$$

To calculate the money market yield (MMY):

$$MMY = \frac{(FV - \text{Proceeds})}{\text{Proceeds}} \times \frac{B \times 100}{T} = \frac{DR}{1 - \left[\frac{DR \times T}{B \times 100} \right]}$$

nothing more than the percentage return, expressed on an annualized basis, that we would make if we purchased the bill for a cost of P (proceeds) and held it until maturity – which is of course the definition of yield.

The second formula shown against MMY arrives at the same result without having to calculate P, the cash settlement amount.

The quoted rate on a US T-bill with 50 days to maturity is 8.12%. Its purchase price is therefore $98.87 per $100, as we saw in the earlier example. What is the money market yield?

$$MM = \frac{(100.00 - 98.8722)}{98.8722} \times \frac{360}{50}$$

$$= 0.0821 \text{ or } 8.21\%$$

Using the direct formula:

$$MM = 0.0812 / [1 - (50/360 \times 0.0812)]$$
$$= 8.21\%$$

Again to convert this yield on to a bond basis we would need to multiply the rate by a factor of 365/360 as explained earlier.

Bankers' Acceptances

Bankers' acceptances (BAs), also known as bills of exchange, are a very old type of financial instrument, originally used to finance international trade.

A bill of exchange, or trade bill, is an order to pay a specified amount of money to the holder, either at a specified future date (time draft) or on presentation (sight draft). It is an IOU, usually in support of a commercial transaction.

The drawer (the seller of some goods or service), prepares a bill of exchange ordering the drawee to pay a specified amount to a nominated bank at a specified future date. The drawee acknowledges his obligation to pay by returning the bill with the word "ACCEPTED" above his signature.

A bankers' acceptance, or bank bill, is a bill of exchange drawn on or accepted by a bank. Once accepted, it becomes a negotiable instrument which can be discounted in the secondary market. The bank takes on the credit risk on the underlying commercial transaction.

In London the creation of bank bills has for centuries been the speciality of merchant banks, or accepting houses. Accepting banks endorse trade bills for a fee and take on the credit risk of the drawee by guaranteeing their payment at maturity. The majority of bankers' acceptances nowadays are in support of international trade, and are actually drawn on the banks themselves.

An importer wants to buy goods from abroad on credit. If the **Example** exporter is not prepared to take on the risk, the importer will ask his bank to issue a letter of credit (LC) in favour of the supplier.

In the LC, the exporter's bank will guarantee payment for the goods on a certain date, provided the exporter has presented satisfactory shipping documents. When the goods are shipped, the supplier sends the LC and the required documents to the issuing bank, together with a time draft which, if the documents are in order, the latter must "accept."

Rather than wait for the money, the supplier may discount the accepted bill at his local bank, which in turn will either hold it as an investment, or sell it on in the secondary market.

When the BA matures, the importer has to pay the accepting bank; but even if he fails to do so, the accepting bank is obliged to pay the bearer of the maturing bill. Consequently, creating BAs requires a great deal of specialized knowledge for the accepting bank.

The majority of BAs in the USA are created by international subsidiaries of money-centre banks. In the past, most of the business arose in support of imports and exports in and out of the USA itself. After the 1974 oil crisis, however, Japan started to use this market to finance its imports of oil. Nowadays many of the BAs created in the USA finance third-country trade, where neither the importer nor the exporter is a US firm.

The Secondary Market

Most BAs are backed by documentation such as invoices, bills of lading or independent terminal or warehouse receipts. This documentation is held by the accepting bank, so the instrument actually discounted in the market is simply a note specifying the name of the accepting bank (the credit risk) and only briefly describing the nature of the underlying transaction.

Figure 21.2 illustrates a typical acceptance note.

Fig 21.2

Sample bankers' acceptance

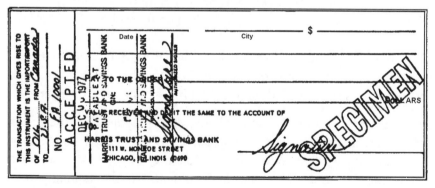

Source: Stigum (1983)

Most BAs are in bearer form. They may be drawn for various maturities and amounts.

BAs are normally created and traded in lots of $1 million, although sometimes the accepting bank will break up a BA into smaller units of $500,000 or $100,000 to sell on to small money funds, private individuals and bank trust departments.

Like T-Bills, US bankers' acceptances and UK bank bills are quoted in the market on a bank discount basis, or discount to par.

Eligible Paper

The creation of BAs is often preceded by a letter of credit in support of a commercial transaction, so the finance provided is pretty much "self-liquidating"; that is to say, it will be met by the eventual sale of goods or services. However, BAs are also created out of less formal contractual agreements.

During the inflationary 1960s and 1970s, various attempts were made in the USA, the UK and elsewhere to control the growth of the money supply through bank credit rationing rather than by raising interest rates. Banks on both sides of the Atlantic were severely constrained in the amount of domestic lending they could do, and were penalized for exceeding the targets set. This led the banks to discover two ways of by-passing the controls:

- channelling lending through the Eurocurrency markets which were not subject to such controls;
- extending working capital loans through so-called Finance Bills (or Working Capital BAs) and selling the BAs thus created in the secondary market.

BA finance became a major way of satisfying credit demand through the back door, earning the banks fee income and avoiding central bank penalties.

Finance bills are a major source of working capital for companies which lack the credit rating necessary to issue commercial paper (see next section, pages 185–188).

The result of course was that the official definitions of the money supply no longer reflected the growth in liquidity within the economy. To close this loophole, both the Federal Reserve and the Bank of England made these bills "ineligible" for re-discount at the central bank, and the sale of such bills subject to reserve requirements.

An eligible acceptance in the USA is a BA which the Fed is prepared to buy from banks, and which does not incur a reserve requirement. The conditions for eligibility are complex, but in broad terms they stipulate that the acceptance should fund short-term (up to six-month) commercial transactions of a certain type.

In the past, banks with a temporary need for funds could sell BAs and other eligible paper into the Fed's Discount Window – i.e., the Fed would provide cash by rediscounting the paper. Nowadays, the window is little used, but eligible BAs can be used as collateral in repurchase agreements ("repos") with the Fed, so they remain a useful potential source of funds in a tight market.

Eligible BAs issued in the USA tend to track T-bill rates quite closely. In the three-month maturity area the spread above the yields available on T-bills is normally in the region of 15–25 basis points (0.15%–0.25%). When there is a lot of surplus cash around on the market, the spread can narrow to only a few basis points. When money is tight or yields are volatile, spreads can widen to a full percentage point or more.

Much the same applies to eligible bills in the UK. Eligible bills can be sold to the Bank of England when liquidity is in short supply. To be eligible in the UK, a commercial bill must carry two "good British names," one of which must be that of the acceptor.

Ineligible acceptances are still common, but they are more expensive for the borrower.

- The accepting bank passes on the reserve costs by charging a higher rate on the instrument.
- The bank also charges commission for creating and issuing the securities, depending on the creditworthiness of the customer and the supply of business (normally in the range of 25–200 basis points).
- The bank must load the yield to allow for their lower market liquidity.

From the trader's point of view the distinction between eligible and ineligible paper is obviously important, as it affects its liquidity. Thus dealers quote price runs on eligible paper only, with a normal bid/offer spread of 10 basis points. However, for the buy-and-hold investor, the distinction is less relevant, as in either case the risk is on the accepting bank.

Commercial Paper

Large firms with good credit rating can issue commercial paper (CP) in the money markets as an alternative to bank loans.

Commercial paper is an unsecured promissory note issued for a specified amount and maturing on a specified date.

CP is a negotiable instrument usually in bearer form, as illustrated in Figure 21.3.

The fact that CP is unsecured means that no assets are pledged, and the only back-up to support the issue is the earning power and liquidity of the borrower's balance sheet.

Traditionally, CPs are to the large corporation what CDs are to banks – a means of raising working capital. Nowadays many banks issue CP as wells as CDs, depending on which market is hungrier for a given name, but of course only recognized banks and deposit takers can issue CDs.

Fig 21.3

Sample commercial paper certificate

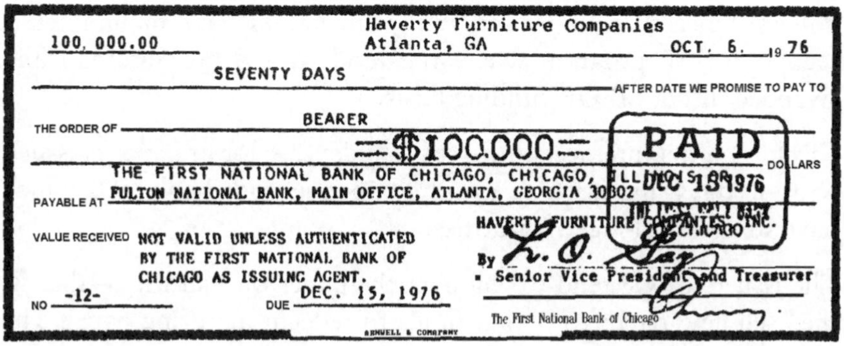
100,000.00
Haverty Furniture Companies
Atlanta, GA
OCT. 6. 19 76
SEVENTY DAYS
AFTER DATE WE PROMISE TO PAY TO
THE ORDER OF BEARER
$100,000
DOLLARS
PAID
DEC 15 1976
PAYABLE AT THE FIRST NATIONAL BANK OF CHICAGO, CHICAGO, ILLINOIS OR FULTON NATIONAL BANK, MAIN OFFICE, ATLANTA, GEORGIA 30302
VALUE RECEIVED NOT VALID UNLESS AUTHENTICATED BY THE FIRST NATIONAL BANK OF CHICAGO AS ISSUING AGENT.
HAVERTY FURNITURE COMPANIES, INC.
By
Senior Vice President and Treasurer
NO -12-
DUE DEC. 15, 1976
The First National Bank of Chicago

Source: Stigum (1983)

Unlike CDs, CP does not pay interest explicitly. Why one type of paper should pay interest and the other not is a matter of history. In pure investment terms, as we have seen, it makes no difference since both types of paper with the same credit quality must produce comparable yields, although there may be tax reasons for preferring one to the other.

The market is, generally speaking, a wholesale market for large institutional investors such as pension funds, money market funds, insurance companies, bank trust departments and major corporations. Sometimes CP is sold in units of as low as $25,000 to appeal to the smaller investor.

CP yields are normally slightly higher than those available on T-bills, because of the increased credit risk and the reduced liquidity.

The US Market

CP originated in the US in the 19th century. Because most banks were restricted to operating within a single state, the issue of CP became the main method for large corporations of tapping large amounts of working capital from across the country.

Nowadays the main issuers are industrial corporations seeking funds for working capital, and banks looking for a readily available source of money to fund their lending operations. There has also been a growth in the use of CP by municipal authorities, and by the branches of foreign banks.

Foreign issuers are very active in the US market. The first foreign issue was by Electricité de France in 1974 to pay for oil imports in dollars. Since then many top European names have maintained a regular US-CP program where the funds raised are automatically swapped into a LIBOR funding basis.

CPs have a maximum maturity of 270 days. A lot of paper is issued with 30 days' maturity, to avoid competing with bank CDs which have somewhat longer maturities.

The issuers of CP tend to roll over the paper on maturity – that is, they sell new paper to obtain funds to redeem maturing paper. The risk to both the issuer and the investor is that changes in the market may make it very expensive (or nearly impossible) to sell new paper on the required day.

To avoid this risk, most CP issues are backed by a standby line of credit from a bank. Under this sort of arrangement, the issuer can activate the line of credit if it is unable to sell the CP at the arranged terms. A revolving line of credit provides a guaranteed arrangement from the bank for a number of years. In today's credit-conscious markets, the availability of a standby line has become a condition for entry into this market.

Large CP issuers like Sears, Ford and General Motors place their paper directly with investors. However, about half the volume of new issues is channelled through dealers like Goldman Sachs and AG Becker, who use their distribution power to retail the paper, in return for a placement fee.

> **US CP is quoted and traded on a bank discount basis, in the same way as T-bills and bankers' acceptances.**

A secondary market exists, but most paper tends to be sold to investors who hold it to maturity. Dealers stand ready to buy back the paper they handle, but only after adding a fairly wide spread.

The yield differential between A1-P1 and A2-P2 rated paper can be as narrow as 15 points or as wide as 200 points, depending on how scarce credit is. The implication is that the name of the issuer is a very important factor in the pricing. Consequently, CPs are nothing like as liquid as T-bills, and somewhat less liquid even than CDs. Few dealers take sizable trading positions in CP.

Euro-CP

The first Euro-CP (ECP) was issued in London by Alcoa in 1970, at a time when US corporations were looking for alternative sources of dollar funding.

For the investors, which are mainly institutions, it provides a flexible form of investment with a good range of maturities. For the issuer, ECP attracts a range of investors and is fairly cheap to set up. However, the quality of the name remains important and it can be a difficult market for low-rated corporations to raise funds.

Activity in this market tends to be erratic as it remains under strong competition from both the US domestic and the Eurodeposit markets, which still represent the traditional sources of short-term corporate funding.

Like the US domestic paper, ECP is normally in bearer form and with maturities ranging from 30 to 180 days.

ECP is priced on a discount to yield basis, like CDs, and NOT on a discount to par, as with US-CP.

The founders of the ECP market thought they would make life easier for the investor by pricing ECP on a yield basis. The formula adopted is identical in structure to the one used for CDs, as introduced in Chapter 19 (see Figure 19.2, page 165).

Fig 21.4

Present value of ECP with tenor of 12 months or less

$$\text{Proceeds} = \text{FV} \times \frac{(\text{Coupon} \times \text{original life}) + (\text{B} \times 100)}{(\text{YTM} \times \text{days remaining}) + (\text{B} \times 100)}$$

where:

FV = Face value
B = Basis (360 or 365)
YTM = Yield to maturity (in percent, i.e., 5% is 0.05)

Since the coupon rate = 0, the formula simplies to:

$$\text{Proceeds} = \text{FV} \times \left[\frac{(\text{B} \times 100)}{(\text{YTM} \times \text{days remaining}) + (\text{B} \times 100)} \right]$$

Summary

Following on from Chapter 19, we have examined the remaining discount securities – treasury bills, bills of exchange and commercial paper. In particular, we noted that these securities are quoted on a "discount to par" basis, and studied examples which illustrated their main features and uses.

By way of revision, please be sure that you are familiar with **Keywords** the following terms and their definitions:

- discount to par
- discount rate
- time/sight draft
- letter of credit
- eligible and ineligible bills
- discount-to-yield conversion.

The exercise in Chapter 22 will give you practice in pricing discount securities.

Exercise:
Pricing Discounts

1. US treasury bills are quoted on a so-called bank discount basis, which is not the same thing as the yield-to-maturity on a CD. The formula for the settlement amount is given in Figure 21.1, page 180.

   Calculate the purchase cost, in US dollars, of the following T-bills.

   (a) Issue date: 1 April 1993
       Settlement date: 1 April 1993
       Maturity: 30 days
       Face value: $100,000
       Quoted price: 2.83% (Actl/360)

   (b) Issue date: 15 August 1990
       Settlement date: 30 August 1990
       Maturity: 15 November 1990
       Face value: $1,100,000
       Quoted price: 6.76% (Actl./360)

2. Exactly the same calculation is used for US commercial paper, short-term debt securities issued by corporates, banks and municipal authorities in the US.

   Calculate the purchase cost in dollars of the following USCP.

Issuer:	Motorola Finance
Rated:	A2-P2
Issue date:	1 April 1993
Settlement date:	1 April 1993
Maturity:	30 days
Face value:	$100,000
Quoted price:	4.45%

3. UK treasury bills use the same purchase cost calculation as US T-bills, except that the year basis is 365, rather than 360 days. Bills issued by UK banks work on the same basis.

   Calculate the purchase amounts for the following paper.

   (a) | | |
   |---|---|
   | Instrument: | UK T-Bill |
   | Settlement date: | 10 August 1991 |
   | Maturity: | 10 November 1991 |
   | Face value: | £1,000,000 |
   | Quoted price: | 12.6624% |

   (b) | | |
   |---|---|
   | Instrument: | UK bank bill |
   | Issuer: | Barclays Bank |
   | Underlying transaction: | Beet exports |
   | Settlement date: | 10 October 1989 |
   | Maturity: | 1 March 1990 |
   | Face value: | £200,000 |
   | Quoted price: | 6.65% |

4. The quoted discount rate on a T-bill is not the rate of return on the instrument. This exercise shows why this is the case.

Today you buy $100,000 nominal (the "face value") of a US treasury bill which matures in 90 days' time. The quoted rate is 5.76%. What is the settlement amount for this bill, and what is the yield on the investment if you held it to maturity?

(a) Settlement amount =
Face value $\times [1 - (0.0576 \times 90/360)]$

(b) Suppose that instead of buying the T-bills, you simply deposited the settlement amount calculated in (a) for 90 days at an interest rate of 5.76%. How much would you have at the end of the period, in principal plus interest?

Future value =
Answer to (a) $\times [1 + (0.0576 \times 90/360)]$

(c) After 90 days, the T-bill would repay exactly $100,000. Comparing this with the return achieved over 90 days on the deposit described in question (b), would you say that the yield on the T-bill is more or less than 5.76%?

(d) We can work out the return on the T-bill, assuming we hold it to maturity.

Yield =
$$\frac{\text{Face value} - \text{Answer to (a)}}{\text{Answer to (a)}} \times \frac{360}{90} \times 100$$

This is also known as the money market yield. Note that it is a simple annualized rate of return calculation, without compounding, and based on a 360-day year.

(e) Suppose you repeated the exercise in (b) above, but this time used the rate worked out in (d) rather than 5.76%. How much do you think you would have in principal plus interest at the end of 90 days?

■ ■ ■

"In essence the FRA is a bet on a future rate of interest."

Forward Rate Agreements

Overview

In this chapter, we look at Forward (or Future) Rate Agreements (FRAs). These are contracts between two parties which fix the rate of interest that will apply to a notional future loan or deposit:

- for an agreed amount, in an agreed currency;
- to be drawn or placed at an agreed future date;
- for an agreed term.

Definition

In essence, the forward rate agreement (FRA) is a bet on a future rate of interest.

The buyer of an FRA will be compensated in cash by the seller for any rise in the reference interest rate, over and above the agreed contract rate. Future borrowers, seeking to hedge against higher future borrowing costs, are therefore natural buyers of FRAs.

On the other hand, the seller of an FRA will be compensated for any fall in interest rates. Therefore prospective depositors, seeking to hedge against future falls in interest rates, are natural sellers of FRAs.

The FRA is a derivative instrument in that its market price is derived from rates in the cash deposit markets, as we shall see. It is very similar to an interest rate futures contract, but with no margin calls.

The following are the key features of the instrument:

- **Cash settlement.** Compensation is paid in cash at the beginning of the notional loan or deposit period, known as the "settlement date."

- **No obligation to borrow or lend.** The buyer of an FRA is not obliged to borrow, and the seller is not obliged to lend funds at any time. The prospective borrower or depositor can go anywhere in the market, seeking the best rate at which they can raise or place funds quite independently of the FRA contract.

- **Lock-in rate.** Like a forward FX contract, there is no upside in an FRA hedge: if future interest rates fall the buyer will have to compensate his counterparty, thereby forgoing any benefit from lower interest costs. If interest rates rise it is the seller who compensates the buyer. Through the FRA, future borrowers and lenders effectively lock into at a fixed future rate of interest.

- **Low credit risk.** Because there is no exchange of principal, the credit risk on an FRA is just the potential cost of finding a replacement counterparty, should the original one fail. The risk is therefore on any profits made on the FRA, rather than on the notional amount; it will be a fraction – typically between 2% and 4% – of the notional amount.

- **Cancellation and assignment.** An FRA is an irrevocable contract between two parties and can be cancelled only with the agreement of both parties. The same applies to an assignment of an FRA to a third party. This is like a forward exchange contract and means that FRA positions are often closed with offsetting contracts.

Figure 23.1 illustrates a typical FRA contract form. The terms in the form are defined as follows:

- **Contract currency and amount:** the currency and amount of the notional loan or deposit.
- **Contract period:** the term of the notional loan or deposit. The period from *settlement date* to *maturity date.*
- **Settlement date:** the date when the *contract period* commences and cash compensation ("settlement amount") is paid.
- **Maturity date:** the date when the *contract period* ends.
- **Contract rate:** the agreed rate of interest for the *contract period.* The FRA price.
- **Fixing date:** two business days before the *settlement date* when the LIBOR reference rate on which the settlement amount will be calculated, is established. For domestic currency FRAs, the *fixing date* is normally the same as the *settlement date.*

The British Bankers Association has published a set of *Recommended Terms and Conditions* (the so-called *FRABBA Terms*) which mean that a client dealing on BBA terms automatically deals on these terms unless explicitly stated otherwise in the contract.

Fig 23.1   **An FRA contract note. Terms are defined in the text**

HAMBROS BANK

Hambros Bank Limited
41 Tower Hill
London EC3N 4HA

Tel (0171) 480 5000

XYZ Limited
Somewhere
London

September 5 1996

CONFIRMATION OF FORWARD RATE AGREEMENT

We are pleased to confirm that the following forward rate agreement (FRA)" made between ourselves, transacted according to FRABBA Recommended Terms and Conditions dated August 1996.

CONTRACT CURRENCY AND AMOUNT   US$........

FIXING DATE

SETTLEMENT DATE

MATURITY DATE

CONTRACT PERIOD (DAYS)

CONTRACT RATE

SELLER'S NAME

BUYER'S NAME

PLEASE SIGN THE ATTACHED COPY OF THIS INVOICE AND RETURN IT FOR THE ATTENTION OF FRA DEPT., 41 TOWER HILL, LONDON EC3N 4HA.

For and on behalf of
Hambros Bank Ltd.

Registered in England No. 964058. Registered Office: 41 Tower Hill London EC3N 4HA.

Source: Hambros Bank Limited

FRA Fixing Rates based on market LIBOR rates are established daily by the BBA and broadcast to the market on Telerate page 3750.

FRA Settlement

The compensation or "settlement amount" is calculated using the formula shown in Figure 23.2.

FRA settlement formula

Fig 23.2

$$\frac{(L - R) \text{ or } (R - L) \times D \times A}{(D \times L) + (B \times 100)}$$

Where:

L = LIBOR (BBA settlement rate)
R = Contract rate (in percent)
A = Contract amount
D = Days in contract period
B = Day basis (360 or 365)

The formula is easy to interpret. The numerator calculates the additional interest cost potentially incurred by the buyer if the actual market rate (L) turns out to be higher than the contract rate (R); or the loss of interest to the seller if the actual rate is less than the contract rate.

But note that the compensation payment is made at the *beginning* of the notional loan or deposit period. Therefore the settlement amount is discounted to its present value at the current market rate.

Market Pricing

The FRA is quoted as a two-way price, with a bid and an offer, as with deposit rates.

Figure 23.3 reproduces a typical contributor page in the Reuters market information network. Prices are quoted on the market screens regularly for standard or "fixed" dates. Typically, the market maker quotes a three-month series (1x4, 2x5, 3x6, etc) and a six-month series (1x7, 2x8, 3x9, and so on). Broken dates are also available, but the spread may be wider. Some FRA traders are prepared to quote much shorter dates than one month.

Fig 23.3

Reuters page TOPFRA, showing FRA prices

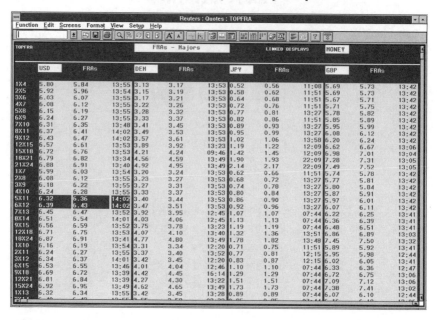

Note: The bid rate is quoted first, followed by the offered rate. In the London market, the offered rate may be quoted first but the meaning is clear: the market user always pays the higher rate!

Source: Reuters

Where Do the Prices Come From?

Earlier in their development, FRAs were calculated from the "forward–forward" LIBOR rates. The example below illustrates the arbitrage pricing of a forward loan.

Example

Consider a market maker who is asked to quote a rate for six-month dollars in six months' time. In order to lock in a fixed forward lending rate today, the market maker could borrow for 12 months and, since he is not required to provide the funds yet, he can deposit these funds for six months. Eurodollar rates at the time are as follows:

	6 MTHS (183 days)	12 MTHS (365 days)
USD	8.50–8.40	8.50–8.40

The break-even rate charged for the 6x12 forward loan would have to be such that the interest earned on the six-months cash deposit plus the interest earned on the forward loan just covers the cost of borrowing for 12 months. That is:

6 mth depo, compounded into fwd loan = Cost of 12 mth loan.
$(1 + 0.084 \times 183/360) \times (1 + F \times 182/360) = (1 + 0.085 \times 365/360)$

Rearranging the terms in the above equation, we obtain an arbitrage expression for F, the forward–forward rate, expressed as a ratio:

$$F = \frac{(0.0850 \times 365) - (0.084 \times 183)}{[1 + (0.084 \times 183/360)]} \times \frac{1}{182}$$

$= 0.082483$ or 8.2483%

Forward–forward interest rate

Fig 23.4

$$\frac{(R_L \times D_L) - (R_S \times D_S)}{(D_L - D_S) \times \left[1 + \left[\frac{(R_S \times D_S)}{B \times 100}\right]\right]}$$

Where:

R_L = Rate from start date to the far date (long period) in percent.
D_L = Number of days from the spot to the far date.
R_S = Rate from the spot to the near date (short period) in percent.
D_S = Number of days from spot to the near date.
B = Day basis (360 or 365).

The FRABBA Terms stipulate that the reference rate used in calculating the settlement sum is always the LIBOR rate, for both buyers and sellers of FRAs. Therefore, in the early days, FRA traders used to calculate break-even rates from this formula, always using the long period LIBOR and the short period LIBID, and add a small spread either side to give a two-way price. Nowadays FRA prices themselves are derived from the interest rate futures market, which is both more liquid than the Eurodeposit market, and as a derivative more closely related to FRAs.

Note that even without a bid/offer spread on borrowing long and depositing short, a flat yield curve produces an FRA price lower than either bid rate in the deposit market.

In a flat yield curve environment FRA rates will be lower than current cash rates and therefore easier to sell to corporate borrowers.

This is normal, because the receipt of interest on the short-dated deposit comes before the payment of interest on the longer-dated borrowing, and can therefore be placed on deposit to generate additional interest. This contributes to an overall lowering of funding costs in the second six months and a lowering of the forward–forward (or FRA) rate.

Using FRAs

In today's market, the FRA can be jobbed like any other instrument: traded strategically – for example, by going long of FRAs if an interest rate rise is expected; traded just on the spread; or perhaps arbitraged against futures when conditions allow.

Hedging future loans or deposits, or future mismatches in interest-sensitive instruments, is however more important from the corporate point of view.

Decision Rules

If you are a prospective borrower and you expect interest rates to move against you, use the FRA.

Example A corporate borrower seeks interest-rate protection for a six-month period beginning in six months' time – a 6x12 forward–forward position. The amount of the proposed borrowing will be $5,000,000, and forecasts are for an increase in rates over the period of the loan, which will be indexed on a three-month LIBOR basis.

The company is quoted FRA prices from two banks, as follows:

FRAs	BANK A	BANK B
6x9	6.21–6.15	6.23–6.18
9x12	6.28–6.22	6.30–6.25

The customer buys a "strip" of two FRAs at 6.21 and 6.28 from Bank A, both prices being cheaper than Bank B. The average rate of interest for the six-month borrowing period will be approximately 6.25% p.a.

The company should continuously monitor the hedge, in the light of its changing cash position, and if the trend in rates changes over the next six months it should consider reversing the hedge, running unhedged, or using an alternative instrument.

If interest rates move up to, say, 7%, the borrower will receive a cash payment on the settlement of the first FRA.

Using the compensation formula defined earlier:

$$\frac{5,000,000 \times (7.00 - 6.21) \times 91}{[(91 \times 7.00) + (360 \times 100)]}$$

$$= \$15,027.16$$

If rates continue up to 7.375% p.a. at the settlement of the second FRA, the compensation then payable to the borrower will amount to another $13,598.96 (using the FRA rate of 6.28%).

The overall effect is to produce an average borrowing rate 6.25%, which is clearly better than the market.

The Risks Involved

The risks involved in FRAs can be seen from two points of view:

- **The dealer bank:** The bank covers its FRA book in the futures market or in the interbank FRA market. Standard position risk is thus a feature, as with any other financial instrument. If the dealer has sold an FRA and interest rates subsequently rise, he will sustain a loss on his position which is proportional to the contract period of the FRA. A small secondary risk (the 2–4% mentioned earlier) is that if rates move in the bank's favor, when the bank comes to claim compensation from the client, he may not be there. A small dealing line is therefore required.
- **The customer:** The risk to the customer is also two-fold. First, will the bank be there to provide cash compensation when it is due? More significant however is the lock-in risk, which prevents the customer from benefiting from favorable rate movements.

Mismatch Risk

Because the FRA is a hedge totally independent of the underlying transaction, a risk exists that the hedge may not be fully effective, because the rate setting process for the underlying loan is independent of the reference rate setting for the FRA. This may be because the instrument being hedged is not linked to LIBOR sufficiently closely; for example, a hedged US commercial paper rate exposure.

Summary

In this chapter, we have examined forward rate agreements in some detail. We defined the principal features of the instrument, such as its low credit risk and its cash settlement, and saw how this settlement is calculated. We then looked at ways in which FRA rates are related to the underlying deposit markets, and explored a typical case in which the instrument is used. Finally, we noted the risks involved in FRA dealing.

Keywords   Please make sure you are familiar with the following keywords before proceeding to the FRA exercise in Chapter 24:

- cash settlement
- FRABBA Terms
- forward–forward rate
- settlement date
- settlement amount
- contract rate
- contract currency and amount
- fixing date
- maturity date
- contract period
- mismatch risk.

Exercise: FRA Dealing

1. A dealer has borrowed funds for six months at an interest rate of 10.3/8% and has lent funds for one month at an interest rate of 9.7/8%. The amount involved is US$5 million. The dealer now has a five-month forward exposure gap.

   To match or cover the exposure created by the "gap" or "mismatch" will require the dealer to lend US$5 million for five months, in one month's time, and hedge the position now with an FRA.

   Five banks are quoting FRA rates for "1s against 6s" as follows:

BANK A	10.39 – 34
BANK B	10.40 – 35
BANK C	10.43 – 38
BANK D	10.44 – 39
BANK E	10.41 – 36

   (a) Calculate the dealer's break-even forward–forward rate of interest.

   (b) Identify the best FRA price at which he should deal to cover the exposure.

   (c) Calculate the settlement amount which would be received/paid by the dealer if, at the settlement of his FRA, the LIBOR fix was 10.75%.

2. A dealer has lent funds for three months at an interest rate of 9.9/16% and has borrowed funds for one month at an interest rate of 9.3/8%.

The amount involved is US$15 million. The dealer now has a two-month forward exposure gap.

To cover the exposure created by the mismatch will require the dealer to borrow another US$15 million for two months, in one month's time, and hedge the position now with an FRA.

Five banks are quoting FRA rates for "1s against 3s" as follows:

BANK A   9.59 – 54
BANK B   9.60 – 55
BANK C   9.58 – 53
BANK D   9.61 – 56
BANK E   9.57 – 52

(a) Calculate the dealer's break-even forward–forward rate of interest.

(b) Identify the best FRA price at which he should deal to cover the exposure.

(c) Calculate the settlement amount which would be received/ paid by the dealer if, at the settlement of his FRA, the LIBOR fix was 9.5/16%.

3. A dealer has lent funds for six months at an interest rate of
    10.9/16% and has borrowed funds for one year at an interest
    rate of 11%. The amount involved is US$25 million. The
    dealer now has a six-month forward exposure gap.

    To cover the exposure created by the mismatch will require the
    dealer to lend another US$25 million for six months, in six
    months' time, and hedge the position now with an FRA.

    Five banks are quoting FRA rates for "6s against 12s" as
    follows:

    BANK A   10.94 – 87
    BANK B   10.93 – 86
    BANK C   10.92 – 85
    BANK D   10.91 – 84
    BANK E   10.90 – 83

    (a) Calculate the dealer's break-even forward–forward rate of
        interest.

    (b) Identify the best FRA price at which he should deal to
        cover the exposure.

    (c) Calculate the settlement amount which would be received/
        paid by the dealer if, at the settlement date, the LIBOR fix
        was 10.3/4%.

4. A dealer has borrowed funds for six months at an interest rate of 10.13/16% and has lent funds for one year at an interest rate of 11.1/8%. The amount involved is US$20 million. The dealer now has a six-month forward exposure gap.

To cover the exposure created by the mismatch will require the dealer to borrow another US$20 million for six months, in six months' time, and hedge the position now with an FRA.

Five banks are quoting FRA rates for "6s against 12s" as follows:

BANK A   10.92 – 83
BANK B   10.87 – 78
BANK C   10.89 – 80
BANK D   10.91 – 84
BANK E   10.85 – 77

(a) Calculate the dealer's break-even forward–forward rate of interest.

(b) Identify the best FRA price at which he should deal to cover the exposure.

(c) Calculate the settlement amount which would be received/ paid by the dealer if, at the settlement of his FRA, the LIBOR fix was 11.1/2%.

■ ■ ■

"Futures contracts are traded on organized exchanges by open outcry, so amounts traded, delivery dates and prices are public knowledge."

Interest Rate Futures

In this chapter, we examine financial futures contracts. These are agreements to buy or sell, on an organized exchange:

- a standard amount of a specified financial instrument;
- for delivery on a specified month in the future;
- at an agreed price between two parties.

Introduction

While financial futures are a relatively recent phenomenon, commodity futures such as wheat or soya have been traded at the Chicago Board of Trade (CBOT), the Chicago Mercantile Exchange (CME) or the New York Commodities Exchange (COMEX), for more than a century. Agricultural producers, eager to protect their income from sharp drops in cash prices during periods of over-supply, are able to fix in advance the price at which future crop deliveries will be made. The buyers of such contracts are speculators, looking to profit from price rises in the cash market, or commodity users looking to fix their production costs.

Futures contracts are highly standardized assets traded in organized exchanges by open outcry. This is very different from the practice in the over-the-counter (OTC) cash or forward markets, where amounts, delivery dates and price are negotiable and confidential between the two counterparties.

The first financial futures were foreign exchange contracts, introduced at CME in 1972. The first interest rate futures contract was a GNMA Collateralized Depository Receipt (CDR) and a Treasury bill contract, both of which began trading at CBOT in 1975. These were followed, in 1977, by the CBOT Treasury bond contract and numerous other contracts. Some of these interest rate contracts, like the US T-bond, proved immensely successful while others never really took off. By the early 1980s, various exchanges had introduced futures on equity indices such as the S&P 500 in the USA or the FT-SE 100 in the UK.

Financial futures are in essence the same as commodity futures, the only difference is that the underlying asset is not some physical commodity but a financial asset. Moreover, the asset may not necessarily be a physical security, like a bond or a T-bill. It may only be a price index, rate of interest or rate of exchange. In such cases, there cannot be physical delivery. Instead, a cash settlement amount is calculated based on the market reference price, similar to the way an FRA might be settled.

The major financial futures exchanges today include those already mentioned, together with LIFFE (the London International Financial Futures Exchange), SIMEX in Singapore, DTB in Frankfurt and MATIF in Paris. Other exchanges, notably in Tokyo, Sydney, Toronto provide important facilities in various "niche" markets.

Users of financial futures divide broadly into:

- **hedgers,** who use futures to cover their risk on positions in the underlying assets;
- **speculators,** who use futures to create highly leveraged positions in a market.

Only about 1% of futures contracts typically reach delivery; the vast majority are "closed" before. This reflects not only the extent to which the speculators outnumber the hedgers but also the way futures tend to be used as temporary hedges.

Most exchanges publish regular analyses of *open-interest* positions held by these groups.

Open interest is the net number of contracts (either long or short) which are outstanding at any one time.

Open-interest figures are monitored closely by all players, as they provide important indicators as to the character and stability of the market.

It is often argued that excessive speculative interest in financial futures contributes to present-day volatility in today's markets. The other side of this coin is that without the speculators there would not be sufficient liquidity to allow hedgers to benefit from these instruments in their everyday business.

Contract Specification

The rest of this chapter provides an introduction to short-term interest-rate futures contracts and their trading methods. Figure 25.1 details the specification of one of the most traded contracts – the three-month Eurodollar futures.

For all futures contracts, the relevant exchange sets the delivery dates; for financial contracts there are typically four delivery months per year – March, June, September and December. At any one time, the next eight contracts will usually be on offer, so one can deal out to about two years ahead. In the case of Eurodollar futures, it is possible to deal in Chicago up to seven years ahead. It must be stressed that the "far" contract months are very much less liquid than the "near" ones, so it is not always possible to get a worthwhile price in a far month.

Fig 25.1 **The three-month Eurodollar interest-rate futures contract traded at the Chicago Mercantile Exchange**

Delivery Day/ Exercise Day/ Expiry Day	Third Wednesday of delivery month
Last Trading Day	11.00
	Two business days before expiry
Quotation	100.00 minus rate of interest
Minimum Price Movement	0.01
(Tick size & value)	($25.00)
Initial Margin	$675–$945 depending on expiry
(Straddle Margin)	($200)
Trading Hours	07.20–14.00 (Chicago)

Three-Month Eurodollar Interest Rate Future
Contract Standard
Cash settlement based on the Exchange Delivery Settlement Price.
Exchange Delivery Settlement Price
Based on the interest rates for three-month Eurodollar deposits being offered to prime banking names between 09.30 and 11.00 on the last trading day, stated by a random sample of 16 from a list of designated banks. Having disregarded the three highest and three lowest quotes, the settlement price will be 100.000 minus the average of the remaining 10 rates.

The contract size, or unit of trading, is preset by the relevant exchange for each market. Contract sizes are chosen so as to give an approximately equal change in cash value per unit change in the futures price.

Thus, the Eurodollar contract is for a notional US$1 million three-month (strictly, 90-days) deposit commencing at a predetermined future date and fixed at the agreed rate of interest.

The price of the contract is quoted not as a rate of interest but as 100 *minus* the rate of interest. Figure 25.2 illustrates a typical listing of Eurocurrency futures prices.

Three-month Eurodollar futures prices

Fig 25.2

13/09	13:13 GMT		[TELERATE FUTURES SERVICE]						PAGE 999
3 MONTH EURO $ – CME									
[MONTH]	TRADE	BID	ASK	HIGH	LOW	OPEN	PR SETT	VOLUME	OPENINT
SEP 96	9443	B9443	A9444	9444	9436	9437	9436	67742	291344
OCT 96	B9429	B9429	A9430	9429	9419	9419	9419	2993	11522
NOV 96	9420	B9419	A9421	9420			9409	348	3109
DEC 96	9414	B9413	A9414	9416	9399	9400	9399	151893	482408
MAR 97	9400	B9400	A9401	9403	9384	9384	9383	179295	349558
JUN 97	9385	B9384	A9385	9387	9366	9367	9366	79832	251469
SEP 97	9370	B9370	A9371	9371	9351		9351	41863	185039
DEC 97	9354	B9354	A9355	9355	9335		9335	16418	142841
MAR 98	9348	B9348	A9349	9350	9330		9330	10209	126740
JUN 98	9340	B9340	A9341	9342	9321		9321	8629	96370

[FOR REGULAR TRADING HOURS SESSIONS FOR CME LIBOR AND T-BILL FUTURES]
[PLEASE SEE TELERATE PAGE 52050]

Source: Dow Jones Telerate

The buyer of a Eurodollar futures is the potential depositor of a three-month fixed deposit at a rate of 100 minus the contract price.

Thus, the buyer of a Sep contract at 91.73 effectively locks himself into a US$1 million notional deposit for three months, commencing on some date during September, at a rate of 8.27% (=100.00 – 91.73).

This convention may seem strange, but it was adopted in order to make trading in Eurocurrency futures similar to trading in three-month T-bill futures. In the bills, market prices are quoted on a percentage discount basis from the face value of the bill, and the buyer of the bill futures is the potential investor.

The minimum price movement on the Eurocurrency futures (a "tick") is 1 basis point or 0.01% per annum. On a 90-day deposit of US$1 million, this represents an interest amount of:

$$0.01/100 \times 90/360 \times 1,000,000$$
$$= \$25.00.$$

This is the "tick value" of the contract. Similarly, at IMM (International Money Market – the financial futures arm of the Chicago Mercantile Exchange), the 90-day T-bill contract is for a principal amount of $1,000,000. The minimum price movement is also 1 basis point, equal to $25 in cash. The one-year T-bill contract, on the other hand, has a principal value of $250,000, but its tick value is also $25.

Tick value = Minimum price tick/100 × contract period/360 × contract size

Trading Procedures

All futures trades must take place through the exchange, and are struck either electronically or by open outcry. Only floor members are able to trade on an exchange; a seat on the exchange can be owned by an individual or a company – and is itself a tradeable commodity. At the time of writing, a seat on one of the major exchanges could fetch about USD0.5 million or more.

Within certain constraints, a member may trade in any pit on the exchange. One often sees traders in a quiet pit moving across to a different one and join in the market action. Members may trade for customers or for their own account, but may not do both at the same time. While off-exchange users give depth to the market, it is the "locals" – the exchange members – who provide the short-term liquidity, going in and out of positions many times during a trading session.

In order to make a deal, a trader who does not have a seat on the exchange ("non-member") phones a broker who is a member. The broker in turn calls down to the floor-trader, who reports back later to confirm that the order has been "filled." Provided the number of contracts in the trading order is not large, normally the whole process would take not more than a couple of minutes.

The Clearing House

Once a deal has been struck on the floor of the exchange, both sides want to be assured of the counterparty's ability to fulfil their obligation. To avoid the need for each participant to have credit limits for all potential counterparties, all futures exchanges interpose the clearing house (CH) after a deal has been struck.

Example

If Trader A has bought 50 March contracts from Trader B at 91.20, both parties treat the deal as having been done with the CH. Thus the house has sold 50 contracts to A and bought 50 contracts from B. Now A has no exposure to B, and vice versa; both take only the risk of the clearing house, which is well secured by the *margins* both A and B will be required to place with the CH by way of collateral.

The clearing house is effectively the counterparty to every deal, so its own net position in a particular contract is always flat: for every buyer A, there is a seller B.

The other advantage of always trading with the same counterparty is that contracts for the same delivery month become *fungible*. If I buy 25 contracts, and then sell 25 contracts, the CH will, if requested, set off the two trades against each other to leave me with a net flat position (plus a profit or loss). I no longer need to settle each of the contracts at maturity: they have in fact ceased to exist.

Margining

The CH effectively guarantees the performance of all contracts, whatever the credit standing of its holder. It is able to do this by requiring all traders to place *initial margin* against their net open positions. The margin amount is calculated so as to enable the CH to cover traders' potential losses in the event that market prices move by the maximum permitted limit during one session (*limit price* move). Limit price ranges or initial margins can be altered by the exchange as market conditions warrant it.

At the time of writing, the initial margin on the Eurodollar futures at LIFFE is $625.00 per contract. This is only 0.06% of the contract value, so futures trading offers an opportunity to create highly leveraged positions. Straddles and spread trades, which involve simultaneously buying and selling into different months, or trading closely related products, generally require substantially lower margins than outright positions.

Margin amounts vary considerably across different markets depending on the price volatility of the contract. Thus, bond futures contracts tend to attract significantly higher margin percentages than the short-term interest rate contracts.

A non-member wishing to open a position must pay his initial margin into a margin account set up by his broker, who is a member of the exchange. In addition to this, each day his net open positions will be marked to market at the *exchange settlement price*, which is an average of the last few trading prices during the day (effectively the market closing price), calculated by the exchange.

If the price has moved adversely, the trading losses will be debited from the margin account, and the client must deposit additional *variation margin* to restore the minimum margin requirement. Conversely, if the position has made a profit, the trader will receive variation margin from the exchange, which he can take out of the margin account.

Variation margin is the daily cash sum that the trader will pay out to, or receive from, the exchange, depending on whether his position has moved against him or in his favor.

Example

		Margin A/C balance
Day 1:	Long 10 Sep Eurodollar contracts @ 93.04	
	Initial margin is 625×10	$6,250
Day 2:	Settlement price rises to 93.28 (up 24 ticks)	
	Profit = $24 \times 10 \times 25.00$	
	= $6,000	$12,250
	Trader takes out $6,000	$6,250
Day 3:	Settlement price falls to 93.10 (down 18 ticks)	
	Loss = $18 \times 10 \times 25.00$	
	= $4,500	$1,750
	Trader receives variation margin call of $4,500	$6,250

The CH is thus confident that it has sufficient funds at all times to fulfill its obligations with all its counterparties. The CH will automatically close out any positions on which margin calls have not been met on time. By marking to market and settling all positions daily, the CH effectively settles and rewrites all futures contracts at the prevailing market prices.

A futures contract may be viewed as a strip of one-day contracts on a forward rate.

In most exchanges initial margins can be satisfied with interest-bearing instruments possessing a high degree of liquidity, such as treasury bills, which reduces the cost of margins. However, variation margin calls must be met in cash, on which the CH does not pay interest.

Some US exchanges work on the basis of *maintenance margins*, where variation margin is not called as soon as the initial margin level has been breached, but only when a lower threshold level has been reached. At that time a call is made for sufficient funds to get the trader back to the initial margin level. The idea is to avoid having to make lots of small margin calls.

Comparison with FRAs

The Forward Rate Agreement, in common with all over-the-counter (OTC) contracts, is a bilateral contract that solely involves the two parties. It has the following properties:

- **Flexibility:** amount, period and settlement process are all negotiable between the two parties.
- **Confidentiality:** no obligation to announce the terms of the transaction.
- **OTC market:** FRA deals can be struck by telephone or dealing screen from each party's own office.
- **No margin:** Usually no money changes hands until settlement, although private investors are often required to place some collateral with their bank.
- **Credit risk:** each side is taking a risk on the counterparty, so each side must accept an element of credit risk, albeit a small one.

- **No right of offset:** Each FRA transaction is a contract in its own right. It cannot be netted against other FRA deals with the same counterparty, cancelled or assigned to a third party, without the specific agreement of both parties.

In contrast, futures contracts have some distinctive features. These are summarized below and discussed in more detail later in this chapter.

- **Standard terms:** fixed amounts, maturity dates, settlement procedures.

- **Open outcry:** All deals must be transacted by open outcry at a specific physical location – the relevant trading pit in a recognized exchange or electronically through the exchange's dealing system. Because of this, a futures trade cannot be kept secret. There is only one market price at any one time. This is a real advantage for the smaller trader, who may not in a position to get a good price in the equivalent cash or OTC market.

- **Marked-to-market:** a percentage of the deal amount – the initial margin – must be paid upon making a deal. Margin funds are held by the clearing house as a good faith deposit. Further margin calls (variation margin) may be required by the clearing house on a daily basis, depending on the movement of market prices.

- **Low credit risk:** After a deal is struck, the clearing house stands in the middle, acting as the seller to every buyer and buyer to every seller. The clearing house can guarantee the performance of every contract through its control of margin funds.

- **Fungibility:** Because all contracts for the same maturity date are identical in every respect, long and short positions in futures may be netted out.

Cash Prices and Futures Prices

Many futures contracts must be settled at maturity against deliverable securities. For example, in the case of futures on government bonds, any of a specified range of bonds are deliverable.

However, for many financial futures even that link is tenuous. For example, it is not possible to make physical delivery against stock index futures such as the S&P 500. Settlement of these contracts is made by cash equivalent at the *exchange delivery settlement price*, or EDSP, which is an average of the last prices quoted for such contracts on their Last Trading Day.

Nowadays, many contracts that do have an actual underlying security are also settled in cash rather than through physical delivery. These include the three-month Eurocurrency contracts which originally required the delivery of a deposit for the principal amounts at a recognized bank, but now settle purely in cash terms. On the last trading day, the outstanding position is simply closed by marking it to market at the EDSP, and any balance left on the margin account is remitted back to the trader. On the Eurocurrency futures contract the EDSP is an average of the cash market three-month LIBORs prevailing on the Last Trading Day. This, on the Last Trading Day the futures market and the cash market converge to one and the same. Before the Last Trading Day the futures price is a price on a three-month forward deposit effective in March, June, September or December.

The connection between most futures contracts and their underlying cash instruments is maintained by powerful arbitrage forces: if futures prices exceed cash prices plus their cost of carry, then arbitrageurs would purchase the cash security, and hold it against short positions in the futures, a strategy known as cash-and-carry arbitrage. Conversely, if futures prices are below their cash equivalent plus the cost of carry, then it may be possible to hold short cash positions against long futures positions.

However, with some instruments it is difficult or expensive to short the cash markets. In those markets, distortions between cash and futures prices may take time to be arbitraged out. This is not a problem with Eurocurrency futures, where traders can easily cover futures position by creating matching forward–forward gaps using Eurodeposits, or equivalent FRAs.

Summary

In this chapter we have discussed financial futures in detail, in particular the interest rate futures contract. We defined its properties and saw how they are traded, and then looked at the concept of margining by means of an example. Finally, we compared interest rate futures with forward rate agreements.

Keywords Before moving on, please make sure that you are familiar with the following terms and their definitions:

- futures contract
- hedgers
- speculators
- open interest
- tick value
- clearing houses (CH)
- fungible contract
- initial margin
- variation margin
- exchange delivery settlement price (EDSP).

26

Exercise:
Interest Rate Futures

1. A borrower will roll-over an existing loan of US$3 million for a further three-month period in three months' time.

    Three-month rates on the interbank market are currently 9.875%–9.75% p.a., and the relevant Eurodollar futures price is 90.20.

    The borrower believes that interest rates will increase.

    If in three months' time, the three-month rate is 10.25% and the Eurodollar futures price is 89.69, calculate:

    (i)   The net increase in the cost of the borrowing:

    (ii) The amount in ticks by which the Eurodollar futures price has moved:

    (iii) The profit if the borrower had sold Eurodollar contracts at 90.20:

    (iv) The net benefit/cost of the new borrowing:

2. An investor will re-invest US$7 million in three months' time for a period of three months. Interest rates are currently 10.000%–9.875% p.a. for three months' money. The Euro-dollar futures price is 90.20.

    If in three months' time, the interest rate is 9.25% for three-month deposits and the Eurodollar futures price is 90.85, calculate:

    (i)   The net fall in the return on the three-month deposit:

    (ii) The number of ticks by which the Eurodollar futures price has moved:

    (iii) The profit if the investor had bought Eurodollar futures contracts at 90.20:

    (iv) The net benefit/cost of the new investment.

3. An investor will re-invest US$5 million in three months' time for a period of three months. Interest rates are currently 11.125%–11.000% p.a. for three-month money. The Euro-dollar futures price is 89.26.

    If in three months' time, the three-month market bid rate is 9.5% and the Eurodollar futures price is 90.23, calculate:

    (i)   The net decrease in the return on the three-month deposit:

    (ii) The amount in ticks by which the Eurodollar futures price has moved:

    (iii) The number of futures contracts the investor ideally should have bought or sold:

    (iv) The profit if the investor had bought or sold the number of contracts calculated in (iii) at the Eurodollars futures price of 90.23:

    (v)   The net benefit/cost of the new investment.

4. A borrower will roll-over an existing loan of US$10 million on 8 March. Today is 30 September. The rate of interest for the existing loan is 9.5% p.a. for six months. Today's Eurodollar futures price for March delivery is 90.05.

If on 4 March the interest rate is 10.75% for six-month money and the March Eurodollar futures price is 89.10 calculate:

(i) The net increase in the cost of borrowing:

(ii) The number of ticks by which the Eurodollar futures price has moved:

(iii) How many Eurodollar futures contracts the borrower ideally should have bought or sold:

(iv) The profit on the futures position if the borrower had bought or sold the number of contracts calculated in (iii):

(v) The net benefit/cost of the new borrowing.

Money Markets Practice

There follows a set of questions of the type you might see in the ACI *Introduction to FX and Money Markets* examination.

In exam conditions, each question receives 1 mark for a correct answer, zero for no answer and minus 1/4 mark for a wrong answer.

Attempt as many questions as you can in half an hour. After this you can go over the remaining questions in your own time. Suggested answers are given in Appendix 3.

1. You are quoted the following one-month rates for Eurodollars by four different banks. What is the best rate for you as a depositor?

   a) 6 5/8 - 1/2

   b) 6 13/16 - 11/16

   c) 6 11/16 - 9/16

   d) 6 3/4 - 5/8

2. In the example above, the spot date is Thursday, 28 April. What is the one-month maturity date?

   a) 28 May

   b) 30 May

   c) 31 May

   d) 2 June

3. You have US$10 million which you place on deposit for one-month at the rate identified in the first question. What is the principal and interest due at maturity?

   a) US$10,055,729.17

   b) US$10,061,302.08

   c) US$10,060,462.33

   d) US$10,668,750.00

4. In the Eurodeposits markets, what is spot normally? Is it:

   a) One working day forward

   b) Two working days forward

   c) The duration for the deal

   d) None of these

5. You have US$10,000,000 which you wish to convert into pounds sterling, and place on deposit for 20 days. Spot rates are 1.4250/1.4260 and the interest rate is 8%. What is the principal and interest due at maturity?

   a) £7,048,732.94

   b) £10,800,000.00

   c) £7,043,362.98

   d) £10,044,444.44

6. If the 90-day rate is 3.10% and the 180-day is 3.50%, what is the 120-day rate using straight-line interpolation?

   a) 3.20%

   b) 3.21%

   c) 3.23%

   d) 3.30%

7. A negative yield curve is one in which:

   a) Longer rates are lower than short

   b) Forward exchange rates are at a discount

   c) Short-term rates are lower than long

   d) Forward exchange rates are at a premium

8. What advantage is there in the purchase of a certificate of deposit compared to the placing of a fixed deposit?

   a) It *normally* pays a higher rate of interest

   b) It eliminates counterparty risk

   c) It is a negotiable instrument

   d) There is no advantage

9. A sterling eligible bill is quoted at 10%. Its tenor is 90 days. What is its yield?

   a) 10.0000%

   b) 10.2564 %

   c) 2.4658 %

   d) 10.2528 %

10. You buy 90-day treasuries with a yield of 3.91%. The face amount is US$10,000,000. What do you expect to pay for them?

a) US$9,900,000.00

b) US$10,000,000.00

c) US$9,903,196.26

d) US$10,097,750.00

11. A dollar CD is quoted at 5 3/8%. Its tenor is 182 days. What is the true annual yield?

a) 5.30%

b) 5.45%

c) 5.38%

d) 5.23%

12. A CD was issued at 7%, which you now purchase at 5 3/4%. Would you expect to pay:

a) The original face value

b) More than the original face value

c) Less than the original face value

d) Too little information to decide

13. If the interest earned on a 10-million-Euro-D-mark deposit for 60 days is DM 83,333.33, what was the interest rate?

a) 10%

b) 5%

c) 8.33%

d) None of these

14. Money market intervention by a central bank will tend to:

a) Drain liquidity out of the market if the bank is selling securities

b) Add liquidity to the market if the bank is buying securities

c) Both of the above

d) Neither of the above

15. You have borrowed for a period of three months US$10 million at 4%; US$5 million at 5% and US$2 million at 5.5%. What is the average rate of your long position?

  a) 5%

  b) 4%

  c) 4.8333%

  d) 4.4706%

16. You are asked to quote a 1×7 USD FRA: the contract period starts in 30 days and runs for 182 days. The spot-30-day rate is 8% and the spot-212-day rate is 8 9/16%. What rate would you quote for the FRA on a break-even basis?

  a) 7.85%

  b) 8.47%

  c) 7.22%

  d) 8.60%

17. Using the previous example, suppose that you sold the FRA with a contract amount of $1 million, and that on the settlement date the relevant BBA Rate is fixed at 7%. What would be the settlement amount?

  a) You receive $7,812.42

  b) You receive $4,150.35

  c) You pay $7,812.42

  d) You receive $7,709.01

■ ■ ■

"The trick is to catch the large movements in the rates when they come, and learn to do very little when they don't."

Simulated Dealing – Second Session

Objectives

The purpose of the session is to give you practical experience of trading and running a book in Eurocurrency deposits.

In this particular scenario you will be dealing US dollar deposits from quotations made to you by a number of market makers, and by making a market yourself by quoting two-way prices. News items will flash up on the screen giving you a general indication of the direction of the market.

Success in this session will depend on your ability to determine the following.

- Based on how the market is moving, should you be net long- or short-funded? That is, should the maturity of your borrowing be longer than that of your lending or vice versa?
- When should you open, increase, decrease or square out your position?
- When you receive a quotation should you deal at that rate, or should you ask for another quotation from a different market maker?
- What rates should you show, given your position and the market trend?

The Scenario

As in the previous session, you will trade over about 15 hours – in real-time, this will last about 20 minutes after which the system will shut down automatically.

> **You can deal round the clock and run overnight positions, but for revaluation purposes the cut-off time each day will be midnight, London time (GMT).**

At the end of the session, you should square out your position completely – all your gaps should be covered. You will be given a range of statistics on your dealing performance which can be compared against benchmarks set out at the end of this chapter.

It is important to tackle this session in the prescribed way. The key objectives are to develop an understanding of the profit or loss and the funding gaps created by your deals. You should be trying to achieve:

- a fast response to price quotations (do you like them or not ?);
- an accurate response to quotations (are you hitting the right side of the price?);
- a good understanding of your position (are you long- or short-funded overall?).

Starting the Session

We will assume from here that you have already installed the software on your PC, and that you are familiar with the start-up procedure from the previous session.

From the start-up screen, press the 📂 button and select MONEY1.WLD from the list of files, or you can do this by selecting **Open** from the **File** drop-down menu. When the file has finished loading, the display will change to something like the screen shown in Figure 28.1.

Before you start the simulation, select **Market** from the **Reports** drop-down menu. This allows you to read a brief economic summary of the trading scenario you are about to start.

When you have read the text, close the **Market** window.

Pressing the ▷ button will start the simulation.

If you have already started the simulation, hit the ❚❚ button to pause it until you have read the instructions below. Then click ▷ when you are ready to start trading.

The Depo Screen

The main windows created in this sessions are shown in Figure 28.1.

Fig 28.1

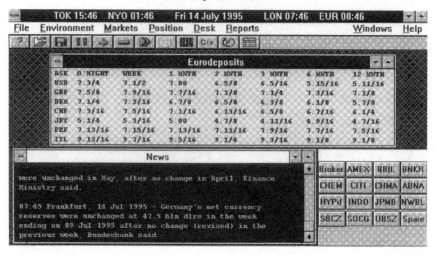

The deposit screen

| TOK 15:46 | NYO 01:46 | Fri 14 July 1995 | LON 07:46 | EUR 08:46 |
| File | Environment | Markets | Position | Desk | Reports | Windows | Help |

Eurodeposits

ASK	O'NIGHT	WEEK	1 MNTH	2 MNTH	3 MNTH	6 MNTH	12 MNTH
USD	7.3/4	7.1/2	7.00	6.5/8	6.5/16	5.15/16	5.11/16
GBP	7.5/8	7.9/16	7.7/16	7.3/8	7.1/4	7.3/16	7.1/8
DEM	7.1/4	7.3/16	6.7/8	6.5/8	6.3/8	6.1/8	5.7/8
CHF	7.3/16	7.5/16	7.1/16	6.13/16	6.5/8	6.7/16	6.1/4
JPY	5.1/4	5.3/16	5.00	4.7/8	4.11/16	4.9/16	4.7/16
FRF	7.13/16	7.15/16	7.13/16	7.11/16	7.9/16	7.7/16	7.5/16
ITL	9.13/16	9.7/16	9.5/16	9.1/4	9.3/16	9.1/8	9.1/8

News

were unchanged in May, after no change in April, Finance
Ministry said.

07:45 Frankfurt, 14 Jul 1995 — Germany's net currency
reserves were unchanged at 47.5 bln dlrs in the week
ending on 09 Jul 1995 after no change (revised) in the
previous week, Bundesbank said.

Broker	AMEX	BBIL	BNKR
CHEM	CITI	CHMA	ABNA
HYPd	INDO	JPMB	NWBL
SBCZ	SOCG	UBSZ	Spare

The Clocks

The clocks on the bar at the top of the screen show the time in
Tokyo, New York, London and Continental Europe. The simulation date is shown in the middle of the bar. When the simulation is
running, the clocks pulsate. Each financial centre is open from
08:00 to 17:00 local time.

**You can deal round the clock but the date will change at
midnight, London time (GMT).**

The clocks provide useful information about the state of the worldwide currency market – market depth depends on the number of
buyers and sellers active at any one time. The market is deepest at
around 15:00 when London and New York are both open.
Depending on the depth of the market, a large currency transaction
can cause market prices to move against you.

Market Rates

The middle part of the screen is a table with Eurocurrency codes
down the left-hand side. Initially, the table shows the interbank
offered rates (ASK) for overnight, spot – 1 week, spot – 1 month
and other fixed dates up to 12 months.

Press the **to toggle between the BID and ASK rates or click the right mouse button on the window**

This part of the screen is inspired by some of the "composite" pages on the Reuters service. Composite pages show the current indication rates contributed anonymously by a number of banks. They are widely used reference pages. As with all market information services, indication rates shown on the screen sometimes lag behind the market. There can be a disparity between the rates you are given by a market maker and the rates shown on the price screen.

News

Messages come into the News window at various times. Only one item is displayed at a time. If you do not have time to read an item fully or want to go back over earlier news, click up or down on the scroll bar to the right of the window, or **PgUp**, **PgDn** on the scroll bar.

Charts

Selecting the option **Charts** from the **Desk** menu opens a window where you can look at the yield curve, spot FX rates, benchmark bond prices or the Eurocurrency futures prices for each currency.

Press the ⎡Ccy⎤ **button to display a different currency on the Charts window**

Press the ⎡⎤ **button to change the price series displayed**

From the toolbar inside the charts window, use the Daily or Tick buttons to view either daily or tick price charts. You also have two buttons to compress or expand the chart horizontally.

Dealing

Asking for a Price

To ask for a quotation select **Deal** from the **Desk** menu (**Alt+d** followed by **d**). A window will open up which shows you the counterparties you can deal with, with their four-letter dealing codes, the size of their limits and how much of their limits have been used. Alternatively, click on a selected button in the phone pad.

A dialog box like the one in Figure 28.2 will appear on the screen.

Fig 28.2

Deposits deal slip

Deal Fixed Income		
To: CITI FRA Swaps ◆ Depo Futures [ ] ⬦	From: CITI Limit: 110,000 Used: -10,000	✔ OK
Currency USD Value date S Maturity 1M	We deal 7.1/4 - 7.1/16 in up to 30,000	✗ Cancel
Deal type L Amount 10M	Deal rate 7.1/16	? Help

The left part of the deal slip is where you enter details of the deal you wish to make. The right of the deal slip is where the simulated counterparty will respond.

Your first decision is to select which fixed-income market instrument you want to deal in. As the Eurodeposits window is the active window, the instrument will automatically be Depo.

To enter the quoted currency, type the Currency code (in MONEY1.WLD this will be **u** or **USD**) and press **Enter**.

The next field is the VALUE DATE, where you enter the date when the funds become available. The next entry is where you enter the MATURITY which is when the funds (together with the interest) have to be repaid.

To enter a spot value date, type **s** (or **spot**) and press **Enter**. You can trade for same-day settlement (enter **tod**) or for settlement tomorrow (enter **tom**).

To enter a fixed maturity, type **o** (overnight), **w** (a week), **1m** (for one month), **2m** (two months), **3m** (three months) etc., and press **Enter**. This must of course be a later date than the VALUE DATE.

Alternatively, to enter the actual date of the forward maturity (a "broken date") type **1 Apr** or whichever date is appropriate. You may enter the year after the month if you require it – e.g., **1 Apr 1995**.

Once you have entered the value date, maturity and the currency, the counterparty will respond with a two-way price, just as if you had asked for a quote on the telephone. He will also indicate the amount for which the price is good (in US$ 000s).

The market maker will not hold his rates indefinitely, so you must decide fairly quickly. His rates may not be the same as those shown on the price screen, depending on which way he wants to trade, so make sure you compare them with the current market prices.

If you do not like the rates, press Cancel to abort or hit the Esc key.

If you want to deal, type **b** (borrow) or **l** (lend). The system will also accept **t** (take) or **g** (give) *but not* "buy" or "sell" as is the convention in the US Fed funds market.

You cannot cancel a deal once you have agreed to give or take at the given rates.

Enter the amount you wish to deal, in thousands, or follow the figure you enter with an **m** to indicate millions – for example **5m** for $5 million. If the amount you enter is very large or very small, a message may tell you that the rates are only good for amounts in a certain range.

As soon as you have entered the deal type and amount, the counterparty will confirm the rate at which you dealt, and the deal will be automatically logged into your position. The limit utilization will also be updated (which will be in USD).

Market Making

When the simulation is running, you will hear a double ringing sound from time to time, and a line button on the phone pad will be highlighted. This tells you that there is an incoming call from a counterparty asking you for a quotation. Click on the button, and a window like the one in Figure 28.3 will appear.

In this version of the software, the dealing convention in the Configuration control of the File menu is set to Offer–Bid, so you should enter the offered rate first, followed by the bid. This is the convention used in London.

Fig 28.3

Price request window

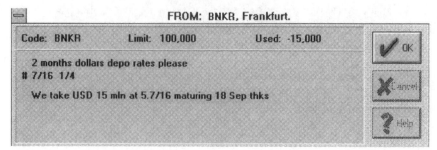

FROM: BNKR, Frankfurt.

| Code: BNKR | Limit: 100,000 | Used: -15,000 |

2 months dollars depo rates please
7/16 1/4

We take USD 15 mln at 5.7/16 maturing 18 Sep thks

✔ OK

✗ Cancel

? Help

You enter your two-way rates under the request. The two rates you enter must be separated by a space.

You can qualify your rates with a maximum amount on which you are prepared to deal in by typing, for example, **in 10m** after your two-way price.

Once you have entered a rate (and an amount if you so wish) the caller will decide whether he will deal with you. If a deal is made, a new message will appear stating the amount and whether they take or give you funds, and the confirmed rate.

The Position Keeper

The simulation comes with a full electronic position. Select **Position (Alt+p)** from the drop-down menu.

Blotter

This window shows the list of deals that have been already executed and are awaiting settlement or maturity. Risk manager automatically settles all deals from the list when they reach maturity, and effects all the required balance sheet adjustments.

Each entry has the following information:

- the time and the date of the trade;
- the currency or reference code of the deal;
- the amount (in thousands). If you are long, the amount is shown as +ve in that currency; and if you are short it will be shown as −ve;

- the settlement and maturity date;
- **THRU**: the counterparty dealing code. If you have dealt on your prices, by answering an incoming call, a **t** will be appended to the code;
- the **RATE** at which you dealt.

Any interest **ACCRUED** on a fixed-income trade.

Ladders

If you select **Ladders** from the list, a window will appear that looks like Figure 28.4.

Exposure ladder

Fig 28.4

USD Exposure							
MAT	**SHORT**	**LONG**	**LIMIT**	**NET**	**YLD**	**VAL1%**	**CUMUL**
CASH			5,000	0		0	0
TOM			75,000	0	6.18	0	0
SPOT			150,000	10,000	6.16	0	10,000
− 1 MTH			100,000	0	5.89	0	10,000
− 2 MTH			100,000	0	5.70	0	10,000
− 3 MTH			100,000	0	5.50	0	10,000
− 6 MTH			100,000	0	5.33	0	10,000
− 1 YR			100,000	0	5.16	0	10,000
− 2 YRS			100,000	0	5.00	0	10,000
− 3 YRS			0	0	4.86	0	10,000
− 5 YRS			0	0	4.72	0	10,000
−10 YRS			0	0	4.62	0	10,000
>10 YRS			0	0	4.59	0	10,000
NET			500,000	10,000		0	

The ladder summarizes for each currency your dealing limits and net position for settlement or maturity on various dates, or date bands.

The ladder starts with your **CASH** (or bank) position and ranges all your deals into various maturity bands. **TOM** shows the net cash flows for values tomorrow. **SPOT** shows amounts for value spot and the other dates are for forward values.

The dots under **SHORT** and **LONG** represent your dealing limits, and the squares show your net position in each maturity band. This display gives you an idea of your position at a glance. If you have exceeded any limits, ! marks will appear under these columns.

The **NET** and **LIMIT** columns show in figures (000s) what the **SHORT** and **LONG** columns represent graphically. The **CUMUL** column shows what your cash position would be at the end of each maturity period given your present portfolio.

> Press the 🖱 button or click on the right mouse button inside the window to toggle the analysis between Liquidity, Exposure and Present Value.

- The **Liquidity** run includes all payables/receivables on various future dates: principal amounts, interest, options premiums, etc.
- The **Exposure** analysis looks only at your net principal amounts (no interest or premiums) and helps you identify quickly where your main exposures lie.
- The **Present Value** analysis looks at the present value of all the forward cash flows identified in the Liquidity run, discounted at the corresponding zero-coupon swap rate shown under **YLD**. The total of these present values, shown against **NET** at the bottom of the table gives you an indication of the net liquidation value of your book.

The different ways of expressing the ladder are especially useful when dealing in the fixed-interest markets.

As the **Exposure** ladder does not include interest amounts payable or receivable, you can look at the **Liquidity** analysis, which includes these. If you have lent (given) US$30 million spot –6 months, the exposure ladder will show –30,000 against spot and +30,000 against –6 MTH maturity band. In the **Liquidity** page, the same position will show the actual settlement amount against SPOT and the maturity amount plus the interest payable on the loan against the appropriate maturity band.

But normally traders do not include the interest flows, as they tend to be small in relation to the exposures created by the principal, and can sometimes obscure the overall picture.

Fixed-Income Book

This page will show your net trading position. Each line of the analysis shows:

- the instrument's currency (CCY) or security reference (**REF**) code;
- the **AMOUNT**, in local currency units (000s);
- the **SETT**lement and **MAT**urity dates;
- the average **PRICE** implied in the position;
- the market price used to revalue the position;
- the mark-to-market profit or loss on the net open position – press the **Ccy** button to toggle between the two.

Performance Assessment

When you have reached the end of your trading session, make sure that you have squared out all your positions. You will get a warning to square positions at 22:00 London time anyway before the system moves on to the next date.

From the Control Panel, select Reports followed by the *Dealing* option, and a screen which looks like Figure 28.5 will appear.

Benchmarks

Here are some benchmarks to help you assess your performance. These are based on the performances of the many dealers who have completed this Dealing Module.

Dealing report window

Fig 28.5

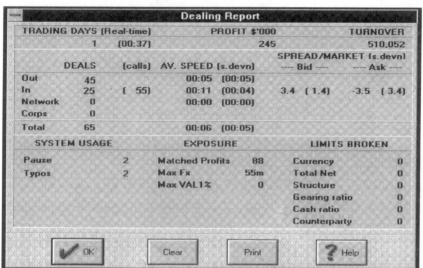

Dealing Report					
TRADING DAYS (Real-time)		**PROFIT $'000**		**TURNOVER**	
1	(00:37)		245		510,052
				SPREAD/MARKET (s.devn)	
	DEALS	(calls)	AV. SPEED (s.devn)	---- Bid ----	---- Ask ----
Out	45		00:05 (00:05)		
In	25	(55)	00:11 (00:04)	3.4 (1.4)	-3.5 (3.4)
Network	0		00:00 (00:00)		
Corps	0				
Total	65		00:06 (00:05)		
SYSTEM USAGE		**EXPOSURE**		**LIMITS BROKEN**	
Pause	2	Matched Profits	88	Currency	0
Typos	2	Max Fx	55m	Total Net	0
		Max VAL1%	0	Structure	0
				Gearing ratio	0
				Cash ratio	0
				Counterparty	0

OK   Clear   Print   Help

Our experience shows that they establish a "profile" of the kind of person who tends to be successful at depo dealing. Of course, we are talking about statistical correlations here, not natural laws – the benchmarks must be applied with a great deal of common sense.

Profits

251+	Excellent
151–250	Very good
51–150	Good
10–50	Fair
Less than 10	Further practice required.

You are, of course, aiming to make a profit in the simulated dealing session. However, from a learning point of view, it is equally important that you should understand exactly how you achieved the result you did, and draw some lessons for the future. If you made a loss, then think carefully about where you went wrong. If you made a profit, ask yourself honestly whether this was the result of good judgement or good luck.

Deals

Out tells you how many deals you made with the simulated counterparties as a market user – i.e., you called them and dealt on their prices.

In deals are transactions where you have quoted rates in response to counterparties requests for rates. The figure in parenthesis indicates the number of calls that were made to you, whether you answered the phone or not. From this figure you can establish how many calls you have "dropped," and therefore how active you were as a market maker.

> **Each in-coming call in which you quoted rates counts as a call, even if the counterparty did not in fact deal.**

Points to Note:

- Low response rates and slow response speeds indicate either lack of practice in market making or uncertainty about your own position.

- You should aim to take more calls than you make, and typically trainees' speed of response to making rates is a little faster than their reaction to someone else's rates.

- Dealing on your own rates is often the most profitable, or at least the most cost-effective, form of dealing – provided of course you know what you are doing!

Average Speed

This shows the average time in seconds that you took to handle your trades, as a market user (**Out**) or market maker (**In**). The time is measured from the moment you press the phone line button to the moment the trade is confirmed or cancelled. But speed alone is not the vital factor – it is of course possible to react very quickly but wrongly.

We recommend that you deal at a "safe speed" – one in which you have control – you know what you are doing and what the results of your actions will be. A reasonable average response time to aim for in the first session is around 15 seconds.

Spread/Market

This shows how close your quotations were to the prevailing market rates, and the dispersion of your quotes around the market rates (in technical terms, the standard deviation). If your rates were significantly out of line, this indicates a lack of comfort with the market-making role.

You should aim to quote close to the market rate, perhaps just 1/16% (5 or 6 basis points) away from the market. However, you should be prepared to shade your rates up or down according to circumstances. Your profit figure will give an indication of how successful you have been with this.

System Usage

Pause: Hitting the ▮▮ button is recorded on each occasion. If it is pressed more than a couple of times during the session, we take this as a sign that the individual is feeling the stress of the market and is not perhaps as comfortable as they might be with interpreting the information presented to them.

Typos: the number of typing errors that are made when entering a deal, giving rise to a message like "I don't understand what you have entered" from *Risk Manager*. This is a useful measure of the propensity of the user to make clerical errors. A high figure here suggests that the user must improve his/her accuracy, as keyboard errors can be a costly source of problems in deal execution and settlement.

Average Deal Size

We suggest that you deal in amounts which produce an average deal size of not more than US$30 million. You should build into and out of positions gradually. Remember that it is easier to correct small mistakes than large ones.

Exposure

% Matched Profits: shows the % of deals matched at profit. This statistic does not attempt to weight profitable trades either by size or price. It is a simple measure designed to capture the trainee's jobbing skill. Looked at alongside the total number of deals done, it shows the extent to which the user has been able to turn positions around profitably.

Max VAL 1%: shows the maximum interest rate exposures (market risk) taken during a trading session. It is measured in cash terms as the profit/loss that would result from a 1% parallel shift in the yield curve. This statistic applies to forward or fixed-interest dealing sessions.

Trading Lessons

There are a number of basic trading rules which have been learned by dealers over the years by trial and error, sometimes at great cost. Here are some of the main ones. Think about your performance in this dealing session, and consider what areas you believe need improvement.

Never break a limit (it may cost you your job)

Dealing limits are there to control risk. Exposing your organization beyond those limits may put at risk the performance and standing of the whole institution, not just your own. There should not be too many problems if you go over a limit by a few thousand dollars in the heat of the moment. But if you must exceed a limit by a significant amount, ask your Chief Dealer first.

K.I.S.S.

This is an acronym coined by McDonald's, the burger chain. It stands for "keep it simple, stupid!"

A good dealer concentrates on one major strategy at a time. He or she will formulate a strategy and cover the position before changing tack. A dealer may test the water first with smaller deals, and only then increase his/her position in stages.

If the trend starts to change, the dealer will start to cover his/her exposure, gradually if the change is uncertain, more aggressively if it is confirmed. Large deals tend to be more difficult to execute, especially when the market is moving quickly – and they may move the market against you.

Know your position

A good dealer does not need to consult the electronic position keeper after every deal to know whether he is essentially long or short funded in a given maturity, or whether he is in profit. The net position should also be kept manually on a deal blotter.

All you need to know is whether you are basically on the right side of the market or not. Most dealers think in terms of (basis) "points made" or "points down": they have an idea of the average rate at which they created a position and monitor market rates to see how far in or out of the money they are. Time spent pouring over the details of the position keeper is time away from the market.

As your experience grows you will be able to retain more and more of what you have done in your head. Experienced dealers have dealt profitably on this simulation over a number of days without once looking at the position keeper!

Look after the short end

As time rolls by, all your deals approach settlement. You should ensure that you always have adequate funding. Don't allow your nostro account to go overdrawn – your correspondent won't like it and they will charge you a penalty rate (certainly the simulation will).

Before the end of the day, borrow the necessary funds in advance and place any surplus funds received at least on overnight deposit, when it arrives. Otherwise you will not earn any interest. You can specify the value date as **today** in the deal slip. This is useful if you have inadvertently allowed a position to settle and you want to move the funds immediately. However, you should try to avoid this: it can be more expensive.

Keep it tidy

If you have been trading actively for a while you may find your position showing various one- or two-day exposure gaps, either in the tom-next or in the far dates.

This is what happens if you continue dealing fixed dates over a number of days. A spot–three-months deal done yesterday can no longer be completely matched by a spot–three-months deal today. You need a deal value tomorrow (tom) and maturing in three months less one day – in other words you need to deal for broken dates.

Gaps created by the passage of time do not usually represent major risks; they just make the gap analysis more difficult to follow. In practice you would close these gaps when convenient, as they approach settlement. You must balance out the inconvenience of having these odd little gaps in your position with the fact that dealing for broken dates can be expensive.

Cut your losses early

It is easy to get obsessed with the prospect of hitting the jackpot and to forget to cut losses before they get worse. Also resist taking a profit before a change in the market trend has been confirmed. Statistically, a dealer who cuts losses quickly and holds on to profitable positions for as long as possible will make profits over the long run, even if he reads the markets correctly only 50% of the time.

Nobody should be too concerned if you do the occasional "bad trade." If you are not allowed to lose money you cannot trade for profit. What matters in the dealing room is your performance over a period of time.

Stay active

If you systematically ignore incoming calls and requests for rates, counterparties will stop calling, and you will become a market user rather than a professional dealer. The dealer has two objectives:

- to make profits for his or her employers;
- to make a market on demand in a manner which promotes the institution's standing in the market.

Bank customers and dealing counterparties demand a fast and efficient service. Calls coming in must be attended to, not ignored. You should respond to a request for rates as quickly as possible. You should participate fully in the market, thus gaining valuable information on current market sentiment.

If you quote wide rates, you can of course protect your position, but you may upset your counterparty, who may go elsewhere next time. If this is a corporate customer, the potential loss of business may be significant.

Remember: your counterparties will reciprocate. If you quote wide spreads then so will they.

In a sense, news information and the composite prices displayed at the top of the screen cannot tell you precisely where the market currently is: by the time they are posted and broadcast, these are already history. When you receive a tele-message, that is where the market currently is: at the end of your telephone line.

The more competitive and active you are in the market, the more market information you will get. In the long run it can pay to quote competitive rates, although it may sometimes be costly in the short-term.

Shading your rates

The fundamental skill in market making is the ability to adjust your prices based on the nature of your position and your reading of the market.

Which way should your spread be adjusted relative to the market price? You have to consider a number of factors (very quickly) to come to the correct decision. If you decide that you want to give funds, you should show a lower offer than the market. If you want to take funds, you should show a higher bid.

Watch your dealing limits carefully when making a market, because within certain boundaries you have little control over what your counterparty will do.

If you have no significant position, then you could test the market by shading your rates in the direction you think it is moving. The caller's response to your rates can provide you with valuable information.

If the caller is prepared to deal at a very uncompetitive rate, or if he declines a keen rate, this could be a signal of a change in market sentiment and it may alert you to cover your own position before the rest of the market catches on.

A given position is not the same thing as a wanted position

The trouble when you quote prices is that your counterparties do not always behave the way you want them to. Sometimes they hit you on the side you did not want to deal, even if the rates you quoted them were uncompetitive.

To get rid of an unwanted position requires the physical effort of calling around and dealing, whereas a wanted position requires no further work. There is a subtle tendency for given positions to become "wanted positions" in the dealer's mind – just because they are there in his book. You must be alert to this danger.

Losing money because you have read the markets wrongly is part of the dealing experience. Losing money because you were given a position which you never wanted in the first place is negligence.

Whenever you are given a position ask yourself this question: "If my counterparty didn't want it, why should I?" If you can articulate one good reason for wanting it, then you are probably OK.

Trading depos is not like jobbing cash markets

This may seem obvious, but many dealers tend to approach depo trading with the same gusto they apply to dealing spot FX – frantically opening and closing positions with lightning speed.

This is sometimes inevitable (if you have lots of callers) but as a trading style it is quite the wrong approach:

- Interest rates lack the volatility of the spot markets, which are sentiment-driven.
- Trends in the rates tend to take longer to build up and also last longer.
- Positions and strategies can be technically more complex to interpret and manage.
- Speculative positions can be traded more cheaply and effectively using off-balance-sheet instruments (such as FRAs and futures) than with depos.

All these things point to a much slower pace of dealing – one that has been described as "cerebral" rather than instinctive. Far from being more boring than the spot markets, money market trading offers more profitable opportunities for a lot less work. The trick is to catch the large movements in the rates when they come, and to learn to do very little when they don't.

Part 4

Forward FX

■ ■ ■

"What is distinctive about the forward FX markets is the time dimension."

The Forward FX Contract

Overview

An outright forward FX deal is a firm and binding contract to buy or sell a given amount of currency for settlement at some future date, at a rate of exchange which is agreed between the parties at the time of dealing. No money changes hands until the settlement date. In this chapter, we look at the structure and uses of forward FX contracts. Key concepts will be:

- the time value of money;
- calculation of forward rates;
- forward margin;
- risks on interest payments.

Introduction

Normally a company that wants to fix a forward exchange rate has a known amount of foreign currency payable (or receivable) in the future. However it is unwilling to risk losing from exchange rate movements.

By covering its exposure, through locking into a known forward FX rate, the company also gives away potential gains from favorable movements in market rates. Both the risk and the potential rewards are passed on to the deal counterparty – usually a bank.

The Time Value of Money

The basic principle of FX dealing is the same whether the delivery date is spot or forward – a buyer wants as much of one currency as possible for the lowest cost in terms of another currency. What is distinctive about the forward FX markets is the time dimension.

If you have money but do not need to use it for a known period, the sensible thing is to place it on deposit or lend it out. The rate of interest you earn is the price of waiting for a given period of time.

Covering any time gap between cash available and cash payable has a price in terms of interest received or paid – or interest forgone. Similarly, the price of a dollar in terms of another currency for value in two days' time is likely to be different from its price for delivery in three days or in three months.

The table in Figure 29.1 illustrates the relative volume of spot and forward FX in 1995.

Turnover of spot and forwards by currencies traded

Fig 29.1

	Spot		Forwards	
		1995		
£/US$	3.6	3.1	9.2	8.3
US$/DM	11.9	11.8	9.2	9.7
US$/yen	5.9	5.7	10.9	11.3
US$/Swiss franc	1.6	1.7	3.5	3.7
US$/French franc	0.8	0.9	4.3	4.5
US$/Canadian $	0.6	0.5	1.8	1.9
US$/Australian $	0.4	0.4	1.2	1.2
US$/lira	0.4	0.4	2.9	2.9
US$/peseta	0.2	0.2	1.8	1.8
US$/other EMS	0.7	0.8	4.9	5.1
US$/other	1.2	1.2	2.9	2.9
£/DM	3.3	2.8	0.4	0.4
£/other	0.4	0.4	0.9	1
DM/yen	2.1	1.9	0.3	0.3
DM/other EMS	4.6	4.8	0.8	0.9
Ecu-denominated	1.1	1.1	3.2	3
Other cross-currencies	2.2	2.3	0.7	0.8

Shares of total net turnover, adjusted for double counting of domestic interbank business, are given in italics.

Source: Bank of England, March 1996

The Forward Margin

The following case study shows how the time value of money concept applies to the forward rate of exchange.

ABCO of New York has imported goods from Germany for sale in the US. Payment is in D-marks. If the invoice was for immediate settlement, then the dollar cost of the goods could be calculated from the spot FX rate.

But payment is not due until three months (90 days after spot). ABCO does not have the marks now and intends to pay its supplier out of its US sales proceeds. If the dollar weakens over the three months then ABCO could find itself paying out more, in dollar terms, to the supplier than it makes from sales.

ABCO could do one of two things to fix its import costs in advance:

(i) Ask its bank for a forward FX rate to buy marks for delivery in three months. On the value date it will have earned the dollars to deliver to the bank, who will hand over the marks at the agreed rate of exchange. The company can work out its profit margin on the goods in advance.

(ii) Borrow dollars for three months at a fixed rate of interest. With the dollars borrowed, buy marks in the spot market and put them on a fixed deposit for three months. At the end of three months the dollar borrowing (plus interest due) will be repaid from the proceeds of selling the goods in the US. The marks plus interest earned will be used to pay the supplier. Figures 29.2 and 29.3 illustrate the cash flows involved at each point.

Fig 29.2

Cash flows on the spot date

Fig 29.3

Cash flows three months later

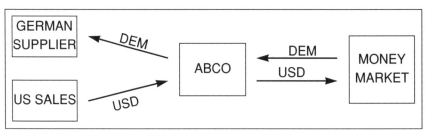

Given market rates for the transactions under option (ii), we can work out all the cash flows involved, and the effective forward rate of exchange locked in by ABCO. Let's work with some simple numbers:

Cost of borrowing USD for 90 days   10% per annum
Deposit rate on DEM for 90 days   8% per annum
Spot USD/DEM rate   2.0000

The interest rate differential between USD and DEM is 2% per annum, equivalent to 1/2% for 3 months. This is a net cost to ABCO, which is borrowing dollars at the higher rate and lending marks at the lower rate.

So the effective cost of buying DM2.0000 spot will be increased from USD1 to:

USD1 + 1/2% of a dollar

= USD1.005

FX rates are typically expressed as marks per dollar, so instead of increasing the USD cost by 1/2% we reduce the net amount of DEM by the equivalent amount. The effective rate of exchange is:

USD 1.005   :   DEM 2.0000
USD 1   :   DEM 2.0000/1.005
       :   DEM 1.9900

ABCO would realise DM1.9900 net for every dollar paid, instead of the DM2.0000 it can obtain spot. The "forward margin" – the 1 pfennig difference between the two rates – represents a net cost of carrying on "warehousing" DM funds for 90 days. It is equivalent to 2% per annum.

If the cost of borrowing dollars and the return on a DM deposit were the same, there would be no "time value" in forward dollar–marks. The effective forward rate would be the same as the spot rate.

Forward FX Formulae

The principles behind the calculations so far can be captured in a very simple formula (see Figure 29.4).

Fig 29.4 **Forward margin – the simple formula**

Forward margin = Net cost of carry =

$$\left[\frac{\text{Counter-currency interest rate}}{100} - \frac{\text{Base currency interest rate}}{100} \right] \times \text{Spot rate} \times \frac{\text{No. of days}}{360}$$

The forward margin is the amount the spot rate needs to be adjusted to obtain a forward exchange rate. Applying the figures in Case A to this formula, the forward margin is:

$$\frac{(8.00 - 10.00)}{100} \times 2.0000 \times \frac{90}{360}$$

$$= -0.0100$$

If both Eurocurrency rates are based on a 365-day year, then the divisor would be 365 instead of 360.

FX Risk on Interest Flows

The above formula is very easy to use. But it ignores the exchange risk on interest payments and should therefore only be used for "ball-park" calculations.

ABCO has an interest cost in dollars to meet in three months. This will be partly met by interest earned on D-marks, but there would be an exchange risk (a smaller one), since the rate used to convert the D-marks interest into dollars at maturity will probably change.

The solution is to avoid converting the interest earned on the marks into dollars. Suppose that ABCO has to pay exactly DM2 million to its German supplier in three months. We can calculate the amount of marks that ABCO would have to deposit now to produce DM2 million in three months.

DM2 million deposited today at 8% for 90 days produces a future sum of:

Principal + Interest

2,000,000 + (2,000,000 × $\frac{8.00}{100}$ × $\frac{90}{360}$)

= 2,000,000 × [1 + (0.08 × 90/360)]

So, we can produce DM2 million in 90 days by depositing the following sum today:

DM $\frac{2,000,000}{[1 + (0.08 × 90/360)]}$

= DM1,960,784.31

When we move forward in time, we accrue a principal amount by the interest earned on it. When we move backwards, we "discount" the principal amount by a factor incorporating the interest rate.

DM1,960,784.31 is the present value of DM2,000,000 in three months' time, discounted at 8%.

ABCO only needs to buy DM1,960,784.31 in the spot market. At a spot rate of 2.0000 that would cost:

USD $\frac{1,960,784.31}{2.0000}$

= US$980,392.16

These dollars will be borrowed at 10%, and the total repayment amount in three months will be:

Principal + Interest

980,392.16 + [980,392.16 × 10.00/100 × 90/360]

= US$1,004,901.96

Since US$1,004,901.96 payable in three months will produce DM 2,000,000 in three months, the effective forward FX rate achieved is:

DM 2,000,000/1,004,901.96

= 1.9902 (to the nearest point)

The forward margin is therefore:

1.9902 –2.0000

=   –0.0098

The above calculations can be condensed into a general (exact) formula:

Fig 29.5

Forward outright – the exact formula

Outright forward rate =

$$\text{Spot rate} \times \left[\frac{1 \times (\text{Days}/360 \times \text{Counter-currency interest rate}/100)}{1 + (\text{Days}/360 \times \text{Base currency interest rate}/100)} \right]$$

Replace 360 with 365 in the numerator if the counter-currency is quoted on a 365-day-year basis. Replace 360 with 365 in the denominator if the base currency is quoted on a 365-day-year basis.

There are two major inputs in this formula: the spot rate and an expression which represents the net cost of carry. If the cost of carry is constant, the forward rate will move in line with the spot rate. If the cost of carry changes (one or both interest rates move), then the relationship between the spot and the forward rate (the margin) will alter.

The forward margin is the difference between the forward rate produced by this formula and the spot rate.

Forward Rates and Future Rates

We have seen how to create a synthetic forward rate of exchange by buying the currency required in the spot market and "carrying" the funds acquired in the money markets.

A forward FX rate has nothing to do with exchange rate forecasts. It is simply the spot rate plus a cost of carry, all of which are known today.

Suppose the rate for buying marks three months forward in Case A above was lower than 1.9902 – say, 1.9890. Then there would be arbitrage (risk-free) profits to be made by buying marks spot at 2.0000 and selling them forward at 1.9890. The net interest cost of carrying the cash marks through delivery would be only DM 0.0098, leaving a clear profit of DM0.0012 (1.9902 – 1.9890) for every dollar at maturity.

The investment flow created by such an arbitrage "window" would put pressure on the rates to close the gap. Spot dollar would fall, and forward dollar would rise, until the margin between the two is restored to –0.0098.

The Forward Bid–Offer Spread

Consider another case.

B.L. Inc. of New York has exported goods to Germany and has invoiced its client for DM2 million. If payment was immediate, then B.L. Inc. would sell the marks for dollars at the spot rate. But the marks are not payable for three months (90 days from spot). There is a risk that the dollar may strengthen against the mark, reducing the dollar value of the exports.

Case B

Suppose that B.L. Inc. decides to protect itself against this risk. It could use a similar strategy to Case A: borrow D-marks for three months, sell the marks spot to buy dollars, and place the dollars on deposit. At maturity of the D-mark loan, the amount owed will be repaid with the export proceeds, leaving the exporter with a known dollar balance.

Deposit rate on USD for 90 days	9 3/4% per annum
Borrowing cost of DM for 90 days	8 1/4% per annum
Spot USD/DEM rate	2.0000

The interest rate difference is 1.1/2% per annum in the exporter's favour. The dollar deposit rate is higher than the DM borrowing cost, so the DM 2.0000 sold spot will produce USD1 plus interest on a dollar at 1 1/2% per annum net, or USD 0.00375 for 90 days.

The effective exchange rate is:

USD 1.00375   :   DEM 2.000
USD 1.0000   :   DEM 2.0000/1.00375
                   :   DEM 1.9925

By applying the above figures to the simple forward FX formula, the result will show roughly the amount of D-marks by which the spot rate must be adjusted:

$$\frac{(8.25 - 9.75)}{100} \times 2.0000 \times \frac{90}{360}$$

$$= -0.0075$$

This is the simple calculation. In the exercises in Chapter 30 you will be asked to calculate the precise forward rate in this case.

Summary

This chapter introduced the outright forward FX contract. We noted that, as distinct from spot settlements, the time dimension is the crucial factor. In particular, we examined how a corporate might exploit this time dimension to generate synthetic forward rates.

Before moving on, please make sure that you are familiar with the following terms and their definitions:

Keywords

- time value of money
- outright forward FX rate
- forward margin
- cost of carry
- arbitrage profits.

The exercises in Chapter 30 enable you to practice calculating forward rates.

Exercise: Forward Spread

1. Calculate the effective forward rate of exchange for B.L. Inc., and the forward margin representing the DM equivalent of the interest rate difference, using the figures provided in the previous chapter.

    (a) Solution calculating the explicit cash flows. Present value of DM 2 million discounted at 8 1/4%:

    $$DM \; \frac{2,000,000}{1 + [8.25/100 \times 90/360]}$$

    = DM _____

    (b) Answer to (a) divided by 2.0000 is the dollar proceeds of the D-mark borrowing:

    = US$ _____

    (c) Answer to (b) plus interest at 9.3/4% for 90 days gives the amount of dollars receivable at maturity:

    = US$ _____

    (d) DM 2,000,000 divided by answer to (c) is the effective USD/DEM forward rate of exchange:

    = _____

    (e) Answer to (d) –2.0000 is the forward margin:

    = _____

    (f) Solution using the exact formula introduced in Chapter 29:

    $$2.0000 \times \left(\frac{1 + [(90/360) \times (8.25/100)]}{1 + [(90/360) \times (9.75/100)]} \right)$$

    Forward rate USD/DEM = _____
    Forward margin   = _____

2. Suppose that B.L. Inc. was quoted a forward rate of exchange of USD/DEM 1.9936 (on a spot rate of 2.0000) by its bank. If the company had an immediate need for working capital, calculate how many dollars the company could generate today:

(a) By borrowing D-marks at 8.1/4% and converting them into dollars at the spot rate

US$ _____

(b) By selling the D-marks forward to the bank at the quoted rate and borrowing the dollars receivable from the bank at 9.3/4%

US$ _____

The diagram below summarizes the relationship between the USD and DEM interest rates and forward FX rates.

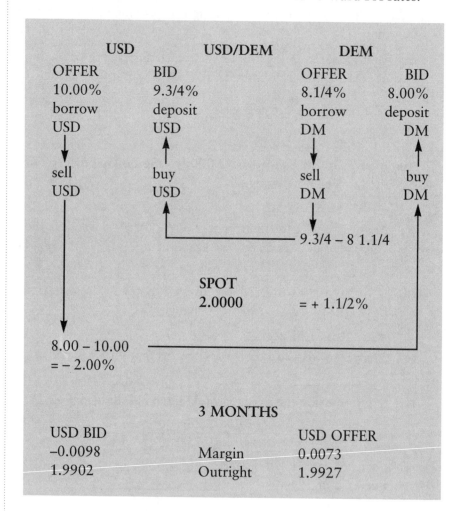

Points to note:

- Base currency (USD) interest rates are higher than counter-currency (DEM) interest rates. The difference between the Eurodollar offered and the Euromark bid rate is therefore greater than that between the dollar bid and the mark offer. So the forward margin on the bid side is numerically larger than that on the offer side.

- You can deduce which currency has the higher interest rate by looking at the structure of the forward margins. If the market maker's forward margin on the bid side is numerically larger than on the offer side, the base currency's interest rate is greater than that of the counter-currency's.

- When a two-way price like 0.0098/0.0073 is quoted the market user knows that the higher price (0.0098) is the price he will have to pay, and the lower price the benefit that he will receive. The 0.0098 margin will reduce the amount of marks the seller of dollars will receive. On the other side, 0.0073 is a benefit to the buyer of dollars.

- The forward bid margin is said to represent 98 "points against" the market user, while the offer margin represents 73 "points in their favor."

In this exercise, all the transactions are for top customers based in the Netherlands. Calculate the effective forward rates of exchange which could be quoted to the customer, if the bank covered its risk at the following spot and money market rates.

SPOT USD/NLG:	2.5000
MONEY MARKETS:	3 MTHS
USD:	7 5/16 - 3/16
NLG:	9 7/16 - 3/8

3. An exporter will receive US$5,000,000 in three months' time (90 days after spot) which it wants to sell.

(a) Solution covering the cash flows explicitly. Present value of US$5 million discounted at 7.5/16% is the amount of dollars that the bank can borrow and service with the US$5 million receivable from the customer in three months:

$$\text{US\$} \quad \frac{5,000,000}{1 + [(7.3125/100) \times (90/360)]}$$

= US$ _____

(b) Answer to (a) multiplied by 2.5000 is the amount of spot guilders that the bank will produce from the dollars borrowed:

= Fl _____

(c) Answer to (b) plus interest at 9.3/8% gives the amount of guilders that the bank can pay to the customer in three months:

= Fl _____

(d) Answer to (c) divided by US$5,000,000 is the effective USD/NLG forward rate of exchange quoted by the bank:

= _____

(e) Answer to (d) – 2.5000 is the forward margin:

= _____

4. An importer wants to buy US$5,000,000 in three months' time (90 days after spot) to pay an invoice.

    (a) Solution covering all the cash flows explicitly. Present value of US$5 million discounted at 7.3/16% is the amount of dollars that can be placed in the money markets today to produce US$5 million for the customer in three months:

    $$US\$ \ \frac{5,000,000}{1 + [(7.1875/100) \times (90/360)]}$$

    = US$ _____

    (b) Answer to (a) multiplied by 2.5000 is the amount of spot guilders that the bank will borrow to buy those dollars:

    = NLG _____

    (c) Answer to (b) plus interest at 9.7/16% gives total the amount of guilders payable by the customer to the bank in three months:

    = NLG _____

    (d) Answer to (c) divided by US$5,000,000 is the effective USD/NLG forward rate of exchange quoted by the bank:

    = _____

    (e) Answer to (d) – 2.5000 is the forward margin:

    = _____

    (f) Solution using the exact formula:

    $$2.5000 \times \frac{1 + [(90/360) \times (9.4375/100)]}{1 + [(90/360) \times (7.1875/100)]}$$

    Forward rate USD/NLG = _____
    Forward margin   = _____

The following diagram summarizes the relationship between interest rates and the forward rates of exchange derived from Exercises 3 and 4.

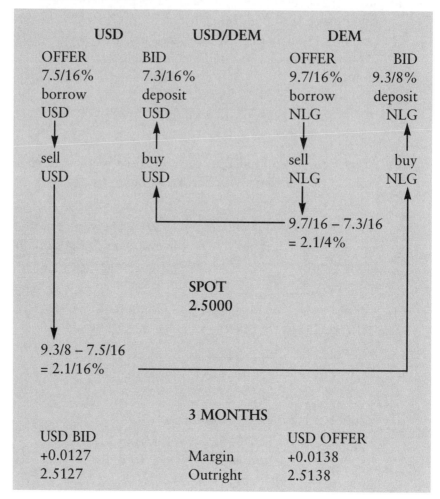

USD		USD/DEM	DEM	
OFFER	BID		OFFER	BID
7.5/16%	7.3/16%		9.7/16%	9.3/8%
borrow	deposit		borrow	deposit
USD	USD		NLG	NLG

sell   buy   sell   buy
USD   USD   NLG   NLG

9.7/16 – 7.3/16
= 2.1/4%

SPOT
2.5000

9.3/8 – 7.5/16
= 2.1/16%

3 MONTHS

USD BID			USD OFFER
+0.0127	Margin		+0.0138
2.5127	Outright		2.5138

Points to note:

- Base currency (USD) interest rate is lower than the counter-currency's (NLG). The difference between Eurodollar offered rate and the Euroguilder bid is less than that between the dollar bid and the guilder offer. So the market maker's forward bid margin is smaller than the forward offer margin.

- When receiving a quotation like +0.0127/+0.0138, the rate on the left will be a benefit to the seller of forward dollars, while the rate on the right will be a cost to the buyer of dollars. The seller of forward dollars will receive an extra

Fl 0.0127, while the buyer of dollars will have to pay an extra Fl 0.0135.

5. The following transactions are for top international customers. In each case, calculate the effective forward rate of exchange which could be quoted, based on the market rates given.

(a) An importer in the USA needs to pay JPY130 million yen in 2 months' time (62 days after spot).

SPOT USD/JPY	128.50 / 65
Money Markets:	2 MTHS
USD	7 5/8 – 9/16
JPY	5 3/4 – 5/8

Effective USD/JPY forward rate: _____

(b) An importer in Britain needs to pay US$1 million in six months' time (184 days after spot).

SPOT GBP/USD	1.9430 / 40
Money Markets:	6 MTHS
USD	7 19/32 – 9/16
GBP	13 1/8 – 1/16

Note: Eurosterling rates are quoted on a 365-day year basis, whereas Eurodollar rates are on a 360-day basis:

Effective GBP/USD forward rate: _____

(c) A Japanese exporter will receive FRF5 million French francs in three months' time (92 days after spot). They would like you to quote them a FRF/JPY forward rate.

Spot Rates (Against USD 1):	
FRF	6.0490/05
JPY	141.75/95
Money Markets:	6 MTHS
FRF	8.2500 – 8.1250
JPY	4.0625 – 4.0000

Three months' forward FRF/JPY _____

6. The monetary authorities in Erehwon have offered to sell dollars to the market 360 days forward at USD/WON 4.50. The spot rate is fixed at USD/WON 4.30.

    The idea is that local banks buying dollars forward will cover their exposure by selling the dollars spot to the central bank, helping to restore the country's foreign currency reserves. Given the following money market rates, will the commercial banks take up this offer?

Money markets:	12 MTHS
Eurodollars	8.1/2 – 8 3/8
Domestic won	10.3/4 – 10.1/2

    Note: Both money markets are based on a 360-day year.

■ ■ ■

"The natural users of outright FX contracts are international corporations looking to cover commercial FX exposures."

Market Practice

Overview   In this chapter, we cover the processes involved in executing outright forwards deals, in preparation for the exercises in Chapter 32.

Forward Prices

Most market information services show forward rates not as outright rates of exchange but as margins, in points, above or below the spot rate. Figure 31.1 shows a typical page.

Fig 31.1   **Typical spot and forward market price screen**

	SPOT	1MTH	2MTH	3MTH	6MTH	12MTH
GBP	1.5853/63	26/23	51/47	73/68	125/120	615/605
DEM	1.6588/95	53/51	101/98	150/147	305/300	615/605
CHF	1.3660/70	64/59	122/117	174/169	337/327	645/615
NLG	1.8600/20	1/+2	1/+1	2/1	3/2	6/3
FRF	5.6200/30	38/58	110/130	185/210	350/390	545/645
JPY	124.53/63	37/32	66/61	96/91	195/85	405/385
ITL	1229.7/0.7	36/46	82/92	118/138	220/260	375/475
BEL	34.69/74	4/1	6/4	9/6	19/12	45/30
CAD	1.2410/20	17/20	35/38	52/55	96/101	170/190
ECU	1.2510/15	6/9	10/14	16/21	40/46	103/118

Often the forward points do not have a sign in front of them. To derive the outright rates, the convention is:

Subtract the points from the corresponding spot rates if the left-hand forward margin is numerically larger than the right-hand margin.

e.g.:	SPOT	2 MTHS	OUTRIGHT
CHF	1.3660/70	−0.0122/−0.117	1.3538/53

Add the points if the margins are larger, left to right.

e.g.:	SPOT	3 MTHS	OUTRIGHT
FRF	5.6200/30	+0.0185/+0.0210	5.6385/40

A minus sign in front of the left-hand margin and a plus sign in front of the right-hand margin indicates that you subtract the left-hand points from the spot bid but add the right-hand points to the spot offered.

e.g.:	SPOT	1 MTH	OUTRIGHT
NLG	1.8600/20	−0.01/+0.02	1.8599/22

Forward outright spreads tend to get a little wider the further you go forward – a reflection of the market thinning out.

Executing an Outright Forward Deal

The natural users of outright FX contracts are international corporations looking to cover commercial FX exposures. Banks often employ people in the dealing room – Corporate Dealers or Corporate Salespeople – who do not necessarily run positions but specialize in servicing customers.

Here is a typical conversation between a corporate dealer at IB **Example** Corp and its customer on 10 December:

Customer: "This is XYZ Inc. I'd like an outright price for six months dollar/Swissy in $10 million please."

IB Corp: "One moment please."

The corporate dealer will check the current forward points from his forward interbank trader, or a broker. He will then get a quote from the spot desk. From these prices he calculates the outright rates for the customer, as follows:

	BID	OFFER
Spot rate	1.4600	1.4605
less forward points	400	395
Forward outright	1.4200	1.4210

These are the finest rates the bank would quote. The corporate dealer may shade the prices a little, depending on the quality of the customer and whether he thinks XYZ is a likely buyer or seller of dollars.

IB Corp: "Sir, our rates are 1.4200/1.4220 for 10 million on a spot rate of 1.46 figure five."

XYZ Inc: "OK, at 1.4200 I sell $10 million. Please settle the deal with our accounts at your London branch."

IB Corp: "All right, so I buy $10 million for value 12 June at 1.4200, and I sell 14,200,000.00 Swiss francs. I'll confirm the deal by fax today. Thank you very much for the business and goodbye for now."

If the customer had simply asked for a six-month forward rate, the dealer might have quoted just the forward points, and the customer would have had to calculate the outright rates for himself. The interbank market quotes forward rates as points rather than out-rights, as we shall see.

Forward Cross-Rates

Situations arise in which a customer needs to know the outright forward rate between two currencies, neither of which is the US dollar. This would be a forward cross-rate. Case C shows how a cross could be calculated, again using the money markets.

Case C
A company in Germany has imported goods from Switzerland and has to pay 1 million Swiss francs in 9 months (273 days after spot).

SPOT RATES (TO THE DOLLAR):

CHF	1.3145 / 1.3150
DEM	1.3585 / 1.3590

MONEY MARKETS:	9 MTHS
CHF	7.9375 –7.8750
DEM	8.0625 –8.0000

The company is selling the goods in Germany so it borrows marks at the bank's offered rate of 8.0625% for nine months, repaying the borrowing with the D-mark sale proceeds.

The treasurer then buys US dollars at the spot rate of 1.3590 and sells the dollars for Swiss francs at the spot rate of 1.3145. This effects a spot CHF/DEM cross-rate of 1.03385 (1.3590/1.3145).

The Swiss francs obtained are placed on deposit for nine months at 7.8750%. Putting these rates into the exact formula:

Forward outright rate =

$$1.03385 \times \frac{1 + [(273/360) \times (8.0625/100)]}{1 + [(273/360) \times (7.8750/100)]}$$

$$= 1.03524$$

The forward CHF/DEM margin is $1.03524 - 1.03385 = +0.00139$ (+13.9 pips). The cross-rates in terms of DEM/CHF would be:

SPOT	9 MTHS
1/1.03385	1/1.03524
= 0.96726	= 0.96600

The forward margin would be:

$0.96600 - 0.96726 = -0.00126$ (−12.6 pips).

Forward Crosses from Outrights

If there are forward rates quoted to the USD (i.e., we don't want to calculate them from the money markets), then the procedure is as follows:

We want to calculate the three-month outright forward DEM/FRF **Example** in the following rates:

	SPOT	3 MTHS
FRF	5.6200/30	185/210
DEM	1.6588/90	150/147

The first step is to calculate the forward outrights, as usual:

	3 MTHS
FRF	5.6385/5.6440
DEM	1.6438/1.6443

Now we can calculate the crosses from these rates in the usual manner. In this case, the base currency is the same, so we "divide across" (offer/bid and bid/offer):

	3 MTHS
DEM/FRF	3.4291/3.4335

To calculate forward crosses, you never operate directly on the forward margins.

Summary

In this chapter, we looked at the processes of dealing outright forward FX. In particular, we saw how the outright forward rate is derived from market information services. We also looked at how forward crosses are derived from outright rates.

Keywords

Before moving on to the exercise in Chapter 32, please be sure that you are familiar with the following terms and their definitions:

- outright forwards FX dealing
- forward cross rates.

Exercise: Outright Prices

1. Listed below are various banks' spot and forward FX rates. Identify the best rate available for each transaction, and the bank you would deal with.

Example: DOLLAR/MARK (USD/DEM)

	BANK A	BANK B	BANK C
SPOT	1.6827/38	1.6828/39	1.6825/35
6 MTHS	25/20	24/19	26/21

Purchase US dollars forward from bank C. Spot rate: 1.6835; forward margin: –0.0021; outright rate: 1.6814.

(a) DOLLAR/LIRA (USD/ITL)

	BANK A	BANK B	BANK C
SPOT	1240.12/62	1240.50/12	1240.00/62
2 MTHS	1000/1200	975/1188	1013/1213

Purchase US dollars forward from bank _____

Spot rate _____ Forward margin _____

Outright rate _____

(b) DOLLAR/YEN (USD/JPY)

	BANK A	BANK B	BANK C
SPOT	152.00/50	152.00/25	151.90/15
3 MTHS	36/33	37/34	38/36

Purchase yen forward from bank _____

Spot rate _____ Forward margin _____

Outright rate _____

(c) CABLE (GBP/USD)

	BANK A	BANK B	BANK C
SPOT	1.6330/40	1.6331/39	1.6332/42
1 MTH	39/36	42/38	39/36

Purchase sterling forward from bank _____

Spot rate _____ Forward margin _____

Outright rate _____

(d) DOLLAR/MARK (USD/DEM)

	BANK A	BANK B	BANK C
SPOT	1.6829/43	1.6824/42	1.6825/40
1 MTH	−3/+2	−4/+1	−2/+3

Purchase D-marks forward from bank _____

Spot rate _____ Forward margin _____

Outright rate _____

(e) DOLLAR/BELGE (USD/BEL)

	BANK A	BANK B	BANK C
SPOT	34.45/55	34.46/56	34.47/57
6 MTHS	15/18	12/15	15/17

DOLLAR/PARIS (USD/FRF)

	BANK A	BANK B	BANK C
SPOT	5.6370/85	5.6365/80	5.6375/90
6 MTHS	69/74	70/75	68/73

Purchase US dollars forward from bank _____

USD/BEL spot rate _____ Forward margin _____

Outright rate _____

Sell USD forward to bank _____

USD/FRF spot rate _____ Forward margin _____

Outright rate _____

Outright FRF/BEL cross-rate (buy French francs, sell Belgian francs) _____

(f) ECU/USD

	BANK A	BANK B	BANK C
SPOT	1.2268/78	1.2267/77	1.2270/80
3 MTHS	58/56	57/55	59/57

DOLLAR/YEN (USD/JPY)

	BANK A	BANK B	BANK C
SPOT	154.77/87	154.79/89	154.81/91
3 MTHS	38/35	39/36	40/37

Purchase US dollars against ECU from bank _____

ECU/USD spot rate _____ Forward margin _____

Outright rate _____

Sell US dollars against yen to bank _____

USD/JPY spot rate _____ Forward margin _____

Outright rate _____

Outright ECU/JPY cross-rate (sell ECU buy yen)

■ ■ ■

"Sometimes, use of the money markets is more competitive than bankers' forward rates for companies exposed to exchange risk."

Forward Cash Management

Using the money markets

Interest rates and competitiveness

Summary

In the previous chapter, we examined the processes involved in typical outright and cross-rate forwards deals. Here we turn to examples of how a company may hedge its exposure to exchange risk by using the money markets instead of bankers' forward rates. In particular we will look at:

- use of the money markets;
- interest rates and competitiveness.

Using the Money Markets

Sometimes a commercial company exposed to exchange risk can engineer more competitive forward rates by covering its exposures through money market operations rather than using forward rates quoted by their bankers.

There are several reasons for this. Firstly, banks may shade their prices against the customer. Secondly, the money market rates the company can obtain may be very different from those implied in the forward FX rates quoted by market makers. The next case study illustrates this.

Case D A British company has to pay US$250,000 to the USA in three months (90 days after spot) for raw materials. It will process these in the UK at a cost of £45,000, financed by a bank sterling overdraft. It will sell the finished goods to Holland and receive US$349,250 in three months.

The matching dollar payment for the imports and the dollar receipt from the re-export removes much of the exchange risk.

Foreign currency payables and receivables often provide substantial natural hedges for each other.

But there remains a net currency exposure: the company is long US$99,250 three months forward (= US$349,250 −US$250,000). And it also has a sterling overdraft cost. The treasurer has a number of alternative financing routes:

(i) Ignore exchange rate fluctuations and sell the balance of dollars for sterling at the spot rate applicable in three months.

(ii) Ask the bank for a forward rate at which the balance of dollars can be sold for sterling.

(iii) Borrow dollars against the future receivables, sell the dollars for sterling at the current spot rate, and use the sterling as working capital in place of the overdraft.

The treasurer decides that option (i) is too risky – the entire profit on the deal could be wiped out by an adverse exchange rate movement. To reach a decision between (ii) and (iii), he has to calculate the results of each option using the rates quoted by the bank.

CABLE SPOT AND FORWARD:

	SPOT	3 MTHS	OUTRIGHT
INTERBANK	1.8990/00	250/244	1.8740/56
COMMERCIAL	1.8970/20	261/232	1.8709/88

Sterling overdraft: 3.00% over base rate (currently 14.00%)
3 mths sterling "retail" deposit: 13.1/4%
3 mths Eurodollar rate (commercial): 10.00 –9.5/8%

Route (ii)

The bank quotes a commercial forward rate of 1.8788 at which it will buy the US$99,250. This will produce for the company, in three months' time:

99,250/1.8788
= £52,826.27

The overdraft cost will be 17% (14 + 3%) per annum on £45,000. Over 90 days the total repayment amount (principal + interest) will be:

£45,000 × [1 + (90/365 × 0.17)]
= £46,886.30

So the net profit to the company from this financing route, in three months, is:

£52,826.27 – 46,886.30
= £5,939.97

Route (iii)

The treasurer borrows the present value of US$99,250, calculated on the USD commercial borrowing rate of 10%, for 90 days:

$$\frac{99,250}{1 + (10/100 \times 90/360)}$$

$$= US\$96,829.27$$

He then sells these dollars at the commercial spot rate of 1.9020 and receives:

96,829.27 / 1.9020
= GB£50,909.19

GB£45,000 of this will pay for the processing costs. The balance (GB£5,909.19) will be placed on deposit at 13.25% for three months, providing a net profit of:

GB£5,909.19 × [1 + (90/365 × 0.1325)]
= GB£6,102.25

On the face of it, option (iii) seems preferable: by reducing its sterling borrowing, the company has gained a far larger interest rate differential than is implied in the forward FX rates.

In practice arranging a relatively small Eurodollar loan at a fixed rate of interest would be time-consuming and perhaps more expensive.

Interest Rates and Competitiveness

Case D illustrates a common misconception among exporters: that high domestic interest costs undermine their competitiveness in world markets.

This would be true if the company had invoiced in sterling, but not when invoicing in dollars: it used the foreign currency receivable to service cheaper borrowing in foreign currency, which was then converted into local currency.

If the company had continued borrowing in local currency, most of the higher financing costs would have been offset by selling the dollars forward at 1.8788 instead of at the spot rate of 1.9020. The forward points are in the exporter's favor *because* domestic interest rates are higher.

Summary

In this chapter we looked at one case in which bankers' forward FX rates are not necessarily the best option for a company wishing to hedge against exchange rate movements. In particular, we saw how high domestic interest rates need not undermine an exporter's competitiveness if foreign currency receivables are used to service cheaper foreign currency borrowing.

Keywords

Before moving on, please be sure that you are familiar with the following concepts:

- the benefits of matching foreign currency payables and receivables;
- the effect of high domestic interest rates on exporters.

FX Swaps

Overview In this chapter, we examine FX swaps, which are in fact more common forward FX instruments than outrights. After defining the main characteristics of the instrument, we will look at the following areas:

- covering outright FX with swaps;
- the structure of a typical FX swap;
- swaps dealing;
- market making in swaps.

Definition

About one-half of all FX business is for value spot, the rest is forward. Most of the forward business, however, is in the form of FX swaps rather than outrights.

An FX swap is a contract to buy an amount of currency for one value date at an agreed rate, and to simultaneously resell the same amount of currency for a later value date, also at an agreed rate.

About 94% of FX swaps are interbank, rather than between banks and corporate customers: the swap is primarily a market maker's funding instrument.

A Funding Instrument

In Chapter 31, pages 279–280, we described a typical outright forward FX deal between XYZ Inc. and their bankers, IB Corp. XYZ sold the bank US$10 million against Swiss francs for value six months forward (184 days from spot) at USD/CHF 1.4200.

XYZ has covered its exchange risk. But the bank has now taken on a risk: if the dollar strengthens, IB Corp has a cheap source of dollars, but if it weakens IB Corp will end up paying "too much" for those dollars.

If IB Corp wanted to cover this risk it could borrow dollars, use these dollars to buy Swiss francs spot, and place the francs on a fixed-term deposit maturing on the date when the customer comes to collect them. Figure 34.1 summarizes the resulting cash flows.

IB Corp's cash flows: covering a forward position in the money market   Fig 34.1

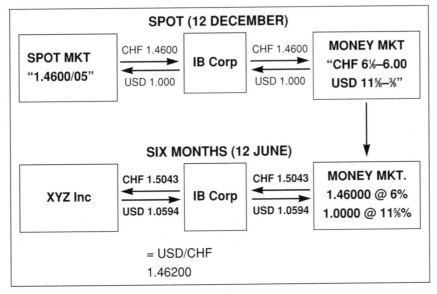

The net cost will be the spot rate plus the cost of borrowing dollars for six months at 11.5/8%, less the 6.00% interest earned on the Swiss francs over the same period.

IB Corp can calculate all the cash flows precisely when it books the deal, so in theory it could cover all its forward deals in this way. In practice there are some problems:

- markets in some Eurocurrencies lack the depth to borrow or lend large amounts without moving the rates;
- each customer's forwards deal would increase the bank's balance sheet by the size of the deal, since the bank has to open an outward deposit and take in an equivalent amount of funds in the other currency.

Covering the risks on outright forward transactions in the money markets would put pressure on a bank's capital adequacy ratios, since each forward transaction adds on to the balance sheet the credit risk of a money market operation. In contrast, the risk on FX deals is mainly a "replacement risk," which is a fraction of the amount exchanged.

A much cheaper alternative is to cover the forward outright transaction by means of an FX swap, which keeps the whole operation off-balance sheet.

Covering with FX Swaps

As before, the first step is for IB Corp to "cover the spot", the most volatile part of the risk taken. Having bought US$ 10 million forward from XYZ, it should sell US$ 10 million in the spot market.

Now IB Corp is long US$ 10 million "in the six months" and short US$ 10 million spot. It can bridge the time gap between these two cash flows by executing a swap with another counterparty (Other Bank Ltd):

IB Corp buys US$ 10 million at 1.4600 (sells SwFr14,600,000) for value spot and simultaneously sells US$ 10 million at 1.4200 (buys SwFr14,200,000) for value six months.

Figure 34.2 shows how the cash flows are covered by the spot deal and the swap.

Fig 34.2   **IB Corp's cash flows: covering a forward position with a swap**

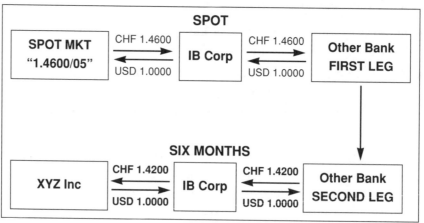

The first leg of the swap funds the spot FX transaction. The second leg produces the required Swiss francs for the customer in six months' time.

The swap funds the time gap from the spot date (when IB Corp buys the Swiss francs) to the forward date when the customer takes delivery of the Swiss francs and pays the dollars. There are no net movements in the bank's balance sheet.

The general structure of the swap is shown in Figure 34.3.

Structure of an FX swap

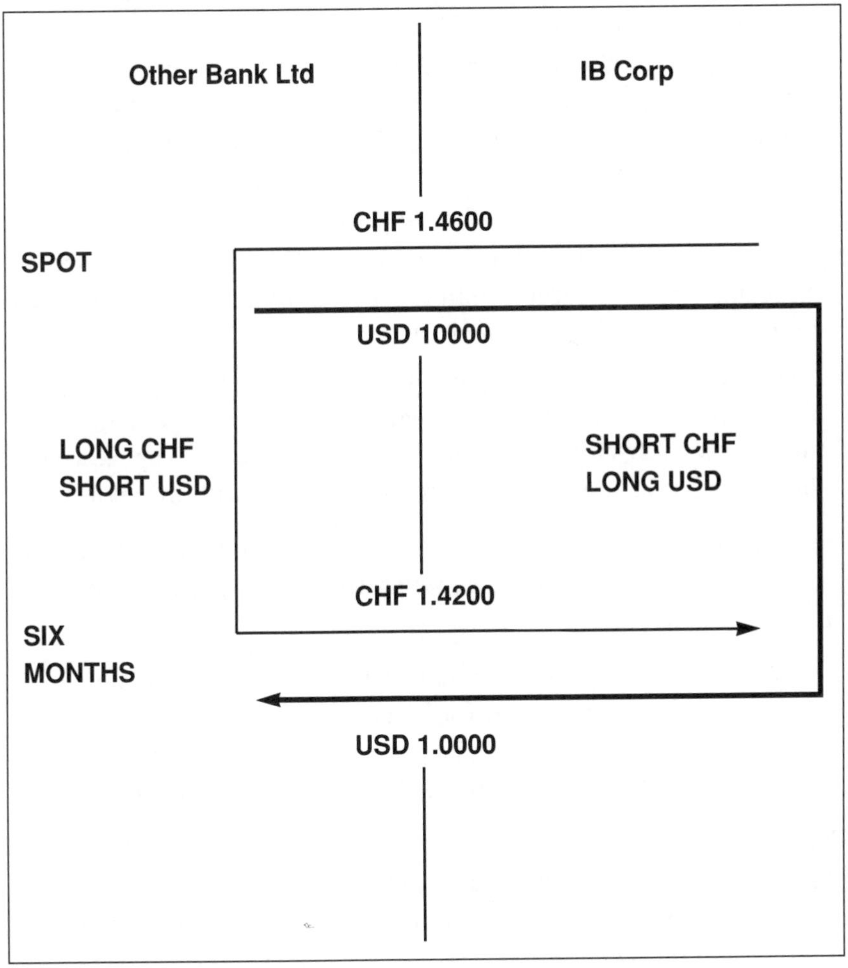

Fig 34.3

Other Bank Ltd | IB Corp

SPOT — CHF 1.4600

USD 10000

LONG CHF
SHORT USD

SHORT CHF
LONG USD

CHF 1.4200

SIX MONTHS

USD 1.0000

There are two ways of looking at the FX swap in Figure 34.3:

- Looked at horizontally, it is a pair of offsetting FX transactions for different value dates, written at the same time and on the same deal ticket.

- Looked at vertically (over time), one party is borrowing a currency for an agreed period of six months, and lending a different currency over the same period. The FX swap is actually a pair of money market operations dressed in FX clothing!

Other points to note:

- When the swap matures (on settlement of the second leg) IB Corp receives SwFr14,200,000 for US$10 million. At the start of the swap it paid SwFr14,600,000. IB Corp has in effect paid SwFr400,000 net for borrowing dollars against lending Swiss francs. In effect, IB Corp has paid 400 points to cover its funding risk on a US$10 million transaction. It "bought-and-sold the dollars, spot against sixes at 400 points against it."

- In the swap, the net interest cost to IB Corp is expressed in exchange points, rather than % per annum, and the interest amount due is paid net in Swiss francs.

- The swap itself does not create an exchange position for IB Corp. Any exchange gains on the first leg, from a stronger dollar, will be more or less offset by losses on the second leg of a swap, since the outright forward rate will tend to move in line with the spot rate.

How could IB Corp buy US$10 million from Other Bank in the spot leg of the swap at 1.4600, when that is the market's spot bid rate for dollars?

The point about swaps is that what really matters is not so much the actual rates of exchange used for calculating the cash flows at each leg, but the *difference* between two rates of exchange – the forward points. These reflect the cost of funding an outright position.

The forward points are therefore swap rates. If it costs IB Corp 400 points net to borrow dollars, and carry Swiss francs for six months using the money markets, it should cost no more (probably less) to do this using the swap market.

As we shall now see, in practice the spot rate used to calculate the cash flows in a swap is typically set by the market maker anywhere between the market bid and offer rates at the time of booking the deal.

Dealing in FX Swaps

Dealer Conversation

In this conversation, IB Corp is dealing a swap with Other Bank Ltd on 10 December to cover its funding gap created as a result of the outright forward deal with XYZ Inc:

IB Corp: "Hi friends, how's your forward dollar-Swissy please?"

Other Bank: "One moment please . . .
                . . . "we deal 75/73, 138/135, 294/291 and 400/395.""

IB Corp: "At 400 I buy and sell $10."

Other bank: "OK, that's done. I sell $10 million for value 12 December at 1.4600 and buy $10 million for value 12 June at 1.4200. My francs to UBS Zurich please and my dollars at maturity to Chase New York."

IB Corp: "OK, I will take my dollars at Chase New York as well and my francs to our nostro with your Zurich office."

Other bank: "That will be done. Thanks for the deal and good day."

Points to Note

- Unless the market maker is asked to quote for a specific date, he will normally quote rates for one, two, three and six months, in points.
- The swap rate is agreed first and the market maker then decides which spot rate to use to calculate the amounts payable at each leg of the deal. The spot rate used is normally somewhere inside the current market spread. Using the bid or the offered spot rate does not affect the cost of the swap, which is the number of points.

- Some dealers might say "at 400 I do 10" or "at 400 yours 10", referring to the direction of the dollar flows at the far date of the swap. But it is better to play safe and spell things out properly.

- IB Corp needs to lend Swiss francs and borrow dollars for six months. We know, from the structure of the forward points – high number on the left/low number on the right – that USD interest rates are higher than CHF rates. So there will be a net interest cost to IB Corp of 400 points: "points against" IB Corp, "points in favor" of Other Bank.

Hitting the Right Side

Once you hit a swap rate you have established a legally binding contract. Some simple rules will help you avoid mistakes.

> **RULE 1: Establish the base currency.**

In the dollar-Swissy swap between IB Corp and Other Bank, the base currency is the dollar. So the swap rate represents points of a Swiss franc per dollar.

> **RULE 2: In an FX swap quotation, the market maker always sells the base currency spot and buys back the base currency forward at the rate he shows on the left-hand side.**

This is true whether the quotation is direct or reciprocal. In the case above, Other Bank sells dollars (buys Swiss francs) spot and buys them back (re-sells the Swiss francs) forward at the rate shown on the left. On the other side, Other Bank is prepared to buy dollars spot and re-sell them forward.

> **RULE 3: As a market user, the larger figure in a two-way price always represents points that you pay, and the smaller figure the points that you earn.**

When quoted 400/395, IB Corp knows that it will pay 400 points (to buy and sell dollars), but it would earn 395 points to do the reverse (sell and buy dollars).

If Euro-Swiss franc interest rates had been higher than Eurodollar rates, the forward points on the left of a quotation would be smaller than the ones on the right. So instead of paying points to buy and sell dollars, as a market user, IB Corp would earn points.

Market Making

The forward market maker shades his prices and widens or narrows his spread in response to changing market conditions in much the same way as the spot trader.

Using the Spread

The first line of defence is the spread, which contains an assessment of the likelihood of reversing an unwanted position.

Example

Someone calls you for a price in 12 months' cable where you do not currently hold a position, nor do you wish to have one. At the time the indication rates in the 12 months are 435/430.

Since you do not know which way the caller will deal, you reply by quoting 437/428.

In effect, you are trying to discourage the counterparty from dealing with you at all, by demanding 437 points for selling and buying the pounds, when the rest of the market is charging only 435, and offering only 428 points for doing the reverse when the market is offering 430.

If the counterparty pays you at 437, you can call someone else and perhaps reverse the position by paying 435 points – so you lock in 2 pips profit.

Conversely, if the counterparty takes your 428, you can reverse the position at 430 in your favor (as a market user) – again locking 2 pips profit.

By widening the spread, you have quoted defensively to protect yourself. Of course, if you persistently quote wide spreads, people will stop taking you seriously as a market maker. They may even begin to widen the prices they quote to you.

Shading the Rate

The second line of defence is to shade both your prices up or down, so as to encourage the counterparty to deal in the way you want them to.

Example

You are asked for a rate in USD/DEM in the three months. The market is currently quoting 42/45 and you feel German interest rates still have some upside, so you expect the points to increase.

This means that you would rather be paying points now so that you can earn more points later. Therefore you quote 43/46.

With these rates you are signalling to the counterparty that you are a seller and buyer of dollars, rather than the opposite, because you are prepared to pay 43 points when the market is paying only 42.

On the other hand, if the counterparty also wants to sell and buy dollars (he too believes German rates will firm up), he will have to pay you 46 points, when others are charging only 45.

If the counterparty takes your 43, then you have got the position you wanted, without having paid too much above the market rate. On the other hand, if he pays you at 46, you may be able to get rid of the unwanted position, paying only 45 points (as a market user) and locking in a 1-pip profit. On the one hand you win, and on the other you don't lose!

Traders talk in terms of shading their forward prices "to the right" or "to the left", rather than up or down, because depending on how the forward rates are structured, you may have to make the figures larger or smaller if you want to be hit on the left-hand side.

In the example, the forward rates reflected higher German interest rates than Eurodollar rates, and in order to be hit on the left-hand side, we moved the prices to the right – up towards the 45 rate rather than the 42 rate.

Had German interest rates been lower than Eurodollar rates, then the three-month rate might have looked like 45/42. That is, the market maker would be *charging* points for selling and buying the dollars, on the left-hand side, rather than paying them.

In this case, if we wanted to be hit on the left-hand side we would also have shaded the prices to the right – that is, down towards the 42 figure, not up.

Confused? Even experienced dealers felt lost, when the D-mark changed from being a low-interest-rate currency into a high-interest-rate currency in the early 1990s. The exercise in Chapter 35 may help you clarify the procedures in your own mind.

Summary

In this chapter, we introduced FX swaps. We saw how, as distinct from outright forward transactions, the swap is primarily a market maker's funding instrument. We then looked at how cash flows are covered by means of swaps, explored the structure of a typical swap deal, and examined the art of market making in swaps.

Before concluding this section, please be sure that you are familiar with the following terms and their definitions: **Keywords**
- FX swap deal
- covering the spot
- points in your favor/points against
- shading the swop points.

The exercise in Chapter 35 provides practice in swaps dealing procedures.

Exercise: Identifying the Price

1. With interest rates in the USA lower than in Belgium, indicate which of the statements below are true:

   (a) There is a net cost of carrying a long position in dollars against Belgian francs, so you would pay more Belgian francs to buy a dollar forward than to buy a dollar spot.

   (b) You would earn points if you bought dollars (the base currency) against Belgian francs spot and resold the dollars forward.

   (c) The market maker sells and buys dollars in a USD/BEL swap at his rate quoted on the left-hand side.

   (d) In a USD/BEL swap quotation you would expect the figure on the left to be higher than the rate on the right – e.g., 325/320.

   (e) In a USD/BEL swap quotation you would expect the rate on the left to be smaller than the rate on the right – e.g., 320/325.

2. In the table below, cross out the statements which do not apply in this case.

MARKET: cable (sterling-dollar)
BASE CURRENCY: sterling
BASE CURRENCY INTEREST RATE: 14%
COUNTER-CURRENCY INTEREST RATE: 9%
TYPICAL SWAP QUOTATION: 459/455

LHS rate	RHS rate
MARKET MAKER	
sells GB£/US$* spot and buys back the US$/GB£* fwd	buys GB£/US$* spot and sells back the US$/GB£* fwd
sells/buys* counter-currency spot and sells/buys* it back fwd	sells/buys* counter-currency spot and sells/buys* it back fwd
swap points are in their favor/against them*	swap points are in their favor/against them*
MARKET USER	
sells GB£/US$* spot and buys back the US$/GB£* fwd	buys GB£/US$* spot and sells back the US$/GB£* fwd
sells/buys* counter-currency spot and sells/buys* it back fwd	sells/buys* counter-currency spot and sells/buys* it back fwd
swap points are in their favor/against them*	swap points are in their favor/against them*

Cross out whichever is inapplicable.

3. Given the market quotations below from five different banks, show which bank you would deal with. (Circle the rate corresponding to your answer.)

(i) **DOLLAR-PARIS (USD/FRF)**

	1 MTH	2 MTHS	3 MTHS	6 MTHS
BANK A	98/108	200/225	323/350	690/722
BANK B	96/109	201/224	326/351	689/721
BANK C	99/107	210/227	324/349	685/719
BANK D	100/106	199/226	326/352	688/720
BANK E	97/108	205/223	325/348	689/723

Sell US dollars spot and buy US dollars six months forward. **Example**
Answer: Bank C at 719 points against you.

(a) Sell French francs spot and buy French francs one month forward.

(b) Buy French francs spot and sell French francs two months forward.

(c) Sell US dollars spot and buy US dollars three months forward.

(d) Buy US dollars spot and sell US dollars six months forward.

(ii) **CABLE (GBP/USD)**

	1 MTH	2 MTHS	3 MTHS	6 MTHS
BANK A	51/48	109/103	170/161	369/352
BANK B	53/50	110/104	171/162	371/354
BANK C	54/51	112/101	173/159	372/355
BANK D	56/52	108/102	167/160	368/351
BANK E	49/46	105/98	168/159	367/348

(a) Buy sterling spot and sell sterling one month forward.

(b) Buy US dollars spot and sell US dollars two months forward.

(c) Sell US dollars spot and buy US dollars three months forward.

(d) Sell sterling spot and buy sterling six months forward.

(iii) OZZIE DOLLAR (AUD/USD)

	1 MTH	2 MTHS	3 MTHS	6 MTHS
BANK A	60/58	128/126	182/179	342/336
BANK B	59/57	126/123	180/178	343/338
BANK C	61/59	128/124	181/179	344/339
BANK D	62/60	129/124	184/180	346/341
BANK E	58/56	130/125	181/177	345/340

(a) Sell Australian dollars spot and sell Ozzie one month forward.

(b) Buy US dollars spot and sell US dollars two months forward.

(c) Sell US dollars spot and buy US dollars three months forward.

(d) Buy US dollars spot and sell US dollars six months forward.

4. If you were a market maker competing against the rates shown in the previous question, what would you quote a counterparty if you were looking to do the following:

(a) Sell US dollars spot against French francs and buy US dollars six months forward.

(b) Buy GB sterling spot and sell GB three months forward.

(c) Sell sterling spot and buy sterling one month forward.

(d) Sell US dollars spot against Australian dollars and buy US dollars two months forward.

■ ■ ■

"By its very nature, the swap market compensates or charges users for the cost of carry."

Other Uses of FX Swaps

Overview In this chapter, we look at additional uses of swaps. In particular, we will examine:

- the use of swaps in the context of cross-currency investments;
- the interest costs implied in a swap rate;
- covered interest arbitrage;
- short-date rollovers.

Covered Foreign-Currency Investments

FX swaps are useful instruments in an investment context, as the next case illustrates.

Case E A German fund manager wants to invest in the US money markets for six months (180 days) to take advantage of higher yields over domestic paper. But moving into dollars would expose the fund to adverse currency fluctuations.

So when buying the dollars spot, the investor must also fix in advance a rate of exchange at which he can "repatriate" the dollars back into marks after six months.

He could buy spot dollars and then re-sell them forward through a separate outright deal (which would mean paying the market maker's bid/offer spread twice). Or he could buy-and-sell the dollars, spot against six months, in the same transaction by means of a swap.

Through the swap the manager is (in effect) borrowing dollars on which he can earn a high yield, and lending the low-yielding D-marks for six months. Of course his counterparty will require compensation, by charging swap points. The fund manager therefore needs to decide whether the return on dollar paper (net of the cost of covering with a swap) is good enough to make the strategy worthwhile.

Let's work with the following rates:

CURRENCY RATES: SPOT   6 MTHS
DEM   1.8000/10   155/152
MONEY MARKETS:
Return on US$ 6-month paper: 10.00%
Return on DM 6-month paper: 8.00%

(a) Funds are invested in US paper

The fund manager buys and sells (say) US$10 million spot against six months, at 155 points against him. The dollars, invested at 10% for 180 days, will generate income of:

USD 10,000,000 × 10/100 × 180/360
= USD 500,000

The swap only covers the exchange risk on the principal. The manager also needs to sell the US$500,000 earned in interest outright six months forward, at 1.7845 (= 1.8000 −0.0155). This will produce:

DM500,000 × 1.7845
= DM892,250.00

The first leg of the swap (buying US$10 million) will cost DM18 million. The second leg (re-selling US$10 million at 1.7845) will only release DM17,845,000. Adding up all the DM cash flows gives the net income from the strategy:

```
  DM   18,000,000
+ DM   17,845,000
+ DM      892,250
+ DM      737,250
```

This income must be compared with the return from investing in DM-denominated paper, his local currency.

(b) Funds are invested in local paper

DM18,000,000 invested locally at 8% for 180 days will produce an income of:

DM18,000,000 × 8/10 × 180/360
= DM720,000

Even taking account of the cost of FX cover, option (a) is more profitable. It produces an annualized rate of return of:

$$\frac{737{,}250}{18{,}000{,}000} \times \frac{360}{180} \times 100$$

$$= 8.19\%$$

This compares with only 8% on the domestic market. The yield on the dollar paper available to this investor exceeds that on domestic paper by more than the interest rate cost implied in the swap rate.

The Implied Cost of Forward Cover

In Chapter 29 we used the following approximate formula for calculating forward points from interest rate differentials (see page 260):

Forward margin =

$$\left[\frac{\text{Counter currency interest rate} - \text{Base currency interest rate}}{100} \right] \times$$

$$\text{Spot rate} \times \frac{\text{No. of days}}{360}$$

Rearranged, this can be used to compute (roughly) the net interest cost implied in a given swap rate (see Figure 36.1).

Fig 36.1

The implied interest cost in a forward margin

Implied interest cost =

$$\frac{\text{Forward margin}}{\text{Spot rate}} \times \frac{360}{\text{No. of days}} \times 100$$

Applying the figures in Case E to this formula:

$$\frac{-0.0155}{1.8000} \times \frac{360}{180} \times 100$$

$$= -1.72\%$$

So, according to this formula, the net return on the dollar investment, including the cost of FX cover, is:

= 10.00 –1.72
= 8.27%

As you can see, the formula overstates the true return on the covered dollar investment by 8 basis points (0.08%), but it usefully provides a quick indication of whether or not the strategy is worth exploring in more detail.

Covered Interest Arbitrage

This refers to the possibility of locking in risk-free profits by taking advantage of misalignments between interest rates and forward exchange rates.

Example

Suppose the above German fund manager was able to borrow marks at 8%. He could swap these into dollars (paying the 155 points), and invest the dollars at 10%. The return on the covered dollar investment (net of the swap cost) of 8.19% could service the cost of borrowing the D-marks and leave a clear 19 basis points profit. If it could be done (allowing for credit lines, capital adequacy and transaction costs . . .), then everyone would jump on the bandwagon. Such opportunities are short-lived; the huge flows of funds generated by arbitrageurs would push market rates back into line.

By its very nature, the swap market compensates or charges users for the cost of carry.

Looking for Arbitrage Opportunities

The following example is designed to allow you to practice searching for arbitrage opportunities on the rare occasions that they arise and to replicate the trading activity which would occur in order to take advantage of them.

Example The following market rates are available:

Foreign exchange	Spot	6 months
USD/CHF	1.2000/05	120/115

Money markets	USD	5.1/4 – 1/8
	CHF	2.7/8 – 5/8

A broker tells us that the 120 forward points look "cheap". Let us see:

(a) We trade at 120 points against us in an amount of US$10 million. This means that we buy spot US dollars and sell forward six months (183 days) forward. The market maker sets the exchange rate for leg 1 at 1.2000 and the forward leg at 1.1880. (1.2000 –0.0120).

(b) Calculating the Swiss franc cash flows:

Spot: US$10,000,000 × 1.2000
= 12,000,000 Swiss francs

Forward: US$10,000,000 × 1.1880
= 11,880,000 Swiss francs

(c) We now invest our US$ in the money markets at 5.1/8% earning interest:

$$\frac{US\$10,000,000 \times 5.125}{100} \times \frac{183}{360}$$

= US$260,520.83.

(d) To avoid exchange risk, we need to cover this interest by selling our US dollars for forward Swiss francs at the outright rate of 1.1880:

US$260,520.83 × 1.1880 = 309,498.75 Swiss francs

In practice, we would arrange with the market-maker to add this deal to the forward leg of our conventional swap to form one forward settlement.

(e) Consolidating the cash flow analysis:

The US dollar cash flows are matched, and we are left with a synthetic lending of 12,000,000 Swiss francs repaying a total of

12,189,498.75 Swiss francs (= 11,880,000.000 + 309,498.75). We can calculate the effective interest earned on these funds:

$$189,498.75/12,000,000 \times 360/183 \times 100 = 3.11\%$$

(f) Finally, we borrow 12,000,000 Swiss francs in the money markets at 2.7/8% to produce profits in Swiss francs through a completely covered structure!

We could have chosen to lock up these arbitrage profits by arranging the money market transactions first and then the swap. Timing is always important, whilst transaction costs and the use of capital and credit lines must also be considered. The FX deals are off the balance sheet but the money market deals eat away at valuable capital resources.

The forward trader quoting the 120 points will soon discover his error; or, indeed, the opportunity may have arisen due to the US-dollar deposit dealer's overbidding for money, or to the Swiss franc dealer's offering cheap funding. Arbitrage opportunities like this often arise due to combinations of different market makers' views of their various markets and products.

Remember: If the forward exchange rate is left uncovered in the structure, then exchange rate fluctuations will affect the profitability of the portfolio of transactions.

Overnight Rollovers

Case H

At the end of the day, on 23 February, a spot dealer has the following position in USD/FRF (all figures in 000s):

CCY	AMOUNT	VALUE	RATE	USD
FRF	−69,270	25 Feb	6.9270	+10,000

At that point the dealer has three options:

(a) Do nothing, so the position approaches settlement

(b) Close the position, with a matching deal

(c) Roll over the position, pushing the value date one day forward.

He decides to roll over the position.

The most common overnight rollover swaps are "tom-next" and "spot-next." These involve buying a currency for one value date and re-selling it for the following day. At the time, the short-dated swaps are quoted as follows:

	SPOT	T/N	S/N	S/WK
FRF	6.9250/70	55/95	50/90	150/180

The dealer decides to buy and sell 69,270 French francs spot-next, at 90 pips against him. After the swap, he has the following deals in his book:

CCY	AMOUNT	VALUE	RATE	USD	
FRF	–69,270	25 Feb	6.9270	+10,000	the spot positions
FRF	+69,270	25 Feb	6.9270	–10,000	first leg of swap
FRF	–69,270	26 Feb	6.9360	+9,987	second leg of swap

The first leg of the swap exactly matches the position for value 25 February. The second leg re-opens it for value 26 February, which will be tomorrow's spot date. The rollover will cost the dealer US$13,000 (= 9.987 million –10 million) and the spot position tomorrow will be opened at a less favorable rate.

The FX swap is the ideal vehicle for rolling forward (or back) an FX exposure.

With an FX swap the time value of money is expressed in exchange points, so the net cost of funding can be added directly to the underlying position rate.

The Bear Trap

The structure of the forward rates in Case H is typical of a situation in which the currency you are shorting is fundamentally weak. Eurofranc interest rates are much higher than Eurodollar rates – a sign that the authorities are struggling to shore up the currency.

Also, overnight Eurofranc rates are higher than rates for one week. You could roll over the position a whole week forward at 180 points against you. To do it on a daily basis over seven days would cost a total of 630 points (= 7 × 90).

Every day that goes by, and the franc is not devalued, you pay 90 points to keep the position open. By the time the franc is devalued, you may have paid away all the potential profit from the position in rollover costs.

In 1983, the Banque de France pushed overnight Eurofranc rates up to 6,000% and the cost of tom-next swaps went up to 10 big figures (FRF 0.1000)! The move was designed to squeeze those who were speculating against the franc.

Ante-Spot Dates

Nowadays most currencies can be traded for value the next day and some can be traded for same-day value. To compute the outright rate of exchange for ante-spot deals you need to work backwards from the spot rates, rather than forward.

Compute the outright rates for value tomorrow and value one day after spot. USD/DEM market rates are: **Example**

SPOT	T/N	S/N
1.8100/10	2.3/1.2	2.8/1.5

With deals for value after spot, the general rules laid down previously still apply. Here we subtract the points because the left-hand rate is numerically larger than the right-hand rate:

Spot	1.81000 / 1.81100
Subtract spot-next	−0.00028 / −0.00015
Value next day	1.80972 / 1.81085

> **For ante-spot rates, the procedure is:**
> - **Reverse the sign of the tom-next margins.**
> - **Switch the two rates around (from 2.3/1.2 to 1.2/2.3).**

Spot	1.81000 / 1.81100
Tom-next turned around	+0.00012 / +0.00023
Value tomorrow	1.81012 / 1.81123

This widens the bid–offer spread for value tomorrow, while still preserving a positive cost of carry for the D-marks.

Summary

In this chapter, we examined the use of swaps in investment contexts, calculated the interest costs implied in a swap rate and looked at covered interest arbitrage, a process which exploits misalignments between interest rates and forward exchange rates. We concluded with a look at the procedures for overnight rollovers and ante-spot deals.

Keywords   Before turning to the swaps exercise in Chapter 37, please make sure that you are familiar with the following terms:

- covered foreign currency investment borrowing
- covered interest arbitrage
- short-dated rollovers
- ante-spot transactions.

Exercise:
Swap Applications

1. **10 March**

   An Australian mining group needs working capital to develop a new coal seam. It has asked its bankers to raise US$100 million on a three-year Eurodollar Floating Rate Note (FRN), which will be swapped into Australian dollars at six-monthly periods. The FRN will carry a coupon of 25 basis points over the six-month Eurodollar LIBOR.

   The first LIBOR fixing, covering 183 days, takes place today. Market rates are currently:

FX RATES:	SPOT	6 MTHS
AUD/USD	1.2870/80	247/240

MONEY MARKETS:	6 MTHS
AUD	12.7/8–5/8
USD	8.3/4–5/8

   Note: Interest on Australian dollars is based on a 365-day year.

   (a) Calculate the effective interest rate cost to the company, in Australian dollars, for the first interest period.

   US$100 million will be swapped into Australian dollars for six months at _____ points against the company/in the company's favor (delete one). The agreed spot rate for the transaction is 1.2875, therefore the first leg of the swap will produce:

A$ 77,669,900 (=100,000,000/1.2875)

and the second leg of the swap will cost:

A$ _____ (round all figures to nearest AUD).

(b) In addition, interest will be payable on the first six months of the FRN at a rate of _____% (LIBOR + 0.25%). The interest amount due is therefore:

US$100,000,000 × 183/360 × _____

=US$ _____

(c) To cover the exchange risk on the interest payable the company needs to buy the dollars forward outright at a rate of _____ which will cost:

A$ _____

(d) Adding up all the cashflows:

A$ _____ first leg of swap

A$ _____ second leg of swap

A$ _____ interest payment

_____

A$ _____ net cost (interest plus exchange cover)

(e) Effective annual cost of covered borrowing:

$$\frac{\text{Net total under (d)}}{77,669,900} \times \frac{365}{183} \times 100$$

= _____ %

(f) Effective cost of the covered dollar FRN borrowing, using the approximate formula:

$$\left[\frac{\text{Forward margin}}{1.2875} \times \frac{365}{183} \right] \times 100$$

+ [(USD LIBOR + 0.25)]

= _____ %

(g) Suggest one reason why the company might proceed with its bankers' proposals, rather than borrow in Australian dollars.

10 September

It is six months since the FRN was issued and settlement of the second leg of the FX swap is due in two days. FX rates are now:

	SPOT	...6 MTHS
AUD/USD	1.2550/60	260/250

(h) As well as fixing the new LIBOR for the next interest period, the bank will roll over the exchange cover, again selling and buying US$100 million spot against six months at ___ points, based on a spot rate of 1.2555.

Net rollover cash flows on 12 September:

A$ _____ maturing second leg of first swap

A$ _____ first leg of rollover swap

_____

A$ _____

10 March

The second interest period on the FRN ends in two days and another swap rollover is required, based on the following rates:

	SPOT	...6 MTHS
AUD/USD	1.2625/35	255/245

(i) Net rollover cash flows on 12 March:

A$ _____ maturing second leg of second swap.

A$ _____ first leg of next rollover swap.

_____

A$ _____

2. In January a Japanese exporter of goods into Italy issues an invoice for 6,250 million Italian lire, payable within 180 days. It has offered the importer a 2% discount on the amount due if payment is received within 90 days.

To cover the exchange risk, the exporter has contracted to sell the lire six months forward to the bank, at a rate of JPY/ITL 9.2500.

Towards the end of March, the Italians say that they are prepared to settle early. Market rates are as follows:

FX RATES:	SPOT	3 MTHS
JPY/ITL	9.1030/50	1500/1560

How can the exporter cancel the FX contract for settlement in June previously arranged with the bank?

(a) To pre-settle the June sale of lire to the bank the company needs to buy and sell/sell and buy (delete one) ITL 6,250 spot against three months on a swap, at _____ points (agreed spot rate: 9.1030). The swap points are against/in favour of the exporter (delete one).

The second leg of this swap cancels the original forward contract, and through the first leg of the swap the company sells the lire received from the importer to the bank, at the agreed spot rate of 9.1030.

(b) Unfortunately, the Italians will now pay 2% less of the invoiced amount, or L6,125 million (= 6,250 x 0.98).

The company therefore has to make up the shortfall of 125 million Italian lire on the contract by purchasing this amount from the bank, at a spot rate of _____

(c) Net cash flow to the exporter in March:

¥ _____ sale of L6,250 million on the first leg of swap.

¥ _____ cost of the L125 million shortfall.

_____

¥ _____

(d) Net cash flow to the exporter in June:

¥ _____ sale of L6,250 million in January, at 9.2500.

¥ _____ repurchase of L6,250 million on second leg of swap.

_____

¥ _____

(e) What is the net cost to the exporter of the 2% discount offered for early payment?

■ ■ ■

"The forward book can be summarized in a maturity ladder which represents the net cash flows on each forward date."

Forward Position-Keeping

Overview   In this final chapter we will examine three different approaches to forward position-keeping, highlighting the relationship between outright forward FX, FX swaps and money market rates.

The Maturity Ladder

The forward book can be summarized in a maturity ladder which shows the net currency cash flows on each forward date or range of dates.

Fig 38.1   **The CHF book of IB Corp**

	CHF BOUGHT/SOLD	Av./RATE	REVAL	P/L (USD)
Spot 1 week	8,908	1.4600	1.4700	(41.4)
1 week–2 weeks	0.0		1.4630	0.0
2 wks–1 mth	10,292	1.4530	1.4625	(46.0)
1 mth–2 mths	0.0		1.4565	0.0
2 mths–3 mths	0.0		1.4500	0.0
3 mths–6 mths	(14,200)	1.4200	1.4345	101.1
6 mths–9 mths	0.0		1.4100	0.0
9 mths–12 mths	(5,000)	1.4120	1.3910	(53.5)
NET	0.0			(40.0)

All amounts in 000s.

Points to note

- On a deal like the US$10 million swap associated with XYZ Inc. (see pages 279–80) the amounts in Swiss francs in the two legs of that deal do not balance, so a maturity ladder like the one shown above would not necessarily add up to zero. Any net cash flow imbalance in a forward book, however, typically reflects net interest payments in favor of or against the bank.

- The cash flows in the above ladder are aggregated into rather wide date bands: for example, all deals maturing between 9 and 12 months are netted into the same "time-bucket."

- This makes it easier to see the wood from the trees, but may obscure important gaps. For example a spot-nine-month deal showing in the 9 MTHS–12 MTHS band may appear to have been be closed by a spot-12-month deal, but it actually leaves a significant three-month forward–forward gap.

Revaluation Approaches

In this section we will outline two common ways of handling end-of-day revaluations.

Method 1

The first step here is to calculate the average outright rate of exchange for all the deals falling within each settlement band. This is the net sum of Swiss franc cash flows divided by the sum of US dollar cash flows within each band. The average rate for each band is then marked-to-market at the corresponding forward outright market rate.

Example

The position in the six months in the maturity ladder shown on page 328 is 14,200 Swiss francs short at a rate of 1.4200 (US$10 million long). Repurchasing the 14,200 Swiss francs forward, at an outright six months market rate of 1.4345, would cost:

14,200 / 1.4345 = US$ 9,898.9

This would leave a net profit of:

US$ 10,000 −9,898.9 = US$ 101.1

Strictly speaking we should present-value this amount by discounting it at a six-month dollar LIBOR. Likewise with all other forward revaluation profits or losses.

This approach is very similar to the one used for revaluing spot positions and tends to be widely used in the "back office" responsible for monitoring dealing room profits – typically the Settlements or Accounts departments. It has the advantage of being simple to operate – all it requires is a set of "closing" spot and forward outright rates of exchange. But it has the drawback that it does not conform with the way the forward traders themselves monitor profits, thus creating possible situations in which the two sets of figures do not agree.

Method 2

Calculate the average swap rate implied in each forward band and revalue each position at the appropriate market swap rate, as shown in Figure 38.2.

Fig 38.2 **The forward CHF Book of IB Corp, revalued against current FX swap rates**

	CHF BOUGHT/SOLD	Av.RATE	REVAL	P/L (USD)
Spot 1 week	8,908	1.4600	1.470	N/A
1 week–2 weeks	0.0			0.0
2 wks–1 mth	10,292	(70)	75	1.9
1 mth–2 mths	0.0			0.0
2 mths–3 mths	0.0			0.0
3 mths–6 mths	(14,200)	400	(355)	35.0
6 mths–9 mths	0.0			0.0
9 mths–12 mths	(5,000)	480	(790)	(76.9)
NET	0.0			(40.0)

The analysis here is quite different. Instead of showing outright rates, the ladder now shows the number of points, in favor or against the dealer, at which each forward position was created. It is marked-to-market against the number of points that must be paid or can be earned to close the position, at current market rates.

For example, the six months position will earn the dealer a total of 400 points, and would now cost 355 points to reverse, leaving a net profit of 45 points per dollar. Calculating the total profit, in US dollars, involves working out the net dollar cash flows that would be left over after squaring this position.

Taking the 3–6 month cash flow as an example:

Net cash flows (in 000s):

	SwFr	VALUE	RATE	US$
Position:				
	14,200	SPOT	1.4600	(9,726)
	(14,200)	6 MTHS	1.4200	10,000
	0		400 pts	274

Revaluation:

	(14,200)	SPOT	1.4700		9,660
	14,200	6 MTHS	1.4345		(9,899)
	0			355 pts	−239
NET	0				35

This approach follows more closely the way the forward dealer works, in terms of points earned and points paid. He can see that the big losses in this book are in the 12-month position. Clearly, this exposure requires his immediate attention.

Although this approach is appealing, it can in certain situations be quite inaccurate. First, the US$35 thousand should be discounted to a present value equivalent, as with Method 1.

More importantly, note how the movement in the spot rate, from 1.4600 to 1.4700 would give rise to a shortfall of US$66 thousand on the spot date (= −9,726 + 9,660). Of course, six months later this shortfall will be more than offset by a surplus of US$101 thousand (= +10,000 −9,899), leaving a net profit of US$35 thousand. In the meantime, the shortfall must be funded, and the costs of funding it should be charged to the desk that created them. This phenomenon is referred to as the "spot risk" on a forward book – the funding cost or benefit on a swap arising purely from a change in the spot rate.

The Swiss franc FX ladder would be mirrored by a corresponding ladder in US dollars and a third approach would be to treat each of the two ladders as a separate money market position. The forward cash flows within each ladder would then be present-valued using appropriate discount rates and the net profit/loss on the FX book would be the sum of the PVs for each ladder. Figure 38.3 illustrates this approach.

In Figure 38.3, the CHF cash flows generate the counter-amounts shown under the USD cash flow column (at the historic rates shown under the Av. RATE column in Figure 38.1). These cash flows are then present-valued using current interest rates for each currency, which are consistent with the revaluation exchange rates shown in Figure 38.1. The NPV of the CHF ladder is +859 thousand francs, which equates to +USD 584 thousand at the current spot rate of 1.4700. Set against the −USD 624 NPV of the dollar cash flows, the NPV of the two sides of the FX book is USD 40

Fig 38.3 **The forward CHF Book of IB Corp revalued against corresponding money market rates**

	CHF			USD		
	Cash flow	Rate %	PV	Cash flow	Rate %	PV
Spot – 1 week	8,908	0.6932	8,908	(6,101)	13.0000	(6,101)
1 week – 2 weeks	0	0.6932	0	0	13.0000	0
2 weeks – 1 mth	10,292	6.8734	10,233	(7,083)	13.0625	(7,007)
1 mths – 2 mths	0	7.4943	0	0	13.1250	0
2 mths – 3 mths	0	7.5659	0	0	13.1875	0
3 mths – 6 mths	(14,200)	8.1001	(13,647)	10,000	13.2500	9,379
6 mths – 9 mths	0	7.7466	0	0	13.7500	0
9 mths – 12 mths	(5,000)	7.8735	(4,635)	3,541	14.0000	3,106
NET PV			859			(624)

thousand, which is the same as we calculated in the previous two methods.

This approach highlights the fact that forward FX deals may be decomposed into equivalent pairs of money market positions, which could then be covered in the underlying interest rate markets. In this example, the two markets – forward FX and the associated interest rate markets – have perfectly consistent rates, so there is no advantage in covering in either sector, but this is not always the case in reality, as we have seen.

Summary

In this final chapter, we examined three approaches to forward position keeping. We looked how an overall forwards position can be represented as a maturity ladder, and highlighted the relationship between the FX and money markets.

Keywords Before proceeding, please make sure that you are familiar with the following concepts:

- maturity ladder
- net present values
- spot risk.

Forward and Swaps FX Practice

There follows a set of questions of the type you might see in the ACI *Introduction to FX and Money Markets* examination.

In exam conditions, each question receives 1 mark for a correct answer, zero for no answer and minus 1/4 mark for a wrong answer.

We suggest you attempt as many questions as you can in 30 minutes. After this you can go over the remaining questions in your own time. Suggested answers are given in Appendix 3.

1. The current spot USD/DEM rate is 1.4500. The DEM interest rate for 91 days is 9% and the USD interest rate for this period is 5%. What will the forward points be for this maturity?

   a) 0.0552

   b) −0.0143

   c) 0.0140

   d) 0.0145

2. The spot GBP/FRF is quoted 8.3580/90 and the three-month forward outright is 8.3930/50, what are the forward points?

   a) 35/36

   b) 360/350

   c) 350/360

   d) 340/350

3. If the forward points for one month USD/DEM are quoted 60/55, how is the D-mark being quoted?

   a) at a discount

   b) at par

   c) at a premium

   d) either side of par

4. Consider the following FX rates:

	SPOT	3 MONTHS
USD/CHF	1.6250/60	48/43
USD/FRF	5.3180/00	133/143

   What is the three months CHF/FRF outright forward price?

   a) 3.2875/24

   b) 3.2893/05

   c) 3.2788/27

   d) 3.2880/00

5. Spot USD/DEM is 1.67 70/80 and USD interest rates are lower than DEM. Would you expect the forward points to be:

   a) Added to spot

   b) Subtracted from spot

   c) Neither of the above

   d) Insufficient information to answer

6. In six months' time (180 days) you have a GBP10 million loan maturing which you lent at 6 3/4%. You wish to crystalize now the amount of US dollars that it will be worth, when today's spot rate is 1.6320/25 and the six months' forward points are quoted 55/50. What amount will you receive?

   a) US$16,806,423.97

   b) US$16,863,254.79

   c) US$6,352,829.21

   d) US$16,824,281.25

7. The current spot GBP rate is 1.6500 and the GBP interest rate for 91 days is 8%; the USD interest rate for this period is 11%. What will the swap margin be for this maturity?

   a) −0.0116

   b) 0.0127

   c) −0.0123

   d) −0.0446

8. Which of the following characteristics does not apply to FX swaps?

   a) Consists of a pair of transactions, usually one for spot and one for a forward date

   b) Can replace a pair of money market transactions

   c) Eliminates credit risk with the counterparty

   d) Can be used to exploit arbitrage opportunities

9. Two-month (60 days) USD cash is at 7 7/8–8.00. The spot USD/CHF rate is 1.3505/15 and the two-month forward CHF is at a 155/150 points premium. At what rate can you raise Swiss francs?

a) 1.25%

b) 14.82%

c) 1.16%

d) 1.34%

10. Spot GBP/USD is trading at 1.8500/10. The tom/next rate is quoted 10/5. How should I quote for value tomorrow?

a) 1.8510/15

b) 1.8505/20

c) 1.8490/05

d) Not enough information.

11. Consider the following FX rates:

	SPOT	TOM-NEXT
GBP/USD	1.5705/15	10/12
USD/CHF	1.2250/55	3/2

At what rate could you buy Swiss francs against sterling, for value tomorrow?

a) 1.9242

b) 1.9251

c) 1.9227

d) 1.9249

12. In nine months' time (270 days) you are due to receive DM10 million and you wish to crystalize now the amount of US dollars that it will be worth. Nine-month USD cash is quoted as 4 1/4–4 1/8; nine-month DEM cash as 5.85–5.75; spot is 1.5005 and nine-month forward points are 173/175. On those rates, what is the largest amount of US dollars that you would be able to raise?

   a) US$6,587,615.28

   b) US$6,384,120.00

   c) US$9,579,691.05

   d) US$6,384,332.59

13. If the three-month USD/CHF swap is 5/8 and six months is 35/30, what is forward/forward three against six months swap?

   a) 43/38

   b) 40/38

   c) 38/43

   d) 43/35

14. Spot USD/DEM is trading at 1.7500/10. The one-month swap (30 days) is quoted 100/90 and the two-month swap (60 days) at 170/160. What rate should I quote for a 45-day swap, using straight-line interpolation?

   a) 170/160

   b) 100/90

   c) 135/125

   d) 80/60

15. Spot USD/CHF is 1.4500/05. One-month forwards are 200/210 and two-months 170/160. What swap rate should you quote for 1 1/2 months (assume each month has 30 days)?

   a) 215/235

   b) 15/25

   c) 235/215

   d) 25/15

■ ■ ■

"Time spent poring over the details of the position keeper is time spent away from the market."

Simulated Dealing – Third Session

Objectives

The purpose of this trading session is to give you practical experience of trading forward foreign exchange in the interbank market.

In this particular scenario you will be dealing sterling forwards from quotations made to you by a number of market makers and you will also be making a market yourself. As in the previous two sessions, news items will flash up on the screen giving you a general indication of the direction of the market. Success in this session will depend on your ability to determine the following:

- Based on how the market is moving, should you be currently bought and sold or sold and bought in sterling?
- When should you open, increase, decrease or square out your position?
- When you receive a quotation should you deal at that price, or should you ask for another quotation from a different market maker?
- Depending on whether sterling is strengthening or weakening in the spot market, should you be buying spot and selling forward, or selling spot and buying forward, and why?
- Which way should you shade your rates to encourage counter-parties to deal with you?

The Scenario

Your base currency in this session is sterling. You will have about 15 hours in which to trade – in real-time this will last about 20 minutes – after which the system will shut down automatically.

> **You can deal round the clock, but for the purposes of revaluing your position (see below) each day ends at midnight, London time (GMT).**

At the end of the session you should square out your book completely. You will be given a range of statistics on your dealing performance which can be compared against benchmarks set out below.

It is important to tackle this session in the prescribed way. The key objectives are to develop an understanding of the effects of swap deals on your cash flows, and on your profit or loss. You should be trying to achieve:

- A fast response to price quotations (do you like them or not ?)
- An accurate response to quotations (are you hitting the right side of the price?)
- A good understanding of your position (are you bought and sold or sold and bought overall?)
- An instinct for quoting forward rates effectively.

Starting the Session

We will assume here that you have already installed the software on your PC, and that you are already familiar with the simulation from the previous two sessions.

From the start-up screen press the ![button] button and select **FWDS1.WLD** from the list of files. You can also do this by selecting **Open** from the **File** drop-down menu. When the file has loaded, the display on your screen will look like Figure 40.1.

Before you start the simulation select **Market** from the **Reports** drop-down menu. This allows you to read a brief economic summary of the trading scenario you are about to start.

When you have read the text, close the **Market** window.

Pressing the ![button] button will start the simulation.

If you have already started the simulation, hit the ![button] button to pause it until you have read the instructions below. Then click ![button] when you are ready to start trading.

The Main FX Screen

The main window created in this session is shown in Figure 40.1.

Fig 40.1

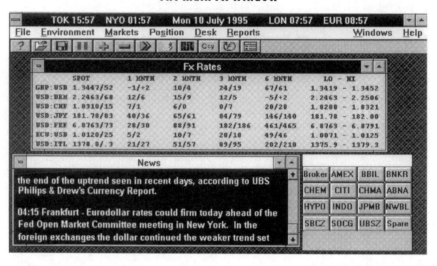

The main FX window

The Clocks

The clocks in the bar at the top of the screen show the time in Tokyo, New York, London and Europe. The simulation date is shown in the middle of the same bar. When the simulation is running the clocks flash. Each financial centre is open from 08:00 to 17:00 local time.

> **You can deal round the clock, but the date will change at midnight, London time (GMT).**

The clocks provide useful information about the state of the world-wide currency market – market depth depends on the number of buyers and sellers active at any one time.

The market is deepest at around 15:00 when London, continental Europe and New York are both open. Depending on the depth of the market, a large currency transaction can cause prices to move against you.

Market Rates

The **FX Rates** window consists of a table with currency codes down the left-hand side. The table shows exchange rates for spot and five standard forward dates. The 12-months rates may be covered up by the **DAY'S SPREAD** indicator showing the day's highest and lowest spot rates.

Press the **to retrieve the 12-month and index rates. Alternatively you may click the right-hand mouse button to the right of the** 6 MNTH **column.**

This window is inspired by some of the "composite" pages on the Reuters service, which show the latest indication rates contributed by a number of banks. As with all market information services, indication rates shown on the screen sometimes lag behind the market. There can be a disparity between the rates you are given by a market maker and the indication rates quoted on this window.

Most currencies are shown in terms of units of currency per US dollar, with the notable exceptions being sterling and the ECU, which are shown in terms of dollars to the pound, and dollars per ECU.

Display Formats

The forward rates are shown as forward margins rather than outright rates. This is the usual convention, as most forward deals are in fact swaps rather than outrights.

By pressing the **button you can toggle to show the bid rates in full, spot and outright forward, then the ask rates in full, and then back to the two-way format.**

Alternatively, you may click the right mouse button anywhere in the window to the left of the 6 MNTH column.

Day's Hi–Low & Trade-Weighted Index

Press the right-hand mouse button to the right of 6 MNTH column to toggle the display to show either the daily high and low for the spot currencies, or the currencies' trade-weighted index. The trade-weighted index relates the value of a currency's spot exchange rate to a group of other currencies, in proportion to the volume of trade between that country and each of the others.

All indices are scaled starting at 100 at some convenient date. For example, if the sterling index is at 80.0, this means that the pound is now worth 80% of its average value when the index was last re-based.

New Alerts

Messages come into the **News** window at various times. Only the latest items are displayed in the screen. If you want to look back at earlier messages, click up or down on the vertical scroll bar to the right of the window.

Charts

Selecting the option **Charts** from the Desk drop-down menu opens a window where you can look at the yield curve, spot FX rates, benchmark bond prices or the Eurocurrency futures page for each currency.

Press the Ccy **button to display a different currency on the Charts window.**

Press the (f) **button to change the price series displayed.**

From the toolbar inside the Charts window use the Daily or Tick buttons to view either daily or tick price charts. You also have two buttons to compress or expand the chart horizontally.

Dealing – Market User

To ask for a quotation select **Deal** from the **Desk** menu (**Alt+d** followed by **d**). A window will open up listing the counterparties you can deal with, along with their four-letter dealing codes, the size of their limits and how much if any of their limits have already been used. Highlight the counterparty you wish to deal with, and press **OK**. Alternatively, click on a selected button in the phone pad.

A deal slip, like the one in Figure 40.2, will then appear on your screen.

FX swaps deal slip

Fig 40.2

The left portion of the deal slip is where you enter details of the deal you wish to make. The right portion is where the counterparty will respond.

On the deal slip, the first choice you will have to make is what type of FX contract you will want to deal – **Outright** forward FX, FX **Swaps** or one of the **SAFE** derivatives. In this session we shall focus on FX swaps.

The first entry at the top of the deal slip is the currency for which you want a price and the second entry is the Value date, where details of the first (or "near date") of the swap are entered. The next entry is the Maturity (or "far date") when the second leg of the swap settles.

To enter a spot start date, type **s** (or **spot**) and press **Enter,** or click on **OK**.

To enter the quoted currency, type the currency code (if you have loaded **FWDS1** the currency in **g** or **GBP**).

For a forward fixed date, type **1m** (for one month), **2m** (two months), **3m** (three months) etc., and press **Enter**. This must of course be a later date than the VALUE DATE.

Alternatively, to enter the actual date of the forward maturity (a "broken date"), type **1 Apr** or whichever date is appropriate. You may enter the year after the month if necessary.

The market maker will respond with a two-way price, just as if you had asked for a quote on the telephone. The market maker will not hold his rates indefinitely, so you must decide fairly quickly. His rates may not be the same as those shown on the price screen, depending on which way he wants to trade, so make sure you compare them with the current market prices.

If you ask for an amount which is less than the equivalent of GBP1 million, the market maker will consider that the amount is less than a market amount, and re-quote the rates by widening the spread.

If you do not like the rates, click on **Cancel** and the deal slip will be cleared. If you want to deal, enter against **Deal Type** either **bs** (buy spot and sell forward) or **sb** (sell spot and buy forward). You cannot cancel a deal once you have agreed to deal at the given rates.

> **Unless otherwise specified, the system will assume that you are buying or selling base currency (sterling in the case of FWDS1).**

Enter the amount you wish to deal, in thousands, or follow the figure you enter with an **m** to indicate millions – for example **5m** for 5 million. If the amount you enter is very large or very small, a message may tell you that the rates are only good for amounts in a certain range.

> **Sometimes in** `FWDS1`**, you may need to sell US dollar amounts (e.g., to mop up small dollar balances). To do this type the currency code USD before the amount. For example USD 250 means you deal in $250,000.00.**

Deal Rate and Outright Rate

As soon as you have entered the **Deal Type** and **Amount**, the counterparty will confirm the deal rate and the deal will be automatically logged into your position. The counterparty limit utilization information will also be updated.

Dealing – Market Maker

When the simulation is running you will hear a double-ringing sound from time to time, and a line button on the phonepad will highlight. This tells you that there is an incoming call from a counterparty asking for a quotation. Click on the button and a window like Figure 40.3 will appear.

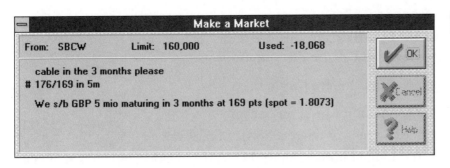

Fig 40.3

Underneath the message is where you enter your rates. You must enter two rates separated by a space or the "/" character.

If the caller does not specify which forward date he is interested in you should enter rates for 1, 2, 3 and 6 months, as is the convention. Each two-way price should be separated by a space.

You can qualify your rates with a maximum amount you are prepared to deal in by typing, for example, **in 10m** after your two-way price.

Once you have entered a rate (and an amount if you so desire) the caller will decide whether he wishes to deal. If a deal is made a new message will appear stating the amount and whether the counterparty wishes to buy/sell or sell/buy.

The Position Keeper

The simulation comes with a full on-line position keeper. Select **Position (Alt+p)** from the drop-down menu.

Deal Blotter

Selecting **Blotter** from the **Position** drop-down menu shows all the deals awaiting settlement.

As each swap consists of two FX deals, each with a different value date, every swap transaction will be recorded as a pair of deals in the **Blotter**. The first deal of each swap will be the near dated leg, normally settling on the spot date; the second deal will be the forward leg. Place the mouse on the scroll bar to the right of the window to scroll up and down the **Blotter**. The simulation auto-matically settles all deals when they reach maturity, and effects all the required balance sheet adjustments.

Every deal is stamped with:

- the time and date it was made;
- the currency or reference code of the deal;
- the amount in thousands; if you are long, the amount is shown as +ve in that currency; and if you are short it will be shown as –ve; to toggle between the base currency and counter-currency amounts press the Ccy button;
- the settlement and maturity date;
- **THRU:** the counterparty dealing code – if you have dealt on your prices, by answering an incoming call, the code will be appended with a **t** (short for Tele);
- the **PRICE** and/or **RATE** at which you dealt – for swaps the rate for the first leg will be shown in full and that for the second leg will only show the forward margin, in points;
- any interest ACCRUED on a fixed income trade, or FX points accrued on forward FX trade.

Ladders

The first screen you see is a maturity analysis (or "maturity ladder") of all your deals. It will look like the screen shown in Figure 40.4.

The **Exposure** ladder begins with your cash position and ranges all your forward cash flows into various maturity bands. **TOM** shows all the deals settling tomorrow. **SPOT** shows deals settling on the spot date. **–1 MNTH** shows all the deals settling between the day after spot and one month, and so on.

The dots under **SHORT** and **LONG** represent dealing limits, and the squares show your net position in each maturity band. This display gives you an idea of your position at a glance. If you have exceeded your limits !!! marks will appear.

The **NET** and **LIMIT** columns show in figures (000s) what the **SHORT** and **LONG** columns represent graphically. The **CUMUL**

Maturities in the position keeper

Fig 40.4

MAT	SHORT	LONG	LIMIT	NET	YLD	VAL 1%	CUMUL
GBP Exposure							
CASH			3,846	0		0	0
TOM			41,514	0	13.33	0	0
SPOT		$$$	83,029	30,000	13.32	0	30,000
– 1 MTH			55,353	0	13.24	0	30,000
– 2 MTH			55,353	0	13.27	0	30,000
– 3 MTH			55,353	0	13.32	0	30,000
– 6 MTH	$$$		55,353	–30,000	13.40	0	30,000
– 1 YR			55,353	0	13.56	–131	0
– 2 YRS			55,353	0	13.75	0	0
– 3 YRS			0	0	13.89	0	0
– 5 YRS			0	0	14.06	0	0
–10 YRS			0	0	14.24	0	0
>10 YRS			0	0	14.53	0	0
NET			276,763	0		–131	

column shows what your cash position would be at the end of each maturity period, given your present portfolio.

When you first go into the **Ladder** option, the ladders will be for USD. Press the [Ccy] button, or click on your right mouse button to select the GBP ladder so that you can see your sterling cash flows.

> Press the [⟳] button or click the right mouse button inside the window to toggle the display between Exposure, the actual Liquidity ladder and the Present Values of the cash flows, discounted at the zero coupon rates shown in the YLD column.

● **Exposure** and **Present Value** may not be the same: a buy/sell GBP30 million FX swap in the six months will be shown in the liquidity run as +30 million against SPOT and –30 million against the –6 MNTH band. In the **Present Value** ladder it will be shown as +30,000 against spot and a negative amount against the six months, representing the 30 million repayment discounted back to spot. The difference between the two values, shown in the NET column at the bottom of the ladder represents your net *spot risk* created by the FX swap. In effect, the ladder breaks down the swap in terms of a (relatively small) spot position and an interest rate position.

- VAL 1% in the **Ladder** window shows the effect on the present value of the cash flows in the NET column of a 1% parallel shift down in the yield curve. The risk on your position gap is the product of the amount dealt and the length of the gap.

Fixed Income Book

Your forward FX position will be shown in the Fixed Income window. This window will show your net trading position in each maturity without attempting to net off mismatched maturities. Press the [Ccy] button to toggle between foreign currencies and the USD amounts. If the symbol "–" precedes the amount it indicates, you are short in the near date and will therefore be long in the far date. An amount with the "+" symbol indicates that you are long in the near date and short in the far date.

If the near leg of your position has already settled, the position keeper will carry the number of points already accrued down to the balance sheet, and the **PRICE** column in the book will be the average position rate for the residual position – the portion which has yet to run.

Dealing Performance Assessment

When you have reached the end of your trading session make sure that you have squared out all your positions.

Select **Dealing** from the **Reports** drop-down menu, where you can see your performance statistics and a record of all the deals you have made.

Benchmarks

Here are some benchmarks to help you assess your performance. These are based on the performances of the many dealers who have completed this Forward Dealing module. Our experience shows that they establish a "profile" of the kind of person who tends to be successful at swap dealing. Of course, we are talking about statistical correlations here, not natural laws – the benchmarks must be applied with a great deal of common sense.

Dealing report screen

Fig 40.5

Dealing Report					
TRADING DAYS (Real-time)		**PROFIT $'000**			**TURNOVER**
1	(00:04)	35			343,847
				SPREAD/MARKET (s.devn)	
	DEALS	(calls) AV. SPEED (s.devn)	---- Bid ----		---- Ask ----
Out	13	00:13 (00:05)			
In	0	(0) 00:00 (00:00)	0.0 (0.0)		0.0 (0.0)
Network	0	00:00 (00:00)			
Corps	0				
Total	13	00:13 (00:05)			

SYSTEM USAGE		EXPOSURE		LIMITS BROKEN	
Pause	2	Matched Profits	25	Currency	0
Typos	0	Max Fx	1,201	Total Net	0
		Max VAL1%	241	Structure	2
				Gearing ratio	0
				Cash ratio	0
				Counterparty	0

OK   Clear   Print   Help

Profits

250+	Excellent
150–250	Very good
50–150	Good
10–50	Fair
Less than 10	Further practice required.

You are, of course, aiming to make a profit in the simulated dealing session. However, from a learning point of view, it is equally important that you should understand exactly how you achieved the result you did, and draw some lessons for the future. If you made a loss, then think carefully about where you went wrong. If you made a profit, ask yourself honestly whether this was the result of good judgement or good luck.

Deals

In this dealing session, you are dealing on prices quoted to you and on those you quote yourself. Hence the dealing report will specify a range of deals both **In** and **Out**. We would be looking for you to complete on average at least one deal per simulated hour's trading. There will be no **Network** or **Corp** deals logged.

For reference, **Out** tells you how many deals you have made when simulated counterparties as a market user – i.e., you called and dealt on their prices. **In** refers to the number of deals you made on your own prices.

Average Speed

This shows the average time (in seconds) you took to execute a trade. The time is measured from the time you press the phone line to the moment you either confirm or cancel the trade. But speed alone is not the vital factor – it is of course possible to react very quickly but wrongly.

We recommend that you deal at a safe speed – one in which you have control, you know what you are doing and what the results of your actions will be. A reasonable average response time to aim for in the first session is 15 seconds.

System Usage

Pause: Hitting the button is recorded on each occasion. If it is pressed more than a couple of times during the session we take this as a sign that the individual is feeling the stress of the market and is not perhaps as comfortable as they might be with interpreting the information presented to them.

Typos: the number of typing errors that are made when entering a deal, giving rise to a message like "I don't understand what you have entered" from *Risk Manager*. This is a useful measure of the propensity of the user to make clerical errors. A high figure here suggests that the user must improve his/her accuracy, as keyboard errors can be a costly source of problems in deal execution and settlement.

Exposure

Matched Profits: shows the % of deals matched at profit. For example, if you bought US$10 million at 45 and closed this position with two deals – one for 4 million at 55 and one for 6 million for 20 – the figure reported would be 50%, since only one of the two closing deals was profitable.

This statistic does not attempt to weight profitable trades either by size or price. It is a simple measure designed to capture the trainees' jobbing skill. Looked at alongside the total number of deals done, it shows the extent to which the user has been able to turn positions around profitably.

Max FX ($): shows the maximum net FX exposure attained during the trading session, in US dollars equivalent.

Max VAL 1%: shows the maximum interest rate exposures (market risk) taken during a trading session. It is measured in cash terms as the profit/loss that would result from a 1% parallel shift in the yield curve. This statistic applies to forward or fixed-interest dealing sessions.

Trading Lessons

There are a number of basic trading rules which have been learned by FX dealers over the years by trial and error, sometimes at great cost. Here are some of the main ones. Think about your performance in the first simulated dealing session and consider what areas you believe need improvement.

Never break a limit (it may cost you your job)

Dealing limits are there to control risk. Exposing your organization beyond those limits may put at risk the performance and standing of the whole institution, not just your own. There should not be too many problems if you go over a limit by a few thousand dollars in the heat of the moment. But if you must exceed a limit by a significant amount, ask your Chief Dealer first.

Which currency am I trading?

In the simulated dealing session just completed you may have had problems remembering which currency you are buying and selling. The convention in this simulation is that by default you buy/sell or sell/buy the base currency (sterling with cable deals, otherwise dollars), unless the amount is preceded by the currency name.

If dollar interest rates are lower than sterling but are increasing, then the swap points will become smaller. The obvious strategy is to buy and sell the dollar (sell and buy the pound) at points in your

Example

Fig 40.6

Deal slip for a USD amount

Deal Fx		
To: BNKT ◇ Outright ◆ Swap ◇ FXA ◇ ERA	**From: BNKT** Limit: 130,000 Used: 20,055	✔ OK
Currency GBP Value date S Maturity 1M	We deal 57/54 in up to 30,000	✗ Cancel
Deal type BS Amount USD 10M	Deal rate 54 Outright 1.8073	? Help

favor. If you enter **bs** for buy and sell into the deal slip, you *must* remember to put **USD** before the amount. Alternatively, you should enter **sb**, for sell and buy, then enter a sterling amount.

Suppose that you have filled in the deal slip shown in Figure 40.6.

The market maker has quoted you 57/54 in amounts of up to GBP30 million. He will sell and buy sterling at 57, and buy and sell sterling at 54.

You have entered the following data:

Currency:	UK sterling
Value date:	spot
Maturity:	1 month
Deal type:	buy spot and sell forward
Amount:	10 million dollars

If you ask for an amount which is less than the equivalent of GBP1 million, the market maker will consider that the amount is less than a market amount, and re-quote the rates by widening the spread.

In the deal slip shown in Figure 40.6, the 54 entry against deal rate means that the market maker has bought and sold sterling. The counter-amount is GB£5,533,000 – the (rounded) equivalent of US$10 million at the current spot rate.

If you want to close this position you could complete the deal shown in Figure 40.7.

In this example, you have entered a sterling amount – the computer interprets the number 5533 as thousands of pounds, so the amount is GBP5,533,000.

The lesson is: make sure you know which currency you are dealing in, and make sure that you specify it clearly to your counterparty.

Deal slip for a GBP amount

Fig 40.7

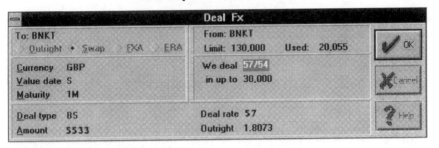

Deal Fx

To: BNKT
Outright ◆ Swap ⟩ FXA ⟩ ERA

From: BNKT
Limit: 130,000   Used: 20,055

✔ OK

Currency   GBP
Value date S
Maturity   1M

We deal **57/54**
in up to 30,000

✗ Cancel

Deal type   BS
Amount   5533

Deal rate 57
Outright   1.8073

? Help

K.I.S.S (Keep it simple, stupid!)

A good dealer concentrates on one major strategy at a time. He or she will formulate a strategy, and close the position before changing tack. A dealer may test the water first with smaller deals, and only then increase their position in stages.

If the trend starts to change, the dealer will start to unwind their position, gradually if the change is uncertain, more aggressively if it is confirmed. Large deals tend to be more difficult to execute, especially when the market is moving quickly – and they may move the market against you.

Know your position

A good dealer does not need to consult the electronic position keeper after every deal to know whether he is essentially long or short of a currency, or whether he is in profit. The net position should also be kept manually on a deal blotter.

All you need to know is whether you are basically on the right side of the market or not. Most dealers think in terms of "pips made" or "pips down": they have an idea of the average rate at which they created a position, and monitor market rates to see how far in or out of the money they are. Time spent poring over the details of the position keeper is time away from the market.

As your experience grows, you will be able to retain more and more of what you have done in your head. Experienced forward dealers have dealt profitably on this simulation over a number of days, without once looking at the position keeper!

Keep it off the balance sheet

As time rolls by, your position approaches settlement. The first deals that will settle will be the spot legs of your swaps.

How do you ensure that you have adequate funding? You could borrow the necessary funds in the money market, and place the currency received on deposit, when it arrives.

But you could arrange the funding through FX swaps – they are, after all, the ideal funding vehicle.

Example Suppose you bought and sold sterling spot against three months. After one day, the first leg of the swap will be for value tomorrow ("tom").

You can roll over this by means of a tom–next swap. In the deal slip, specify:

Start date: **tom** *End date:* **next**

Deal type will be sell and buy (**sb**), since you are long of sterling for value tomorrow and, effectively you want to lend it out for one day, while borrowing the dollars.

You can in the deal slip specify the start date as **today**. This is useful if you have inadvertently allowed a position to settle and you want to move the funds immediately. However, you should never let this happen.

Quite apart from the cost of dealing for same-day settlement (it can be expensive), once an FX deal settles, it creates two deposits, which inflates the balance sheet unnecessarily. Also, since you now have the funds, you are forced to consider for what term the funds could be placed and borrowed, and at what rates of interest. In other words, you become a money market dealer.

Cut your losses early

It is easy to get obsessed with the prospect of hitting the jackpot, and to forget to cut losses before they get worse. Also resist taking a profit before a change in the market trend has been confirmed. Statistically, a dealer who cuts losses quickly, and holds on to profitable positions for as long as possible will make profits over the long run, even if he reads the markets correctly only 50% of the time. Nobody should be too concerned if you have the occasional "bad trade." If you are not allowed to lose money, you cannot trade for profit. What matters in the dealing room is your performance over a period of time.

Appendices

Appendices

APPENDIX 1
KEY FORMULAE

These are the main formulae used in this book. They are reproduced from the ACI formula sheets which you are given when you sit one of the ACI exams.

Converting a straight discount to a true yield

$$\text{TRUE YIELD} = \frac{DR \times 100 \times B}{(100 \times B) - (DR \times T)}$$

or

$$TY = \frac{DR}{\left[1 - \left(\dfrac{DR \times T}{B \times 100}\right)\right]}$$

DR = Discount rate (as a percentage)
T = Tenor (number of days)
B = Day basis (360 or 365)

Calculating proceeds from straight discount

$$FV - \left(FV\left(\frac{T \times DR}{B \times 100}\right)\right)$$

FV = Face value
T = Tenor (number of days)
B = Day basis (360 or 365)

Forward–forward interest rate

$$\frac{(R_L \times D_L) - (R_s \times D_s)}{(D_L - D_s) \times \left(1 + \left(\dfrac{R_s \times D_s}{B \times 100}\right)\right)}$$

R_L = Rate from start date to the far date (long period) in percent
D_L = Number of days from spot to the far date

R_s = Rate from spot to the near date (short period) in percent
D_s = Number of days from spot to the near date
B = Day basis (360 or 365)

NB. Some currencies are quoted from same day value (e.g., domestic sterling)

FRA settlement formula

$$\frac{(L-R) \text{ or } (R-L) \times D \times A}{(D \times L) + (B \times 100)}$$

L = LIBOR (BBA settlement rate)
R = Contract rate (in percent)
A = Contract amount
D = Days in contract period
B = Day basis (360 or 365)

Calculating proceeds of secondary market CD

$$\text{Proceeds} = FV \times \left[\frac{(\text{Coupon} \times \text{original life}) + (B \times 100)}{(\text{YTM} \times \text{days remaining}) + (B \times 100)} \right]$$

FV = Face value
B = Day basis (360 or 365)
YTM = Yield to maturity (as a percent)

Covered interest arbitrage

U = Base CCY interest rate
L = Sterling interest rate (365 days basis) (or other 365 day basis CCY)
C = Counter currency interest rate (360 days basis)
S = Forward swap points (in the same format as spot rate, i.e., 89 discount is +0.0089 and 230 premium is –0.0230) premium (–)/discount (+)
T = Tenor (number of days)
A = Spot value
B = Outright = (A) ± swap

360/360 arbitrage

To produce:

$$U = C - \left[\left(\frac{36000}{T} + C \right) \frac{S}{B} \right]$$

$$C = U + \left[[(U \times T) + 36000] \frac{S}{A \times T} \right]$$

$$S = \frac{(C - U)\,(A \times T)}{(U \times T) + 36000}$$

360/365 arbitrage

To produce:

$$C = \left(\frac{B \times T \times L}{36500} + S\right)\frac{36000}{A \times T}$$

$$L = \left(\frac{A \times T \times C}{36000} - S\right)\frac{36500}{B \times T}$$

$$S = A\left[\left(\frac{365}{360} \times \frac{(C \times T + 36000)}{(L \times T) + 36500}\right) - 1\right]$$

APPENDIX 2
GLOSSARY

ACI The Association Cambiste International, an international body which aims to enhance and extend the professionalism of foreign exchange trading.

Ante-spot transactions A transaction traded for value the same day or tomorrow rather than in two working days.

Arbitrage profits Risk-free profits obtained in some trading situations, by setting one transaction at one rate against another at a different rate, which is sold in a different market.

Bankers' acceptance A commercial bill of exchange which has been endorsed or "accepted" by a bank, so the bank takes on the credit risk on the underlying commercial transaction. Bankers' acceptances (or bank bills) are negotiable in the secondary markets.

Base Currency/Unit currency In a FX deal, this is the currency not normally shown in the quotation. For instance, in a USD/DEM quotation of 1.41, the base currency is the dollar, since DEM1.41 = USD1.

Bear trap Or bear squeeze: a situation in which losses occur due to rollover costs exceeding the potential profits on a short position in a market.

Bearer securities Securities whose title to them is assumed to be their holder, as opposed to registered securities, where the owner's name appears in the certificate or some central register.

Bid-offer spread The difference between the price at which a market maker buys a financial instrument and the price at which he sells it. It reflects the risk of pricing at a given moment; the lower the risk, the wider the spread.

Big figure In an exchange rate of, for example, USD/DEM1.4145, the figure is 1.41. This is assumed, and not quoted, in dealer conversations.

Bill of exchange A note signed by the purchaser of goods or services (the drawee) in favour of the supplier (the drawer), promising to pay the amount invoiced on some future date.

Bretton-Woods Agreement The United Nations Monetary and Financial Conference held in 1944, which sought to stabilise the world monetary system by setting fixed exchange rate parities and by establishing the World Bank and the International Monetary Fund.

British Bankers' Association (BBA) A London-based industry association involved in the self-regulation of many sectors of the Eurocurrency deposits and derivatives market.

Broken dates In money markets and forward FX trading, a price quoted for a date which does not fall within one of the fixed dates regularly quoted by the market.

Broker A financial intermediary whose function is to match, buy and sell orders from principals, for a brokerage fee, rather than taking positions itself.

Bullets Fixed income investments in which the interest and/or principal payable is paid in one single instalment at maturity of the loan.

Cable The name given to a sterling/dollar FX transaction.

Certificates of deposit Receipts for Eurocurrency fixed-term deposits. Unlike fixed deposits, these are negotiable in a secondary market.

Clearing house A legal entity associated with a futures or options exchange which effectively becomes the counterparty to every futures transaction, so there is no need for each market participant to have credit limits with its trading counterparties.

Commercial Paper Unsecured short-term promissory notes issued by rated corporates and negotiable in the secondary markets.

Compounding The process whereby interest earned on an investment may be reinvested to earn interest on interest until maturity.

Contract period The period from the settlement date to the maturity date on a deposit or FRA contract.

Contract rate The agreed rate of interest for the contract period.

Counterparty The other party to a transaction.

Counterparty risk The risk that the counterparty to a transaction may be unable to honour its side of the deal. Also known as credit risk.

Coupon The interest payable at one or more stages during the term of a loan.

Coupon period The number of days between one coupon payment and the next.

Covered interest arbitrage The possibility of locking-in risk-free profits by exploiting misalignments between interest rates and forward exchange rates.

Credit ratings A system of scores awarded by independent ratings agencies to borrowers which assesses their perceived credit risk.

Credit risk The risk that the counterparty to a trade may be unable to honour its obligations. Also known as counterparty risk.

Cross-currency transaction The exchange of one non-dollar currency for another.

Deal blotter A table on which details of transactions are posted so as to establish profit, loss and position averages.

Decompounding The calculation of an effective annual interest rate from a nominal rate, taking into account the compounding period on the loan.

Demand deposits Non-interest bearing or low-yielding banking facilities used mainly for settlements.

Derivatives Synthetic instruments whose market prices are derived from underlying cash securities. FRAs and futures, for example, are derivatives of interbank deposits.

Direct quotation An exchange rate in which the value of a unit of foreign currency is quoted in units of domestic currency. The D-mark exchange rate quoted in terms of marks per dollar is a direct quotation in Frankfurt, but an indirect or reciprocal quotation in New York.

Discount securities A class of financial instruments which do not pay interest explicitly: the investor's return is implied in the difference between the security's price at the time of purchase and its value at maturity.

Discount to par This is the way in which discount securities are issued and traded. For example, if an exporter wishes to raise capital against a bill of exchange of $100 from its bankers, the bank might purchase the bill at a discount of, say, 10%, paying the exporter $90. The figure of 10% is known as the **discount rate**.

Eligible paper A bankers' acceptance or bank bill not incurring a central bank reserve requirement and eligible for re-discounting with the central bank.

Eurocurrency Banking transactions in a currency which are not governed by the domestic banking regulations of that currency, or of the centre in which the transaction is booked. A dollar deposit placed with a London bank is a typical Eurocurrency transaction.

European Currency Unit A currency unit, which came into being with the European Monetary System (EMS), which is made up of a 'cocktail' of European currencies. Its rate of exchange against the US dollar is a weighted sum of the exchange rate of each constituent currency.

Originally used only as a unit of account within European Community institutions, it has now become a monetary unit in international invoicing and financing operations.

European Monetary System (EMS)   A system originated in 1979 designed to manage European exchange rates. The key elements are the Exchange Rate Mechanism, the European Monetary Institute and the European Currency Unit.

Exchange Rate Mechanism (ERM)   A system operated by certain European central banks, which commits them to maintaining the exchange rates of their currencies within pre-determined fluctuation bands against each other, as well as against the ECU.

Fair value   The present value of a security which is calculated by discounting its future cash flows.

Federal Reserve System   The US central bank.

Fed Wire   The computerised system used by banks which are members of the Federal Reserve System to clear dollar funds with each other domestically.

Fixed exchange rate   A currency whose rate of exchange is pre-determined at some fixed parity.

Fixed dates   Standard money market and forward FX maturities routinely quoted by market makers (e.g. 1 month, 2 months, etc).

Fixed deposit   A bank deposit for a stated term to maturity and rate of interest. Eurocurrency transactions are for the most part fixed deposits.

Floating exchange rate   A currency whose rate of exchange is determined primarily by market forces.

Foreign exchange (FX) transaction   The sale of a deposit in one currency against the purchase of a deposit in another currency.

Forward cross rates   Forward rate of exchange between two currencies, neither of which is the US dollar.

Forward discount   The amount by which the forward counter-currency is cheaper than spot. If the 1 month forward USD/DEM is 1.4565 and spot is 1.4540 the forward DEM is said to be at a discount – one mark buys less dollars forward than at spot. Notice that it is the counter-currency which is at a forward discount, not the base currency.

Forward-forward rate   The rate of interest for a deposit or loan which is effective on a forward date (i.e. after spot), or the price of an FX swap for value on a forward date.

Forward margin The difference between an outright forward rate of exchange and its corresponding spot rate.

Forward premium The amount by which the forward counter-currency is more expensive than spot. If the 1 month forward USD/DEM is 1.4515 and spot is 1.4540 the forward DEM is said to be at a premium – one mark buys more dollars forward than at spot. Notice that it is the counter-currency which is at a forward premium, not the base currency.

FRABBA terms The terms and conditions recommended by the BBA in the transaction of FRA contracts.

Fungible In the futures markets offsetting futures positions for the same delivery month do not need to be settled separately at maturity but can be cancelled out. In the bond markets some new issues become indistinguishable from previously-issued tranches of the same securities.

Futures Agreements to buy or sell, through an organised exchange, an amount of a specified instrument or commodity, for settlement on a specified future month, at a price agreed between two parties at the time of opening the trade.

Future value The value of a sum of money on a specified future date, taking into account the interest accrued on it.

Gold Standard An international arrangement whereby countries defined their currency exchange parities against a fixed amount of gold. This existed before the World War I, briefly in the inter-war period and again after World War II. It was gradually abandoned after 1971.

Hedgers Those who cover their financial exposures using appropriate financial assets.

Hitting the bid The agreement by the market user to trade at the market maker's bid price.

Ineligible paper A bankers' acceptance or bank bill which is not eligible for re-discount with the central bank and which, if held by a commercial bank, may attract central bank reserve requirements.

Initial margin A specified amount of cash or acceptable securities which a futures or options trader has to place with the exchange, by way of guarantee, when opening a position.

LIBID London Inter-bank Bid rate: the rate of interest at which London banks will bid for Eurocurrency funds for various maturities.

LIBOR The London Inter-bank Offered rate: the rate of interest which London banks charge for lending Eurocurrency funds to each other. LIBOR is often used as a benchmark for many Eurocurrency transactions.

Lifting the offer The agreement by the market user to trade at the market maker's offered price.

Mark to market The calculation of profit or loss on a position when revalued against a current market price. An estimate of the profit/loss that would be made if the position were liquidated in the current market.

Market amount The normal amount (usually minimum USD$1 million or equivalent) which can be traded at the prices quoted by market makers in the FX or money markets.

Market maker The party to a transaction which quotes two-way prices.

Market risk The risk of making a loss on a financial instrument due to changes in market prices rather than in the quality of that particular instrument. Also known as price or outright risk.

Market user The party to a transaction which deals at rates quoted by the market maker.

Maturity date The date when a contract period ends.

Maturity ladder A tabular/graphical representation of the net cash flows or exposures on a series of fixed income or FX positions.

Mismatch risk In FRAs or futures, the risk that a hedge might not be fully effective because the rate setting process for the underlying instrument is different from the reference rate fixing for the derivative. Also known as basis risk.

Money markets Wholesale financial markets in which governments, banks and major corporations raise or place funds for periods of twelve months or less.

Nostro account From the point of view of bank A, it is bank A's account with bank B.

Open interest In futures trading, this refers to the number of contracts (long or short) which are outstanding at any one time.

Outright forward rate A forward FX rate quoted as a rate of exchange rather than as a margin, in points, above or below the spot rate.

Over-the-counter (OTC) Markets in which currency amounts, settlement dates and prices are all negotiable between the trading parties. Transactions which are not executed through an exchange.

Par The face value of a fixed income security – the principal amount repayment at maturity. When a security trades at par its market price is equal to its face value. Most securities trade at a discount to par or a premium to par in the secondary markets.

Petrodollars   Huge amounts of US dollars earned by Gulf states from exports during the oil price hikes of the 1970s, which were subsequently placed in the Eurodollar market for on-lending to deficit countries.

Position limits   As a way of controlling market risk, position limits exist to control the extent to which a dealer may be long or short in a given market. This limit is determined with reference to the amount of capital a bank can afford to risk on the operation and to the seniority of the dealer.

Reciprocal quotation   An FX quotation in which the price of a country's currency is quoted in units of foreign currency. Also known as an indirect quotation. In the UK, the value of sterling is quoted reciprocally: in terms of DEM, USD, etc., per pound.

Regulation Q   A restriction, enforced by the Federal Reserve until the late 1960s, which limited the interest rates which US banks could pay on certain domestic deposits.

Replacement risk   The risk that a counterparty may be wound up *before* a contract reaches its settlement date, which requires the bank to find an alternative counterparty with which to cover its position.

Repo   Short for sale and repurchase. A transaction in which one party sells a security for value one date and simultaneously agrees to repurchase the same security for value some later date, at an agreed price. Repos are a cost-effective way for dealers to fund long or short positions in securities; the repo rate is the rate of interest effectively charged for funding in this way.

Settlement risk   The risk that a counterparty may be wound up on the settlement date of a trade, by which time the other side may have already issued payment instructions. The risk of loss is on the entire principal amount settled, as well as any profit or loss on the trade. Also known as clean or Herstadt risk.

Shading the rate   The practice of moving your bid and offer rates slightly higher or lower than the market. This is used as a means of defending a position.

Small figure   In a USD/DEM rate of 1.4145, the figures 45.

Smithsonian Agreement   An agreement reached in December 1971 between the Group of 10 which was designed to restore currency stability by devaluing the dollar against gold, and revaluing all other currencies in relation to the dollar.

Speculator   A trader whose purpose is not to hedge an underlying financial exposure but to take calculated risks on market prices for profit.

Spot   A transaction for value or settlement normally in two working days from the trade date.

Spot risk   The funding shortfalls caused on a forward FX position as a result of changes in the spot rate. These shortfalls arise at the settlement of the first legs of two offsetting swaps (at different spot rates) and must be borne until the forward date.

Squaring   The practice of covering one transaction made with another for the same amount and maturity. For instance, a bank may square its long position in US$10 million spot by selling the same amount of dollars.

Swap   An FX swap is a contract to buy an amount of currency for one value date at an agreed rate, and to resell simultaneously the same amount of currency for a later value date, also at an agreed rate.

SWIFT   Society for Worldwide Interbank Financial Settlements: a mechanism for the worldwide transfer of funds between banks.

Technical analysis   The study of market price action: *how* the market moves rather than *why* it moves.

Tick value   The profit or loss, in cash terms, represented by a one-tick change in the market price of a futures contract.

Time value of money   The idea that money today is worth more than money in the future, because the former can be invested so as to earn interest.

Value date   The date in which an FX transaction is settled between the parties, or when a money market transaction becomes effective, i.e., the funds are cleared. Also known as settlement date.

Value of 1%   The profit or loss that would result on a fixed income or forward FX position from a 1% (100 basis points) parallel shift in the yield curve. A unit of risk in some position limit systems.

Variation margin   In futures and options trading, this is the net sum of cash that a trader will receive from or pay to the exchange daily, depending on whether his position was marked to market at a profit or loss.

Vostro account   From the point of view of bank A, a vostro account is bank B's account with Bank A.

Yield curve   A graphical representation of the relationship between interest rates on debt with the same credit quality but different maturities. The shape of the yield curve reflects market expectations about future interest rates.

Yield to maturity   The rate of return that would be made on a fixed income security if it were bought at a given market price and held to maturity.

APPENDIX 3
ANSWERS TO REVIEW QUESTIONS, EXERCISES AND PRACTICES

Answers to review questions and exercises

Chapter 2 – Review Questions

1. C
2. D
3. B
4. D
5. C
6. A
7. D

Chapter 6 – Review Questions

1. C
2. C
3. A
4. C
5. (a) DEM/GBP 0.33835–0.33841
   (b) FRF/USD 0.18995–0.19001
   (c) USD/ECU 0.81070–0.81136
   (d) CHF/DEM 1.21242–1.21286
   (e) JPY/DEM 0.01012–0.01013

6. (a) DM5,000,000 would be received at the rate of 1.3550 and US$3,690,036.90 would be received.

    (b) ¥120,000,000 would be received at a rate of 141.75 and USD would be paid.

    (c) GB£2,000,000 would be received at a rate of 0.5235 and US$3.820,439.35 would be paid.

    (d) SwFr10,000,000 would be paid at a rate of 1.3263 and US$7,539,772.30 would be received.

    (e) L1,000,000,000 would be received at a rate of 1273.8 and US$785,052.59 would be paid.

7. D

8. B

9. (1) B

    (2) A

    (3) D

    (4) A

    (5) F

    (6) C

    (7) E

Chapter 8 – Quoting Spot FX Rates

Case 1: GBP/USD 1.9500/05

Case 2: USD/DEM 1.4604/09

Case 3: USD/DEM 1.4598/08

Case 4: GBP/USD 1.9918/28

Chapter 10 – Cross-Rate Calculations

1. (i)   Bank C at a rate of 1.4956

    (ii) Bank E at a rate of 141.75

    (iii) The CHF/JPY cross rate is 94.78
    (= 141.75 divided by 1.4956)

2. (i) Bank B at a rate of 37.69

   (ii) Bank B at a rate of 1.63000

   (iii) The cross-rate BEF 100/GBP is 1.6277
   (= 100 divided by (37.69 × 1.63000))

3. (i) Bank D at a rate of 1374.25

   (ii) Bank E at a rate of 6.9775

   (iii) The cross-rate ITL (1000)/DKK is 5.0073
   (= 1000 divided by (1374.25/6.9775))

4. (i) Bank D at a rate of 0.7119

   (ii) Bank D at a rate of 7.8072

   (iii) The cross-rate AUD/HKD is 5.5579
   (= 0.7119 × 7.8072)

Chapter 12 – Spot Position Keeping

DAILY POSITION SHEET

CURRENCY: USD/DEM

TIME	CURRENCY BOUGHT (+) CURRENCY SOLD (–)	RATE	US$ SOLD (–) US$ BOUGHT (+)
08:00	–7,262,500	1.4525	+5,000,000
09:00	+4,350,000	1.4500	+3,000,000
09:05	+4,347,000	1.4490	+3,000,000
09:15	4,345,500	1.4485	+3,000,000
10:00	–17,000,000	1.4450	+11,764,705
10:05	+4,333,500	1.4445	+3,000,000
10:25	–34,250,000	1.4440	+23,718,837
11:00	–20,000,000	1.4445	+13,845,621
11:15	+4,335,000	1.4450	+3,000,000
12:00	–7,212,500	1.4425	+ 5,000,000
13:00	–8,500,000	1.4420	+5,894,590
14:30	+15,000,000	1.4430	–10,395,010
15:15	+15,000,000	1.4435	–10,391, 409.
16:00	+4,332,000	1.4440	+3,000,000

CLOSING BALANCES:

		AV. RATE	US$ NET
DM NET			
–38,182,000		1.4442	+26,437,333

CLOSING RATE: 1.4445

NET PROFIT/LOSS   US$6,730.40

Chapter 17 – Deposit-Dealing

1. (a) Bank E @ 8 19/32%

   (b) USD 74,001.74

   (c) Bank B @ 8 9/16%

   (d) 8¾ – 8 19/32

2. (a) Bank E @ 8.8125%

   (b) GBP 157,176.37

   (c) Bank A @ 8.90625%

   (d) 8.671875 – 8.875

3. (a) Bank D @ 9.13%

   (b) Bank B @ 9.11%

   (c) 9.12 – 9.18

4. (a) Bank B or D @ 8 11/16%

   (b) Bank E @ 8 17/32%

   (c) 8 9/16 – 8¾

5. (a) Bank B @ 9 3/16%

   (b) Bank D @ 0.0937%

   (c) 8 15/16 – 9 11/16

Chapter 20 – Pricing CDs

1. (a) Purchase cost in dollars ($103,432.82)

   (b) Interest is accrued on the actual number of maturity (365) on a 360 day basis. There are therefore five extra days of interest to take into account.

   (c) Profit/loss = $143.10
   Return = 5.0498%

2. (a) $1,055,061.39

   (b) $1,046,796.06

3. (a) Profit in dollars = $9,434.28
   Holding period return = 10.53%

(b)   Profit in dollars = $9,902.93
      Holding period return = 11.14%

Chapter 22 – Pricing Discounts

1.   (a) $99,764.17

     (b) $1,084,095.22

2. $99,629.17

3.   (a)   £968,083.81

     (b)   £194,825.75

4.   (a) $98,560

     (b) $99,979.26

     (c)   More

     (d)   5.8442%

     (e) $100,000

Chapter 24 – FRA Dealing

1.   (a)   The break-even forward–forward rate must be 10.3895%

     (b)   To cover the interest rate exposure in one month's time the bank will have to lend; therefore the bank is a seller of an FRA. The highest FRA buying price being quoted is Bank D at 10.39%

     (c)   If the LIBOR fixing for the FRA is 10.75%, then, having sold a FRA to Bank D at 10.39%, the bank in question must pay to Bank D a Settlement Amount of $7,178,46.2.

2.   (a)   The break-even forward–forward rate must be 9.581395.

     (b)   To cover the interest rate exposure in one month's time, the bank will have to borrow; therefore, the bank is a buyer of an FRA. The lowest FRA selling price being quoted is Bank E at 9.57%.

     (c)   If the LIBOR fix for the FRA is 9.3125%, then, having bought a FRA from Bank E at 9.75%, the bank in question must pay to Bank E a settlement amount of $6,339.11.

3.   (a)   The break-even forward–forward rate must be 10.863758%.

     (b)   To square the position in 6 × 12 months the bank will have to lend; therefore the bank is a seller of an FRA. The highest FRA buying price being quoted is Bank A at 10.87%.

(c) If the LIBOR fixing for the FRA is 10.75% then, having sold a FRA to Bank D at 10.87 %, the bank in question must pay to Bank D a settlement amount of $14,234.87.

4. (a) The break-even forward–forward rate must be 10,850875%

(b) To square the position in 6 × 12 months the bank will have to borrow; therefore, the bank is a buyer of an FRA. The lowest FRA selling price being quoted is Bank E at 10.85%.

(c) If the LIBOR fix for the FRA is 11.50% then, having bought a FRA from Bank E at 10.85%, the bank in question will receive a settlement amount from Bank D of $61,465.72.

Chapter 26 – Interest Rate Futures

1. (i) Net increase in the cost of borrowing: $2,812.50

(ii) Futures points movement: 51 ticks

(iii) Futures profit: $3,825

(iv) Net benefit: 1012.5

2. (i) Net decrease in the return on the three-month deposit: $10,937

(ii) Futures points movement: 65 ticks

(iii) Futures profit: $11,375

(iv) Net benefit: $4,383

3. (i) Net decrease in the return on the three-month deposit: $18,750

(ii) Futures points movement: 97 ticks

(iii) Number of contracts: 8

(iv) Futures profit: $19,400

(v) Net benefit: $6,504

4. (i) Net increase in the cost of borrowing: $62,500

(ii) Futures points movement: 95 ticks

(iii) Number of contracts: 27

(iv) Futures profit: $64,125

(v) Net benefit: $1,625

Chapter 30 – Forward Spread

All amounts to the nearest whole number.

1. (a) 1,959,584
   (b) 979,792
   (c) 1,003,674
   (d) 1.9927
   (e) −0.0073
   (f) Forward rate USD/DEM: 1.9927
       Forward margin: −0.0073

2. (a) 979,792
   (b) DM2,000,000/1.9936 = US$1,003,210
       Discounted at 9.75%, this gives:
       1,003,210 / (1 + 9.75/100 × 90/360)
       = US$979,339

       Therefore the bank's forward dollar rate is overpriced.

3. (a) 4,910,235
   (b) 12,275,558
   (c) 12,563,297
   (d) 2.5127
   (e) + 0.0127

4. (a) 4,911,742
   (b) 12,279,355
   (c) 12,569,071
   (d) 2.5138
   (e) +0.0138
   (f) Outright: 2.5138
       Margin: +0.0138

5. (a) 128.06
   (b) 1.8929
   (c) 23.1786

6. A bank buying dollars forward from the government at 4.50 would try to cover the exchange risk by selling the dollars spot at 4.30. The transaction would be funded by borrowing the dollars at 8.1/2% and by placing the won proceeds on deposit at 10.50%. The net interest rate for every spot-dollar sold would be:

$$\frac{(10.50 - 8.50)}{100} \times 4.30$$

= Won 0.086 per dollar.

This income, together with the won 4.30 per dollar obtained at spot, generates only won 4.386 which is not enough to cover the cost of buying dollars forward at the central bank's rate. Therefore, no bank aiming to cover the risk on this operation would take up the offer. Some banks may be prepared to do so if they feel the won may be devalued below 4.50 within 12 months, but that would be a speculative transaction.

Chapter 32 – Outright Prices

1.

	Bank spot rate	Margin	Outright
(a)	A 1240.62	+12.0	1252.62
(b)	A 152.00	−0.36	151.64
(c)	B 1.6339–0	.0038	1.6301
(d)	A 1.6829	−0.0003	1.6826
(e)	B 34.56	+0.15	34.71
	C 5.6375	+0.0068	5.6443
	FRF/BEL 6.1496		
(f)	C 1.2270	−0.0059	1.2211
	C 154.81	−0.40	154.41
	XCU/JPY 188.55		

Chapter 35 – Identifying the Price

1. (a) is true and therefore so is (b). If the dollar is the base currency (c) is always true, no matter what interest rates are. If (b) and (c) are true then (d) must be false: the market maker would not give you 325 points to sell and buy dollars and charge only 320 points to do the opposite. Therefore (e) must be true.

2. GBP/USD

LAS rate	RCS rate
MARKET MAKER	
sells GB£ spot and buys back the GB£ fwd	buys GB£ spot and sells back the GB£ fwd
buys counter-ccy spot and sells it back fwd	sells counter ccy spot and buys it back fwd
swap points are in their favor	swap points are against them
MARKET USER	
sells GB£ spot and buys back the GB£ fwd	buys GB£ spot and buys back the GB£ fwd
sells counter-ccy spot and buys it back fwd	buys counter ccy spot and sells it back fwd
swap points are against them	swap points are in their favor

3. (i)

   (a) Bank D @ 100 in your favor

   (b) Bank E @ 223 against

   (c) Bank E @ 348 against

   (d) Bank C @ 690 in your favor

   (ii)

   (a) Bank E @ 49 against

   (b) Bank B @ 104 in your favor

   (c) Bank D @ 167 against

   (d) Bank C @ 355 in your favor

   (iii)

   (a) Bank D @ 60 in your favor

   (b) Bank A @ 126 in your favor

   (c) Bank B @ 180 against

   (d) Bank D @ 341 in your favor

4. (a) 691/724 or higher: we pay more points (691) to sell and buy the dollar (which is what we want) than any other bank, but we charge more than any other bank to do the opposite (which we don't want).

(b) 174/163 or higher: we pay more (163) points than any other bank to buy and sell the pound, but we charge more to do the reverse.

(c) 48/45 or less: we charge less (48) than any other bank to sell and buy pounds, but we also pay less to do the opposite.

(d) 131/127 or more: we pay more (127) to buy and sell the AUD (sell and buy th e dollar) than any other bank, but charge more to do the reverse.

Chapter 37 – Swap Applications

1. (a) US dollars will be swapped into Australian dollars at 247 points against the company. The second leg of the swap will cost A$79,189,104.

(b) Interest payable at 9.00% for the first period = US$4,575,000.

(c) Company buys US$4,575,000 forward outright at 1.2623, which will cost A$3,624,337.

(d) Net cost of US dollar loan:

A$77,669, 900 first leg of swap.

A$(79,189,104) second leg of swap.

A$(3,624,337) interest payment.

———————————

A$(5,143,541)

(e) Effective interest cost of borrowing US dollars swapped into Australian dollars = 13.21%

(f) The approximate formula gives an effective cost of 12.83% which understates the true cost calculated under (e). One of the reasons for this is that it does not take into account the cost of covering the exchange risk on the interest payable on the dollars. Another reason is that the Australian dollar interest is based on a 365-day year, whereas US dollar interest is on 360 days.

(g) The company might still prefer to raise dollar funds and swap them into Australian dollars because, unlike the Eurodollar market, the domestic Australian dollars market may not be deep enough to raise the funds required without moving the rates against the borrower.

(h) Extending FX cover for a further six months will cost the borrower 260 points. Net cash flows arising from the first swap rollover:

A$(779,189,104) second leg of first swap

A$(79,649,542) first leg of rollover swap.

A$460,438

The apparent gain arose because of the weaker AUD exchange rate. However, this gain will be more or less offset by an equivalent loss once the second leg of the rollover matures.

(i) Extending FX cover for a third six months period will cost the borrower 255 points. Net cash flows arising at the second rollover:

A$(81,333,876)   second leg of swap @ 1.2555–0.0260

A$(79,176,564)   first leg of rollover swap @ 1.2630

A$(2,157,312)

Now the exchange rate has firmed since 10 September, resulting in a loss at this rollover. But this loss may be offset by a corresponding gain at maturity of the current rollover.

2. (a) The exporter will sell and buy ITL6,250 spot against three months on a swap, at 1500 points in its favor

   (b) The exporter will buy ITL125 million from the bank at 9.1030

   (c) Net cash flow to the exporter in March (in JPY millions):

   JPY   686.587   sale of ITL6,250 million on 1st leg of swap

   JPY   (13.732)   cost of the ITL discount

   JPY   672.855

(d) Net cash flow to the exporter in June (in JPY millions):

JPY   675.676   sale of ITL6,250 million in January at 9.2500

JPY   (675.457)   repurchase of ITL6,250 on second leg of swap
──────────────
JPY   0.229

(e) The loss of revenue of JPY13.732 million from the 2% discount has been largely offset by a JPY11.13 million gain on the swap points (JPY686.587–675.457) so the net loss on the early payment discount was only JPY2.602 million.

Answers to practices

Chapter 13 – Spot FX Practice

(Questions marked with * were in the December 1994 ACI *Introduction to Foreign Exchange and Money Markets* exam)

1. C

   Base currencies are not the same:

   We need to sell French francs (buy US dollars, the base) so we use the USD/FRF market offer rate of 5.5560; then buy sterling, the base, and sell the US dollars also at the market offered rate of 1.6260, so the GBP/FRF cross-rate is 5.5560 × 1.6260 = 9.0341.

   We "multiply down."

2. A

   Base currencies are not the same:

   We need to buy lire (sell US dollars) at the USD/ITL market bid rate (for dollars) of 1100.50, and then sell sterling (buy the US dollars) also at the market cable bid rate, so the GBP/ITL cross-rate is 1100.50 × 1.6250 = 1788.31

   Again, we "multiply down."

3. **C**

   Base currencies are the same:

   We need to sell lire (buy US dollars, the base) at the USD/ITL market offered rate of 1101.50 and then buy French francs (sell US dollars, the base) at the USD/FRF bid rate of 5.5550, so the FRF/ITL cross-rate is 1101.50 / 5.5550 = 198.29

   This time we "divide across" (new counter-currency / new base currency).

4. **C**

   L3,750,000 / 198.29 = FrF18,911,694.99

5*. **B**

   We are buyers of French francs (sellers of sterling, the base) so we must hit the highest market bid rate (for sterling), of 8.4793.

6*. **D**

   We are buyers of Swiss francs (sellers of D-marks, the base) so we need to hit the highest market bid rate (for D-marks), of 0.8703.

7*. **D**

   Base currencies are not the same so we multiply the two rates (rather than divide):

   USD/DEM 1.5770 × AUD/USD 0.7060 = AUD/DEM.1.1134
   Therefore DEM/AUD = 1 / 1.1134 = 0.8981

8. **A**

   Base currencies are the same, so we "divide across":

   We need to buy French francs for the customer (sell US dollars, the base) at 5.4430 and then sell the D-marks that the customer will give us (buy US dollars) at 1.5665 so the DEM/FRF rate we can quote is 5.4430 / 1.5665 = 3.4746.

9. **A**

   Base currencies are the same, so we "divide across":

   We need to buy lire to sell to the customer (therefore sell the US dollars) at 1150.50 and then sell the D-marks we take from the customer (buy US dollars) at 1.5665, so the DEM/ITL rate we can quote is 1150.50 / 1.5665 = 734.44.

10. D

Same base currency, "divide across."

We need to sell the lire *that we bought from the customer* (buy dollars) at 1151.00, and buy the French francs (sell dollars) *that we sold to our customer* . . . so the cross-rate is 1151.00 / 5.4430 = 211.46

11. D

DM	RATE	US$
(2,000,000)	1.4510	1,378,359.75
(8,000,000)	1.4530	5,505,849.97
(3,000,000)	1.4522	2,065,831.15
(13,000,000)		8,950,040.87

Average rate = 13,000,000 / 8,950,040.87 = 1.4525

12. B

To close the position we would have to buy the DM13,000,000 (sell the US dollars) at 1.4685, which would cost us 13,000,000 / 1.4685 = US$8,852,570.65, which would leave a debit position in the US dollar account of US$97,470.22.

13. D

14. B

If you have dollars to sell (sterling to buy) you must bid up the market, so 22 / 27 is the right direction. This sends the message to the counterparty: "I am buying sterling / selling US dollars and I am not selling sterling."

18 / 23 sends the opposite signal, so you may end up even shorter sterling (longer dollars). 18 / 27 says "I don't really want to deal with you either way, so I'll quote you a barn-door." 25 your choice says "I am definitely a buyer of sterling (I sell US dollars) but I don't mind selling some more sterling (buying more dollars) and I am definitely keen to deal with you" – not quite our intention.

15. D

Another way of saying this is, "5/20, $10 million by $15 million."

Chapter 27 – Money Markets Practice

(Questions marked with * were in the December 1994 ACI *Introduction to Foreign Exchange and Money Markets* exam)

1. B

   You want to hit the highest bid: 6.11/16.

2. A

   28 April is the spot date (not the dealing date) which is *not* the last working day of the month, so the maturity will be 28 May.

3. A

   Repayment amount = $10,000,000 + (6.68750 / 100 × 30 / 360 × 10,000,000)

   = $10,055,729.17

4. B

5. C

   Sell US$10,000,000 (buy sterling) at 1.4260 and place the GB£7,012,622.72 on deposit at 8% for 20 days.

   Repayment amount = GB£7,012,622,72 + (8 / 100 × 20 / 365 × 7,012,622.72)

   = GB£7,043,362.98

6*. C

   3.10 + { (120 − 90)/(180 − 90) × (3.50 − 3.10) } = 3.23%

7*. A

8. C (It *normally* pays a *lower* rate of interest!)

9. D

   Using the ACI formula to convert a discount rate into a money market yield:

   MMY = 10 / [1 − { (10 × 90)/(365 × 100) }] = 10.2528%

10. C

    The bills are already quoted on a money market yield basis, rather than at a discount rate. One solution is to treat the bill as a zero-coupon CD and apply the CD formula to it:

    Proceeds = 10,000,000 × [(360 × 100) / { (3.91 × 90) + (360 × 100) }]
    = US$9,903,196.26

11. B

True annual yield (bond basis) = 365/360 × 5.375 = 5.45%.

12*. B

The coupon on the CD is higher than its yield, so the CD will be worth more than the original face value.

13. B

This problem requires using the accrued interest formula and solving for R%, the rate of interest.

$$DM83,333.33 = DM10,000,000 \times \frac{R}{100} \times \frac{60}{360}$$

Therefore:

$$\frac{83,333.33}{10,000,000} \times \frac{360}{60} \times 100 = R\%$$
$$= 5$$

14*. C

15*. D

Here, we shall take a weighted average of the rates, each rate weighted by the amount dealt on it:

Average rate = (10/17 × 4.00) + (5/17 × 5.00) + (2/17 × 5.50)
= 4.4706%

16. D

Using the forward–forward break-even formula:

Fwd = [(8.5625 × 212) – (8 × 30)] / [182 × {1 + ((8 × 30)/(360 × 100))}]
= 8.60%

17. A

Settlement = {(8.60 – 7) × 1,000,000 × 182} / {(182 × 7) + (360 × 100)}
= $7,812.42

The LIBOR is below the contract rate, so as a seller you receive this amount.

Chapter 40 – Forwards and Swaps FX Practice

1. D

    Applying the forward FX formula:

    Outright forward $= \text{Spot} \times \text{growth}_{ccy} / \text{growth}_{base}$

    where   Spot $= 1.4500$
    Growth$_{ccy}$ $= \{ 1 + (9/100 \times 91/360) \} = 1.02275$
    Growth$_{base}$ $= \{ 1 + (5/100 \times 91/360) \} = 1.01264$

    $= 1.4500 \times 1.02275 / 1.01264$
    $= 1.4645$

    Forward margin $= 1.4645 - 1.4500$
    $= +0.0145$

2. C

Outright	8.3930	8.3950
– Spot	8.3580	8.3590
= Points	0.0350	0.0360 (i.e. 350/360)

3. C

    High-figure/low-figure means we take the points away, so one dollar forward is worth less DEM than one dollar spot, so the forward DEM is at a premium.

4. A

    Outright rates:

USD/CHF	1.6202/17	(subtract the points)
USD/FRF	5.3313/43	(add the points)
CHF/FRF	3.2875/24	(same base, therefore "divide across")

5. A

    The DEM grows faster than the USD, so the points are added!

6. A

    Repayment on the sterling loan $= 10,000,000 \ + \ (10,000,000 \ \times \ 6.75/100 \times 180/365)$
    $= 10,332,876.71$

    We can sell these pounds forward outright at 1.6265 (= 1.6320 – 0.0055) to crystalize:
    US$16,806,423.97.

7. B

    Applying the forward FX formula:

    Outright $\qquad = \text{Spot} \times \text{Growth}_{ccy} / \text{Growth}_{base}$

    where Spot $\qquad = 1.6500$
    $\qquad$ Growth$_{ccy}$ $\quad = \{ 1 + (11/100 \times 91/360) \} = 1.02781$
    $\qquad$ Growth$_{base}$ $\quad = \{ 1 + (\ 8/100 \times 91/365) \} = 1.01995$

    $\qquad \qquad \qquad = 1.6500 \times 1.02781 / 1.01995$
    $\qquad \qquad \qquad = 1.6627$

    Forward margin $\quad = 1.6627 - 1.6500$
    $\qquad \qquad \qquad = +0.0127$

8. C

    Like any OTC product, there is credit risk, although as a funding vehicle the FX swap has much lower credit risk than a pair of Euro-deposit transactions – which in essence it is.

9. A

    The mechanism is: borrow US dollars (at 8%); sell/buy the US dollars at 150 points in our favor. Spot = 1.3515 and Outright = 1.3365

    Here we need to rearrange the forward FX formula to solve for Growth$_{ccy}$:

    Growth$_{ccy}$ $\qquad = \text{Outright} / \text{Spot} \times \text{Growth}_{base}$

    where Spot $\qquad = 1.3515$
    $\qquad$ Outright $\quad = 1.3365$
    $\qquad$ Growth$_{base}$ $\quad = \{ 1 + (\ 8/100 \times 60/360) \} = 1.01333$

    $\qquad \qquad \qquad = 1.3365 / 1.3515 \times 1.01333$
    $\qquad \qquad \qquad = 1.00208$

    $\qquad$ Growth$_{ccy}$ $\quad = 1 + (\text{Rate}/100 \times 60/360) = 1.00208$
    $\qquad$ R $\qquad \quad = (1.00208 - 1) \times 360/60 \times 100$
    $\qquad \qquad \qquad = 1.25\%$

10. B

Spot	1.8500 / 1.8510	
T/Next	+ 0.0005 / 0.0010	(swap around and change the sign!)
Tom	1.8505 / 1.8520	

11. C

We sell sterling (buy Swiss francs) at the LHS rate, and we shall be multiplying the two bids, so we only need to calculate these two outrights:

GBP/USD   1.5693
USD/CHF   1.2252

GBP/CHF   1.9227

12. D

There are two possible "routes home" here:

(i)
Sell the DM10 million forward outright at 1.5180 (1.5005 + 0.0175) to produce US$6,587,615.28 in 9 months' time, and then borrow the discounted value of these dollars (discounted at 4.25%):

6,587,615.28 / { 1 + (4.25/100 × 270/360) }
= US$6,384,121.41

(ii)
Alternatively, borrow the discounted value of DM10,000,000 (discounted at 5.85%):

10,000,000 / {1 + (5.85/100 × 270/360) }
= DM9,579,691.05

Then sell these D-marks spot at 1.5005 = US$6,384,332.59.

The second route produces the largest amount of US dollars.

13. D

The principle of market making is to know at what cost you can cover; if you know the cost of the hedge you can price the product. The mechanics of creating a forward–forward FX price is as follows:

LHS price, at which market maker sells/buys three × six months:

He covers with buy/sell spot – six months at 35 points against him, then sell/buy spot – three months at 8 points, *in this case also against him*. Total cost = 43.

The trick here is to notice that the three-month forward CHF is at a discount, while the six months is at a premium! This is somewhat unusual and suggests that the USD and CHF yield curves cross somewhere between the three and the six months.

RHS price, at which market maker buys/sells three × six months:

He covers with sell/buy spot – six months at 30 points in his favor, then buy/sell spot – three months at 5 points, *in this case also in his favor!* Total income = 35.

Therefore, market maker's price = 43/35.

14. C

$$100 + \{ (45 - 30)/(60 - 30) \times (170 - 100) \} = 135 \text{ points}$$
$$90 + \{ (45 - 30)/(60 - 30) \times (160 - 100) \} = 125 \text{ points}$$

Actually, this one is not difficult to work out in your head, because 45 days is exactly half-way between 30 and 60 days, so we just add half of the one-to-two months' points difference to the one month rate.

15. B

This one is mean: the one-month forward CHF is at a premium while the two-month is at a discount. So the one-to-two month points difference is 370/370. Since we are looking for a 1 1/2 month rate, take 185/185 away from 200/210 to leave 15/25. I doubt they would put such a mean question in the exam, but you never know . . .

APPENDIX 4
INSTALLING THE RISK MANAGER
DEALING SIMULATION

Hardware Requirements

To get reasonable performance from *Risk Manager for Windows*, you will need the following *minimum* hardware configuration:

- 486 DX 33Mhz PC

- 4 Megabytes of RAM

- 20 Megabytes of free hard disk space

- 3.5″ floppy disk drive

- Colour VGA monitor, keyboard and mouse

- A text/graphics printer.

Obviously, to run *Risk Manager for Windows*, your PC will need to have *Windows 3.1* or higher already installed.

Installing the Software

To install *Risk Manager for Windows* on your hard drive take the following steps:

1. Run *Windows 3.1* or *Windows 95*.

2. Place the diskette supplied into your floppy drive.

3. From the Windows Program Manager click on the **File** menu and select **Run**. At the prompt enter *either*:

    - **a:\setupinstall** if your floppy drive is A;

    - **b:\setupinstall** if it is B.

4. The installation program will give you the option to select the directory into which the software will install. By default, *Risk Manager* will create a directory **C:\RISKMAN** and install the software there.

5. After all the required files have been copied, the simulation will create a *Windows Program Group* called *Risk Manager* with an icon to access the program that has been installed.

At the end of the installation process, please exit and re-start *Windows* to activate the sound driver which has been installed.

APPENDIX 5
FAX REPLY

If you would like further information about the *Risk Manager for Windows*™ (*RM*) dealing simulation included with this book, we have included a fax reply sheet for you to return. Please copy the page overleaf, indicate the areas of your specific interest, and send the completed reply to the fax number given.

Alternatively, you may visit our Website
http://www.riskmanager.com
or call us on +44 171 630 0161.

Risk Manager Fax Reply

To: **Chisholm Roth and Company Ltd.**
London
+44 171 630 0163

From: **Name:**_____

Job Title:_____

Department:_____

Company Name:_____

Address:_____

_____

_____

Telephone:_____

Fax:_____

I would like to receive information on (please tick):

☐ Other simulations comprising the *RM* dealing series and the upgrading service provided by Chisholm Roth and Company Ltd.

☐ Chisholm Roth's in-house training programs using *Risk Manager*.

☐ Registering as a user of *Risk Manager*.

APPENDIX 6
STRUCTURE OF THE ACI EXAMINATIONS

LEVEL ONE
The ACI Foundation Programme

Four subjects – all subjects compulsory

Subject	Forex Assocation Examination Board
Introduction to Foreign Exchange & Money Markets	Forex London
Code of Conduct & Market Practice	Forex Singapore
Back Office Operations	Forex London
Risks & Controls in the Dealing Room	Forex Suisse

LEVEL TWO
Leading to the status of Fellowship (for ACI members) or Associate (for non-members) of the ACI Institute

Six subjects (one compulsory and five options to be chosen from ten)

Subject	Forex Association Examination Board
The ACI Foreign Exchange Simulation	Forex Australia
Options	Forex France (AFTB)
Futures	Forex France (AFTB)
Swaps	Forex France (AFTB)
The Repo Market	Forex Luxembourg
Financial Calculations	Forex Norway
Risk Management using Derivatives	Forex Singapore
Technical Analysis	Forex Suisse
Treasury Risk Management	Forex USA Inc
Fundamental Analysis (Macroeconomics)	Forex RSA (South Africa)
The ACI Diploma (Compulsory)	Forex London

Index